PRAISE FOR THE WASPs

The WASPs

The Hanscome Trilogy

Book III

Dr. Joan Adsit Dickinson

First Electronic Edition: September 2019
First Print Edition: September 2019

eBook and Print Book Design & Formatting by
D. D. Scott's LetLoveGlow Author Services

For my loving daughter Sarah

Artist Rhoda Hanscome Campbell.
Watercolor of a village
in the rolling Spanish hills.
Circa 1953.
Author owned.

Table of Contents

Chapter 1

A Normal Family
October 1865
Toronto, Canada

"Mr. Hanscome, you need to make a decision and fast," said the exhausted mid-wife as she stepped from the bedroom, wiping the blood from her hands onto a once spotlessly clean, white apron. "I'm not one to mince words. Your wife may die if she continues with this birth. What do you want me to do? I can save Mary Sophia or the child, but not both."

"Save Mary Sophia!" he shouted instantly, turning ghastly pale. "It is the only choice. It pains my heart to lose the child, but I cannot and will not survive without her. Nor will our children. I only hope she will forgive me."

"She will not be able to bear any more children. Are you certain?"

"Yes, I am certain. We have been blessed with plenty of children. Please, do what you must to save my wife!"

The door closed ominously. Thomas sat helplessly in a wooden chair and waited for an eternity before it opened again. The nurse carried a limp bundle in her arms, quietly murmuring a *boy* to him as she clomped down the stairs. He rushed into the room only to find his wife silent in their bed. Too quiet it seemed, but as he bent over to kiss her forehead, he felt her faint, rhythmic breath on his face. His body started shaking, and his tears of relief flowed. Then he patiently kept vigil and simply held her hand. This eternity of waiting he could handle. She was alive.

Finally, as the morning sunshine flooded the room, Mary Sophia stirred. She smiled at Thomas, but not for long, as the empty bassinette caught her eye. She knew then she had lost the baby. She closed her eyes again.

"A boy? A girl? How did this happen?" she finally whispered.

"A boy. Please understand that I had to save you, to choose you," begged Thomas. "I love you, Mary Sophia. I am so sorry."

She closed her eyes, again, to absorb the meaning. Another eternity passed before her voice found its strength.

"Oh, Thomas, I would have easily traded my life for my baby, our baby. Thomas, we lost another son." She wept, this time loudly. "I am so angry with you, Thomas! I am angry with the mid-wife! And I am angry at myself for not making my wishes clear! It is my gift to humanity to bear children for a better future. I am but a vessel for this purpose."

"Hush, Mary Sophia. Be angry with me if you want, but I could not live without you. I was selfish. Please don't be so upset. You are forty-three. We should have stopped having children long ago – for that I claim responsibility. Please forgive me. Let's just appreciate the fine family we have."

She said nothing more, but she let her husband hold, comfort and cry with her. He was so thankful for that. She had not pushed him away. It meant she would forgive him and that she loved him, still. They had loved each other since childhood and their love would continue.

Thomas summoned his daughters to tell them the sad news and have them greet their mother.

"Please take away the bassinette and the new nursery items. There will be no more Hanscome babies," he sadly and solemnly declared.

Silence.

Finally, Alice spoke, calmly and clearly.

"Yes. Yes, there will be," Alice said, courageously. *Here it is. The truth. Finally.* She knew this was a bad time to tell her parents, with her mother still in shock and ill, but there never had been a good time.

"What do you mean?" asked Thomas, puzzled.

"I mean there will be another Hanscome birth. I am pregnant. I will have a baby after the New Year." *There. I have said it.* Alice had finally admitted her heinous situation to her family and with that burden lifted, she felt much stronger and stood taller, making her belly obvious to all. No more would she hide. No more would she feel ashamed.

What a surprise! Her father, mother and sisters were stunned by her news. They had noticed Alice was beginning to gain back the weight she had lost during the summer when she became too ill to work. She had grown despondent and finally quit her beloved position at Eaton's Department Store. Her family had no idea that she was pregnant. They thought she was heart-broken.

Oh, how Thomas regretted taking Alice back to his old home in Charleston and, yes, to that damn plantation he loved ever as much as his father's namesake, Thomas Hanscome Walpole, did. Yes, Thomas had known young Walpole would choose his land over his daughter, like every man of planter blood. He was in angst, but held in his tears and, yes, rage.

I am responsible. I failed to protect my precious Alice. I tried my best to save her, to chase young Thomas away, but she simply wanted to be loved too much to see the truth. Why is she so headstrong? Why won't she listen to me, ever? I am her father! Too late now, the milk is spilt.

What were they to do?

"Alice will have to give the baby up for adoption," Thomas said finally to Mary Sophia as he ignored Alice and firmly set his jaw. "I don't believe we can get her quickly married to anyone - unless that rascal Thomas Walpole would miraculously dare to show his face here."

"What do you want to do, Alice?" asked Mary Sophia, ignoring her husband and gently taking her daughter's hand. "Have you written to him? Does he know you are pregnant?"

"I have not written to Thomas, nor have I received any correspondence from him." Then she stared boldly at her father. "It is as you thought, Father. He came to Charleston, ready to depart with me, ready to marry me in Toronto as we have no ridiculous miscegenation laws. Suddenly, as we approached the wharf, he hesitated. He said nothing, just looked at me with such sad eyes and placed the valise in my hand! He would not forsake his precious plantation for me. That was the truth of the matter, the ugly truth of the matter! That was the depth of his affection! And when I knew that, I couldn't stay with him, either. I just wasn't precious enough." Alice's lip quivered and her firm resolve disappeared in tears. This was the first time she had unburdened her broken heart to anyone. Just as quickly, her hysterical confession was replaced by fire and she stood even more erect as she served warning. "My baby is precious, and I will keep it. I love it, even before it's born."

"Alice you cannot keep this child. It will live disgraced, illegitimate, and your reputation will be ruined forever," said her father, who knew too well the inward, deep shame of being a bastard, albeit a wealthy one.

"Do you intend to hide me away and pretend this never happened? Whisk my baby away? Give my child to someone else to love? I will leave then! I will keep my baby." Alice's eyes narrowed in fury and determination. Indeed, she was feeling more powerful than she ever had. She was no longer a child.

"And where will you go?" asked her father, trying to remain calm.

"I will go to Philadelphia. Aunt Mary and Margaretta Forten will help me. I will not be the first woman in our family to hide her illegitimate children, yes, one a mulatto, and to declare herself an honorable widow. As I recall, Ann Downing did just that. And wasn't her real name also Alice – just like mine? Wasn't she the famed Alice Hanscome from Kittery, Maine? And her life was not ruined. She became the much admired Charles Town school directress and an esteemed wife of a doctor. Or is her legend false?" Alice hurled these words at her father, in a rage.

Her words hit him dead center.

Why did we name Alice after the feisty, courageous Alice Hanscome? Will she be forever cursed? Will she ever bend to our wisdom?

But then he remembered how she did listen and didn't marry Harry Howling Wolf. It was his fatherly duty to lead, to protect, to be right. He was the father. Had he erred in his judgment? His firmament felt shaken. Being wrong was weak and despicable. He sighed. Marriage to an Indian was better than no marriage at all. Indians had more rights than mulattos in South Carolina before the War. On the other hand, poverty was poverty. These things he knew. He felt spent and a failure with his first born child. Her sins were his failures. He fell silent, a rarity for him.

"Alice and Thomas, stop this conversation right now," ordered Mary Sophia. "I have another idea. Why don't we claim Alice's baby as our own, Thomas? We have just lost our child, but no one in the community need know. We will simply say our newborn is ill and we cannot entertain. When Alice's babe is born, we will have an adequate explanation for its small size. It's only a few months to wait."

"And you will take my baby from me? Raise it as your own? I am its mother. I will be my child's mother!" Alice shouted.

"Your child will have our name, Alice. It will feel you are its mother, but only know you as its true mother when it is older. You will raise him or her, right here in this house, with a loving family to help you. Do you really want to leave us, move to

Philadelphia? It could be a rough life. And, your baby will be white. How do you think your white child will fit into the Forten's black world? Think of what's best for your child, please."

Silence.

"Are you willing to accept responsibility for Alice's child, Thomas?" Mary Sophia asked.

"I will think about it."

"And Alice, will you consider this solution?" her mother implored. "Please."

"I won't be his or her mother if I stay," lamented Alice. "You will be the mother."

"We haven't much time. The neighbors will be asking about our baby, Thomas," Mary Sophia said.

"We will all reflect on the best decision," said Thomas. "Please rest, Mary Sophia. You need to heal. We will talk later."

What did they decide? They decided it was Alice's choice. And Alice decided to stay. She would raise her child, but the names mother and father would be reserved for her parents. And the lie would become another expedient family secret, like their whiteness. Lies were sometimes the best solutions, weren't they?

January 20, 1866

"It's a boy," Mary Sophia announced to Thomas and the rest of their family. She had helped deliver Alice's baby. "A healthy boy!"

"Isn't he beautiful!" Alice exclaimed, holding her son and presenting him to her family. He was very fair and had a full head of fine, blonde hair.

"Yes, he is handsome," said Anna Louisa.

"Alice, what do you want to name him?" asked her father.

"I've been thinking. I want to call him Arthur, Arthur Randall Hanscome," she replied. "Arthur, because those tales of Camelot have been my constant companion these past few months. I want him to be virtuous and champion his true love, like King Arthur. And Randall for our strong Grandmother Ann."

"And what do you want him to call you?" her mother asked, gingerly.

"Arthur can call me Constantia, my middle name." Then she laughed. "Perhaps Connie might be more manageable. I truly want him to have a special name for me, a name that no one else calls me. I will hold this secret until he reaches his majority at twenty-one. Then he must know I am his mother. Will you help me, dear family?"

"Yes, we will," swore Thomas, Mary Sophia and the girls.

February 14, 1866
Valentine's Day

The Hanscomes baptized their son at St. James Cathedral and announced their wee Arthur to the congregation. Their girls' arrival in red velvet dresses, in honor of St. Valentine who fell in love right before his beheading, created quite a stir. All the other ladies wore their drab gray, black or brown dresses, as befitted the northern climes. Their Charleston Aunt Louisa Rebecca had sent the red velvet fabric with a matching red velvet Valentine's card that read:

> *A gift of love to brighten your winter spirits*
> *and welcome your child of love to our Hanscome*
> *family. We hold you ever in our hearts and pray*
> *there is no beheading on this special Valentine's*
> *Day.*
>
> *Love, Aunt Louisa Rebecca*

Was Louisa Rebecca simply turning a clever phrase or did she surmise that this babe was Alice's gift of love from South Carolina? Had the Lees, Gardens or Inglis' wondered about the long illness, confinement and small size of wee Arthur? If so, no one had the poor manners to question them at the family dinner celebrating his baptism. The hardest part was the telling of the first lie. Now the crisis was over, and the secret was sealed. It was kept so well that over the years the lie became the truth. But isn't that what happens to family secrets?

"Mary Sophia, I want to ask you a question. Do you have any close friends?" Thomas asked.

"That is a strange question, dear. I have your sisters, Elizabeth Sarah, Mary Ann and now my brother William and his wife. I am friendly with women in the Auxiliary at St. James. With our large family and now wee Arthur, I don't have time for friends."

"I'd like us to find time. I'd like us to become part of the Toronto community."

"What prompts this need, after all these years? We haven't had a social life, other than family, since we left Charleston."

"I remember Elizabeth Sarah saying to me on our recent trip to South Carolina that she felt set apart from the community, in Bucks County and in Toronto. She lamented that our children might never find spouses because we were different - not the palest of white, not the straightest of hair or the bluest of eyes. The more I thought about it, the more I think it is we who have closed out others and not vice versa. We are held as different because we stay to ourselves, more than any traits or features we have. If we are part of the group, participate, are welcoming, many of those barriers will collapse."

"And our daughters? Didn't two families reject the engagements of our lovely Martha Sophia and Anna Louisa because of their different appearance? Why would I open my arms to people who rebuffed them?" Mary Sophia was angry.

"You should have seen your daughters shine in Charleston. They grew confident with attention and affection. And for good or bad, Alice fell in love with my father's namesake, that rascal planter Thomas Hanscome Walpole. They found themselves beautiful, and so did others. Yes, we belonged to the mulattos, but no more. The mulattos are a lost society. We chose to be white, now we must claim white society as ours. It is not sufficient just to vote, live in the St. James district or attend the designated white schools. We must jump in, participate in the community, the Anglican Church, give to the community and socialize in the community. If we act as if we belong, we will belong."

"And how do you propose to accomplish this, dear husband?"

"I am accepted as a good businessman. We have plenty of money. I think we should join the Toronto Yacht Club. Elizabeth Sarah was in heaven sailing the schooner in the Sea Islands. Her eyes lit up as she danced to the music in Charleston. Don't you still secretly covet those fine silk dancing dresses?"

"Is it truly me you are selling this idea to?" Mary Sophia asked then laughed.

"Yes, yes, you know me too well, my dear," Thomas said, smiling in return. "I have sold myself on a new beginning. I found a part of me in Charleston that was lost. The fun part. The light part. I love to sail. I love to fish. I love to swim. I love to wager, play cards, laugh and drink with boisterous men. And we could also buy horses and join the equestrian set. I'm told they even had a fox hunt last year, right here in Toronto."

"Oh, Thomas, how can I refuse you?"

"You can't. I love thee, Mary Sophia, mother of my children, but I have missed my playmate. Our children are older. And Alice needs to mother our Arthur, not you. It is our time."

"This is a change, indeed. A second romance for us? I like this idea."

"What do we have to lose? All our children will enjoy playing at the Yacht Club. If we want to join this new era of assimilation, where all are mixing, yes, even the Catholics and the Protestants, the French and the English, this is the time."

"Really? The French and the English, the Catholics and the Protestants all joining in a grand Toronto esprit de corps? I fail to see the acceptance, only the animosity and the pecking order. Next, you'll be claiming we Hanscomes are White Anglo-Saxon Protestants. How ridiculous."

"Well, my father, grandfather and your grandfathers were. Why not? WASPs. I like the tone of it."

"And my Muslim Lucy Moor and my African grandmothers?"

"It's just a smidgeon of color that makes us interesting. My mulatto mother would applaud us. Stop thinking of us as *different*. Think of us as rich, rather than drab common."

"Oh, Thomas, I do love you so. I think you a fool at times, but you do make me smile."

And Mary Sophia more than smiled as Thomas took his bride of twenty-five years to their bed. It was a new beginning for them as a couple.

Life returned to a new normal, and the years passed. They became a *normal family*, a *successful family*, a *good family*, whatever that meant. They joined the Toronto Yacht Club where they played lawn tennis, croquet, whist, swam, danced and sailed in the summers. They boarded horses at the equestrian club. In the winters, they went sleighing and ice skating. And year round, they enjoyed their family music fests and card games. They made friends. They did not talk about their relatives in South Carolina, nor did their new friends speak of their family histories. All families had secrets. Lies of the past became woven into better truths for better futures.

It was a new era. Assimilation.

• • •

Every year, the Hanscomes would take a family vacation by train, boat or both.

"I have a prize for whomever guesses our next vacation destination," Thomas said, enticing his family with a twinkle in his eye, holding his money-filled hand high in the air.

All knew they had to guess correctly, before the conductor yelled *all aboard*, or their father would pocket his money. They only knew their destination would be new. They'd traveled west to Chicago and east to Montreal and even New York City on the new Canadian Southern Railroad.

Trains had enlarged their world, educated them and enhanced trade, and were good for prosperity. Thomas traveled by rail to Pennsylvania to renew his coal business contracts. In Philadelphia, he visited his old sister-in-law, Mary Forten, who lived with Margaretta Forten. He always left sad, as sad as Mary was, but grateful for his large family.

"Time to model your new holiday dresses, girls," called Mary Sophia as she hung the new arrivals from the dressmakers.

Christmas was their favorite family festival, and the modeling of the latest fashions was a traditional part of the excitement and marked the beginning of the social season. Toronto was no longer a dowdy frontier town. Drab grays, replaced by greens, purples, reds and ribbons of every hue, made the holiday parties bright. This year, the twins chose identical, Kelly green velvet fabric decorated with red ribbons. They were so elegant that all the Hanscome women decided to be twins. Their Hanscome entrance at the Cathedral caused quite a stir.

But they were not alone. All the ladies wore voluminous long dresses with bustles, trains of flounces and ruches to draw interest to their backs and low-cut, tight bodices to draw, sometimes too much, attention to their well-bosomed fronts. It was impolite to stare or touch, but admiration was always in vogue. And the men, of course, wore their dark, austere three-pieced suits with crisp top hats, properly removed at church and the dinner table.

Mary Sophia held an annual Christmas tea, touted as one of Toronto's finest. Anna Louisa prepared exquisite English lemon and cranberry tea cakes, buttery shortbreads, flaky biscuits and puffy sweet French pastries in the Lee restaurant days ahead for the event. Their fancy brass girandole candelabra with the crystal prisms from Charleston always graced the table's center.

The Hanscomes invited the city notables to their grand Madrigal feast, complete with a whole boar, the head stuffed and dressed with baked red apples and cinnamon sticks, figgy bread pudding and old English wassail.

They, or their affluence, had been accepted in the community.

William, who also sang Handel's Messiah in the choir at St. James' Cathedral, led the others with his clear baritone as the servers cleared plates only to be replaced with sumptuously filled new ones. The servers sang as they served, and the guests joined in the refrains.

On Christmas Eve, the Inglis' helped them decorate a tall tree with small white candles, gilded pinecones, porcelain birds, and festive paper, popcorn and cranberry garlands. Holiday carolers stopped at the Hanscome door, expecting to be warmed by Thomas' mulled wine, a special recipe he refused to divulge. Soon they were joined by the Gardens and Lees, all bearing gifts. What a full house.

The tree grew fat with presents, one for everyone. The candles were lit and all sang *Oh Come All Ye Faithful.* Toasts were made to the season with eggnog, laced with brandy and sprinkled with nutmeg. After all the gifts were opened, they adjourned to the dining room for their special Christmas goose dinner. But first, they carefully blew out the blazing candles on the magnificent tree. There would be no fires, except for the ones roaring in the fireplaces.

On Christmas Day, the Hanscomes attended the Cathedral services to celebrate the birth of the adored Christ child. And yes, Alice gave thanks for her son, Arthur. She felt she had made the best decision to give him the gift of a normal family life. All was well, *normal,* for a while.

August 3, 1877

"Oh no! Oh no!" cried Mary Ann Hanscome Lee, when she heard the news.

Pray, what happened?

John Garden returned home from work on a summer day to find his Elizabeth Sarah dead. Their son Daniel had found her, lying peaceful in her bed.

"Why didn't I stay home? Why did I allow Elizabeth Sarah to convince me to go to work?" John lamented, beside himself with grief and, yes, guilt.

"Father, she wanted you to work, not wait for her to die," consoled their daughter Joanna. "Her consumption seemed no worse. Please, Father, do not blame yourself," she begged. "Mother knew she was dying. She could barely breathe, and she did not want to be a burden. She was ready. It was too much work for her to live."

"Yes, yes. I knew that, too, but I thought we might have more time together. I wanted more time. Perhaps your mother was ready, but I'm not!" And with that, he held his head with his hands and sobbed.

Were they prepared? No. But was her death sudden? Not really. Elizabeth Sarah had steadily wasted away, until she could no longer rise from bed. Dr. Oliphant said there was no cure for her cancer, and the tuberculosis had already taken its toll. Mary Ann asked the Reverend John Pearson to officiate her sister's funeral and hurriedly purchased two lots at St. James' Cathedral Cemetery. Her husband John Lee suggested she buy plots for the whole family. Mary Ann agreed, but with a sigh.

None of them wanted to accept that death could be lurking behind every cough, fever or ailment and, even sometimes, strike with no warning. Now they were prepared for the inevitable. Elizabeth Sarah's death was a sign to the senior Lees, Hanscomes and Gardens of the obvious. They were getting older. They were all healthy, but death would claim them all, much sooner than later. They were coming to that age when their own mortality could not be denied.

And Thomas? How did he take his sister's death? He needed to accept what he had no control over - the passage of time. He would cherish the image of his sister's bronzed skin sailing on the Stono, eating oysters and grits, dancing at the Brown Fellowship Society balls, her marriage to mulatto planter John Garden and their lovely mansion in Charleston. He appreciated their time alone together as brother and sister on their return trip to Charleston in that fantasy land of their youth. As the years passed, the glory of the Golden Age of Charleston grew even greater in his memory. He tried to block out its demise after the War.

"It is fitting we die together as we have lived," Mary Ann stoically said. "I will miss Elizabeth Sarah, but she welcomed death. She had been bed-ridden too long. Still, I had hoped we could celebrate her sixtieth birthday. I think we should have a party for her anyway. She would like that."

Thomas loved all of his sisters and brothers. He loved his white father and his mulatto mother. But more important than the past was the future, his children's future. He wanted them to thrive, but they were stumbling.

January 20, 1878

"Happy Birthday to you! Happy Birthday to you! Happy Birthday, dear Art..."

Arthur was no longer Wee Arthur or even Little Arthur. He was twelve-years-old and demanded to be called Art. And rightfully so. He had recently celebrated his first Communion and considered himself a young man.

"Blow out the candles and make a wish!" entreated his *Connie*, the name he called his big sister, Alice.

And what did he wish for? Secretly, he wished to be an engineer, but for starters, he would settle for a railroad ticket – to anywhere. He longed to ride the rails. He studied trains - learned how the rotary snow ploughs cleared the tracks in the winter, how the bridges and tunnels were constructed, how the brakes and engines worked, what the engineers and conductors did and, yes, how the coal was loaded. Thomas had a contract to supply the trains with coal and allowed his boys to tag along when he visited the station. While Thomas conducted business, his sons pestered the engineers and conductors. But now, only young Arthur would traipse after Thomas. Art even sought out the tramps in their camps and quizzed them about their travels. By this time, the older two boys had lost interest in trains. William and Harry loved music and the arts.

"Boys, boys! Coal is how we make our living," repeatedly lectured their father. "The point is to gain new coal contracts, work with the suppliers, manage the barges, order, transport and deliver the goods, collect the fees and become, yes, wealthy. I will not be able to support you forever. Gone are the cotton kings of the south and timber princes of the north. Coal is the future. Vast wealth can be ours." However, Thomas's wisdom was lost on his sons, and their eyes glazed over with his continual *Coal is King* speech.

William, twenty-two, had worked with his father since he matriculated, but truly was not enamored with the coal business. William was personable, but he was no salesman. Honestly? He had no ambition. He was content making deliveries with the Hanscome Coal Company wagon and chatting, far too long, with the customers. What else did he enjoy? He read voraciously, played the organ, piano, sang a hearty baritone in the church choir and volunteered at cultural events and city concerts. Did he have an interest in marrying? Apparently not. His spirit required little except laughter. He was a gentleman, content socializing with people.

"Coal, Father, is a dirty, smelly substance. If you must know the truth, I prefer not to be around it," he said, as kindly as possible. He did love his father, but really – *Coal is King*? How could his father entertain such a silly notion? But then, how was his father different from the other businessmen at the yacht club, all bragging about their achievements over too many cocktails? His talk of coal was all too mundane, predictable and boring, thought William. At church, William prayed for an alternative calling:

Dear lord, what is my life's mission? But no answer ever came. Finally, he gave up asking.

And Harry? At seventeen, he had little interest in anything except his sketchbook. He worked after school for his two Uncle Johns. He painted signs and sketched likenesses of new machines for John Garden, food menus for John and Mary Ann Lee, and emblazoned the Hanscome barges and storefront with his fine calligraphy, *Hanscome Coal Company*. Was that his heart's desire? Definitely not. He aspired to be a serious painter. He was not affable, like William. He was quiet and reserved, except on canvas. Girls? He had no interest. He was content alone.

"What has happened to our sons? Ambition is not an evil!" Thomas lamented to Mary Sophia.

Perhaps they'd had too many older sisters cooing and clucking around them. Perhaps they'd had no hardships threatening their existence. Thomas had once been a young dandy, true, but he had changed. At church, he prayed his sons would find their way. Was he making excuses? He didn't know. Thomas hoped he could interest Arthur in his business. Yes, Arthur was a possible business heir.

And the Hanscome girls? Spinsters all. After their initial disappointments in love, they gave up hope that their *interesting* attractiveness would be accepted by other proper families. Well, Naomi at fourteen was still in school, but Mary Sophia's and Thomas' hope for marriages for the older girls waned. Would that change? Probably not. They were in their thirties, and socially, *the die was cast*. Alice was content staying at home with the love of her life, Arthur. Martha Sophia had taken a position at the library and shared with William his love of books. Anna Louisa continued her interest in food and helped the Lees in their restaurant and boarding house. The lovely and musically talented twins, Virginia and Eugenia, would turn thirty this year.

Virginia was engaged several years ago to a young man from an acceptable family who she met at an ice skating club. His fine figure skating had captured her heart. Mary Sophia had been ecstatic; one of her girls would marry. She threw herself into extensive and expensive wedding preparations. However, when Eugenia grew despondent, Virginia canceled her engagement. Just like that. Virginia, too, it turns out, did not want to leave her sister. They were too content with each other. Twins were sometimes inseparable.

"I do believe it is a good thing we bought this huge house, Mary Sophia," reflected Thomas. "I don't believe any of our children will ever leave it."

"Thomas, I worry. What will happen to them when we're gone? Will they be able to afford this home?"

"Don't worry about their welfare, Mary Sophia. I intend to provide for all of them. In the meantime, let's just enjoy our family."

And they did.

Chapter 2

Integration
Summer 1878
Toronto

Bad news and good news arrived from Margaretta Forten. Mary, yes, their sweet Aunt Mary, had died. Margaretta attributed Mary's death to grief. Mary had recently learned her second son, Edmund Quincy Forten, had died in England. He was young, too young. She never recovered. Simply, she had lost too much – her first husband Joseph and daughter Ann on Woodland Plantation, then her second husband Robert and both their sons. Charlotte hurried to her dear stepmother's side from Washington, DC, but to no avail. It was as though Mary looked forward to being reunited with her dear departed ones. Margaretta said she died with a smile on her lips, peaceful.

And Margaretta's good news? Charlotte was to be married to the Reverend Francis James Grimke, a Charleston mulatto and younger half-brother of Charlotte's two white abolitionist friends, Angelina and Sarah, better known as the Grimke sisters.

Thomas smiled when he read the news about the Grimke family, most well-known for their Charleston scandal, similar to the Thomas Hanscome-Nancy Randall love affair. Judge Grimke, his very own father's friend and executor, had two families in Charleston - his planter white family and his slave and mulatto family. It was unheard of for young women of an old, refined planter family to attack their *peculiar institution* of slavery, their source of wealth, and to assert their independence as women. But to the horror of their mother, the Grimke sisters did just that.

They left Charleston in the 1830's to join the Quaker abolitionists in Philadelphia. They were disgusted with slavery and their slave beating, slave-raping angry brother, Henry. After their father died in 1819, his young slave son, Francis, was to have been emancipated, as per Judge Grimke's will. But did that happen? No. Francis' very own, white half-brother Henry kept him a slave until after the War, almost forty years after their father died.

That very same Francis was not to be held down. He rose to graduate from Howard University and Princeton Theological Seminary. In Philadelphia, he was reunited with his half sisters, Angelina and Sarah, who of course introduced him to their friend, Charlotte Forten. He became a Presbyterian minister in Washington DC. Over the years, Francis' life had intertwined with Charlotte's.

What success stories. What a love story. And the best news was that the Hanscomes were all invited to their wedding.

Were the Hanscome girls jealous? If they were, no one mentioned it. They were too excited for Charlotte and hopeful for themselves. She was forty-one years old, considered too old to be a bride. The wedding date was set for December, 1878.

And Thomas? He was pleased that Charlotte had decided to include her *white* relatives, as she called them. Oh how Charlotte had sparred with her Uncle Thomas' decision to change their racial designation. Were they actually related? No. Charlotte was Robert Forten's daughter by his first wife, but Thomas' sister-in-law Mary had raised her stepdaughter Charlotte on their Buck's

County family farm. Thomas was thrilled to be invited. Secretly, he had always wanted to see Washington DC.

When he left South Carolina more than thirty years ago, mulattos and freedmen were not welcome in the Capitol. Then, the *in-vogue* Congressional plan was to export the unwanted freedmen, way too plentiful, back to Africa. *Recolonization* was the perfect solution.

December 1878
Washington DC

The church bells gloriously rang as Charlotte Forten Grimke and the Reverend Francis James Grimke exited his Presbyterian Church. Married! Hundreds of well-wishers lined the church entrance throwing rice, the old southern symbol of prosperity. What a jovial mixture of white and black, old and young, southern and northern. It was a model wedding of integration, yes, the new wave of future equality.

Virginia, Eugenia, William, Harry, Naomi and Arthur Hanscome looked wide-eyed at the spectacle. Unlike their older sisters, who had been to Philadelphia and Charleston, they had never witnessed such an integrated crowd or such a grand wedding. In Toronto, people stuck with their own kind - their own color, their own religion, their own language. Soon, Harry was capturing all with his new camera.

"I am so happy you came to my wedding!" Charlotte said as she warmly greeted her old mentors, John Greenleaf Whittier, Wendell Phillips and William Lloyd Garrison.

"Yes, we all rode together by train from Boston. What a godsend that invention was. At our ancient age, we'd never have survived a journey in winter by carriage or sea. And here we are, seeing our Charlotte married. We wanted you to know how proud your grandfather, James Forten, and your dear father, Robert, would have been to see you marry such a fine man. It is unfortunate that Sarah Grimke has passed. Didn't she introduce you to her half-brother, today your groom, in Philadelphia years ago?"

"Yes, she did, but it wasn't until I returned to Charleston after the war to teach that Francis and I renewed our acquaintance. And it wasn't until I moved to Washington DC that we decided to marry, old as we are."

"We admire you. You have made a difference with your life. The abolitionist cause succeeded. I hope you now have time to continue your fine writing and poetry, dear Charlotte. It is a gift few have," said Wendell Phillips.

"I will, but there is still so much work to be done. Slaves may be freed, but prejudice runs rampant. Lynchings chase our people from their land and the polls, while Francis and I stay safe in our nation's Capitol. At least here the men can vote and receive equal pay for equal work, but women, regardless of color, also need a voice. Next, I will become a suffragette like Sarah Grimke."

"Please, don't get her started on inequities and atrocities on our wedding day, gentlemen," interjected the good Reverend with a smile. "They will be here tomorrow, unfortunately. We do what we can, but not today."

"Yes, of course, Francis. I see Angelina Grimke, your esteemed new sister-in-law, waving from across the room. We shall talk another day, dear Charlotte. Again, our best to you," said William Lloyd Garrison.

Other notables, Washington congressmen and clergy, in turn, were welcomed by the bride and groom. And the Hanscome families were reunited with their Charleston sister, Louisa Rebecca. Where was brother James? He had not been invited. He refused to align himself with the abolitionist crowd.

"Oh, dear sister," cried Mary Sophia as she embraced her sister-in-law, Louisa Rebecca. It had been thirty-three years. When Charlotte Forten returned to teach in Charleston after the war, the two became friends. And Charlotte desperately needed friends. Her abolitionist cause had only closed doors for her in

Charleston. Of course, Louisa Rebecca would be honored to attend her wedding. She only lamented Elizabeth Sarah's absence.

Dark and handsome Harry hardly noticed the flirtatious glances of the young beautiful girls. Instead, he captured the bride and the groom and lined up the older generation Hanscomes for family photographs. Charlotte, the honorary Hanscome, and Francis were first, followed by Louisa Rebecca and William, Mary Ann and John and Thomas and Mary Sophia. Notably absent were Elizabeth Sarah, who had died, and James, persona non grata.

"Mary Sophia, please introduce me to your other children," Louisa Rebecca said. "I've already renewed my acquaintance with Alice, Anna Louisa and Martha Sophia from their trip to Charleston." Louisa Rebecca warmly embraced them all. When she came to young Arthur, she impolitely stared. Finally, she stammered, "Mary Sophia, Art resembles my father with his sandy, blonde hair and blue eyes. I never thought any of us would have such a miracle child. What a gift!"

"Yes, each of our children is a unique blend, but undoubtedly Art is the fairest."

Then Louisa Rebecca greeted her other sister Mary Ann and all the rest of the northern Hanscomes.

Later, when Louisa Rebecca was alone with her husband, William DeCosta, she said, "Did you see young Arthur? I was shocked by his resemblance to a Charleston youth."

"Yes, you remarked Art looked like his grandfather, Thomas Hanscome. Except for his fairness and blue eyes, I really don't see it."

"Yes, I did say that. When I saw Art, I was at a loss for words. In truth, Arthur is the true likeness of another man, a young man."

"And who might that be?" William asked, most curious.

"Thomas Hanscome Walpole."

"Oh!" And now William was equally shocked. "We certainly don't socialize with him, but yes, I see the resemblance, now that you mention it. He has done a good job reclaiming Creekside and is planting cotton again."

"*Oh*, is shockingly correct. I wonder what truly happened to Mary Sophia's pregnancy. It was the reason she couldn't come to Charleston. I do believe that Art is Alice's rightful child."

"And if that is true, of what import is that?"

"None really. None. Except that perhaps Alice should have remained with young Walpole, as his mistress. It is a shame none of my lovely nieces married. At least Alice had a child, someone to love. Do you think I should ask Mary Ann?"

"No, leave it alone, Louisa Rebecca. It serves no purpose," warned her husband. "If Mary Sophia wanted you to know, she would have written you."

Would Louisa Rebecca heed her husband's wisdom?

The wedding came to an end, but the reunion with old family and friends continued as they took in the sights of the Capitol. Did they all stay in the same hotel, ride the same streetcars, eat in the same restaurants? Yes, they did. Due to a law passed in 1872, Washington DC was integrated. It was a center for African American culture and education. Francis Grimke had attended Howard University before he went to Princeton. And Charlotte worked for the Treasury Department where her wages were tied to her position, not her color. Washington DC was the hopeful place to be for the up-and-coming, educated freedmen. The Grimke's integrated guest list was a joy to all who had worked so diligently for freedom. Next, their mission was to eradicate prejudice and integrate the races everywhere.

"Mary Ann, I wanted to ask you a question. Do you think Arthur resembles our father?" Louisa Rebecca asked.

"In that he is fair and blue-eyed, yes, but many of our children have his blue eyes. I think my Drayton actually resembles him more. Why do you ask?"

"This is a delicate issue, but he is the true likeness of a young Charleston man, a man Alice had a serious flirtation with when she was in Charleston."

"Alice had a Charleston flirtation? I was unaware of that. I do know Thomas broke Alice's heart when he refused to allow her to marry *Howling Wolf Harry*." She smiled. "It must be your imagination, sister. I saw our pregnant sister, at least weekly. Alice was never pregnant. But I do want to hear more about her serious Charleston flirtation."

"It must be just a coincidence, Art's resemblance. The flirtation was serious in that Alice stayed at Creekside with young Thomas Hanscome Walpole. Her father went to fetch her, and she refused to leave his side. Then young Walpole was going to Toronto with them, to marry Alice. But in the end, Alice boarded the ship alone."

"That saddens me and hurts my feelings. I never knew that. How could Mary Sophia or Elizabeth Sarah have kept that hidden from me? And Anna Louisa has worked side-by-side with me, for years in our restaurant, and never mentioned Alice's Charleston broken heart. We are family. I thought we were confidants!"

"I wish I had never brought up my silly observation. Perhaps Alice swore her Aunt Elizabeth Sarah and her sisters to secrecy on their return voyage. Please don't feel hurt, dear sister."

"I won't feel left out if you promise to visit us, soon. If you wait for any of our children's weddings, well, that may never happen. And, we don't want to all die before you have a chance to see Toronto."

"I will discuss it with William. His construction business is doing well, so I don't think he would take the time."

"Perhaps James could accompany you," Mary Ann said.

"James is quite busy. His business partnership with William did not work out. You know he divorced Hattie or vice versa. Then he and his third wife Emma had four children, in eight short years. He is barely able to provide for his family. I think he would feel bad if I even asked him."

"That is a shame."

"It is more than a shame, Mary Ann. Poverty has claimed South Carolina and James. But I see James' first wife, Serena, and his daughter, Sarah, frequently. They are still ecstatic about their emancipation, but not their poverty. You know, like us, the source of their wealth had been their slaves. Sarah is busy working on the cause of integration."

"From the looks of Washington DC, it looks like integration has already happened."

"I think this is a sham, purely window-dressing. I do not think integration will ever happen in Charleston. No, not in my lifetime. The white planters have taken back the land that was given to the freedmen. The Negros are sharecropping. And all are smoldering with rage. Is the War over? The south is a powder keg ready to explode, again."

"You could join us in Toronto and claim whiteness," suggested Mary Ann, hopefully.

"We are doing well, and our Jewish DeCosta family is in Charleston. I doubt William would leave."

Chapter 3

The Proper Social Order
1879
Toronto

Charlotte Forten's wedding was an omen for the Hanscomes. The happy new year was rung in with another wedding announcement. But was it a fortuitous match?

"Father, Mother, I want to introduce my betrothed, Rhoda Baldwin Cooper!" a announced a beaming William.

Silence.

What a shock! Yes, William had asked his mother if he could bring a church lady home for Sunday dinner. Mary Sophia thought it might be a lady from the choir or his chamber music ensemble, but he had never shown a romantic interest in anyone before. Marriage? How ridiculous. However, his parents gathered their proper, graceful wits about them, and a quiet dinner ensued. The younger Hanscome children kicked each other under the table, trying to muffle their laughter and excitement. William and Rhoda had everyone's full attention. Yes, indeed.

"How long have you two been acquainted?" Mary Sophia asked, with her most polite smile.

"We met a year ago, at church. Rhoda sings alto in the choir. After the Baldwins moved here from England, they joined St. James' congregation," William replied, grinning from ear-to-ear.

"Rhoda, what do your parents think of this engagement?" Thomas asked, trying to be hopeful.

"We have not told them yet. We thought we'd give you the first honor," beamed Rhoda, unabashedly glancing at her fiancée.

"It is usual etiquette for the man to ask the lady's father first for her hand in marriage," Mary Sophia said.

"Yes, we are aware of that, but since I am a widow, my husband having died in England before we emigrated, this is not my first marriage. Now, I make my own decisions. I thought we might discuss our decision with you, first."

Silence.

Rhoda returned Mary Sophia's smile. It was clear from her tone they were not asking anyone's permission. They were simply declaring their intentions. No, their approval was not sought or considered necessary. William had selected a direct, not unlikeable, but very direct lady to be his wife.

"And do you have children from your marriage to Mr. Cooper?" Mary Sophia asked, trying to be tactful.

"No, my husband became quite ill soon after we married and died within the year."

"I am sorry to hear his life was cut short at such a young age."

"Actually, he was fifty when we married, much older than I, but not too young for death to claim him. My guess is that he was about your age, Thomas." Rhoda met Thomas' gaze directly, eye-to-eye. "I must also tell you I am ten years older than William, thirty-two, no longer a young girl. But we hope to have a family, William and I - certainly not as many children as the Lord has given you, but we would welcome a few."

Silence.

His older sisters lowered their eyes, trying to hide their smiles. What was their younger brother thinking? Rhoda was old! She was closer to their age. And listen to her speak for him, as if he had lost his tongue. Her bluntness bordered on rudeness and, at best, was not proper. This was the most interesting dinner. Yes, indeed. They smiled, intrigued with this new turn of events.

"William, how do you propose to provide for Mrs. Cooper?" Thomas asked, wondering how well this Rhoda knew their William. The truth was William lacked ambition. Pleasant, yes, musically talented, yes, that was their William. Thomas also knew how little he paid him for his coal deliveries – hardly enough to sustain a family.

"Rhoda says we can make this work, Father. She has a small inheritance from her deceased husband, lives with her parents and teaches school. This is a beginning, and I am young. Please don't worry father, money is not important to us. We want you to bless our wedding. We plan to be married next June."

Pray tell, how did this romance blossom? Rhoda had simply fallen in love with the melodic timber and conviction of William's heaven-sent baritone and how his fingers gracefully, strongly and, yes, perfectly, flew over the keyboard. While he was in love with his music, Rhoda was falling in love with him. At times, she watched his skill so intently she forgot to sing her part in the choir. At night, she had torrid dreams of his fingers caressing her body with as great a precision and stamina as he played his music. She awoke from her dreams, flushed, out of breath and finally determined she must have him. Yes, right then and there, Rhoda decided she could not live without his arms around her.

The next night after choir practice, Rhoda waited until the room had cleared, except for William who was still at the organ, straightening his music scores. She didn't think, a rarity for her. Instead, she stealthily crept up to his stool, whisked it around, lifted her skirts, straddled his lap, crushed his ribs and placed her eager lips on his.

And poor William's response? Did he declare Rhoda a wanton hussy and shove her away with great disdain? Oh no, William was inexperienced in the ways of love, but he was no fool. He soon moved her to the floor, found his stride and matched her ardor. And just like his music, William practiced and practiced until he reached perfection. Soon, he didn't know what he loved more, his music or Rhoda.

And Rhoda? She never liked to lose any contest. Soon, William Hanscome was hers.

After their surprise engagement dinner, William left to walk Rhoda home. Mary Sophia and Thomas, in total amazement, retired early to their room. They needed to talk.

"Well, Thomas! Well, well!" Mary Sophia huffed, collapsing on her chaise lounge. "Well!"

"Is that all you can say? *Well*? This won't do. This marriage will never happen!" Thomas shouted. "I will speak with William tomorrow and stop this nonsense engagement."

"Thomas, Thomas. Contain your anger. Look at our family. None of our girls are married. None! Do you want to have bona-fide grandchildren or not? Rhoda is a determined young woman, determined to marry our William. She's English, educated, blue-eyed and fair-skinned, as white as the snow in winter. William is not ambitious, but if anyone can inspire him to provide, it just might be this Rhoda."

Thomas glared at Mary Sophia. They had few disagreements in their married life. Would this be a serious injury to their harmony?

"She may be white, but she has ice running through her veins. If you want to kindly call her *determined* go ahead, but William will lose his gregarious nature within months of a marriage to her. Is that want you want for our son? Shrew is a better adjective for this Rhoda Baldwin Cooper. We need to find out more about her family."

"Perhaps you are working yourself up into a lather for nothing. If you truly want to discourage this wedding, why don't you just allude to our proud mulatto lineage when we meet the Baldwins?" Mary Sophia's rare sarcasm was most cutting.

"Wonderful idea, dear wife. I believe I will do just that!" Thomas' sarcasm was even sharper.

"And why not? You chased off two of Alice's suitors! Then Anna Louisa's and Martha Sophia's suitors' families rejected us. Let this engagement happen. Do not interfere, please," Mary Sophia begged. "I want to have a normal family life. I want grandchildren!"

Did Thomas agree to meet Mrs. Cooper's family? Yes, he did.

"Thank you for the lovely dinner," said Mary Sophia as they settled into the Baldwin's parlor for the after-dinner wedding discussion.

Thank goodness Rhoda's younger brother excused himself. He had monopolized the dinner table conversation with his future plans to own a farm, as his family had in England. Not that he minded working for his parents in the family grocery store. Finally, Rhoda interrupted him, "Enough, dear brother. William and I want to discuss our wedding plans, please, and you are monopolizing the conversation."

"Don't you think a Cathedral wedding will be fitting for our children, since that is where they met?" Mrs. Baldwin asked. "We, of course, as the parents of the bride, will pay for the minister and reception in the Church Hall, but we think it should be a small wedding, just immediate family," said Mrs. Baldwin with a courteous smile. "As you know our Rhoda has been married before. We think a big ceremony would be, you know, improper."

"Oh, Mother, that is so ridiculous," countered Rhoda. "William has not been married and his large family enjoys celebrations. What do you want, dear William?"

"Whatever you want, Rhoda." Yes, William was good at pleasing his fiancée.

"Since you leave the decision to me, let me paint you a picture of my dream wedding." And, just like her father-in-law to be, Rhoda grew expansive and direct in her oratory.

"Tell me if it seems in poor taste. I'd like to wear an ivory, not white, but an ivory long dress and walk down the aisle on your arm, dear father. I'd like your sisters to be bridesmaids, your brothers all groomsmen, along with my brothers. I want the church filled with flowers and the reception lit with hundreds of candles. I want to dance in the moonlight with you, dear William. I know a larger wedding can be an added expense, but since I am teaching, I can help pay for my extravaganza. How does that sound, William?"

"It sounds wonderful. I have the perfect music scores to try out on the Cathedral's new pipe organ."

"But dear, since you will be the groom, someone else will have to play."

"Yes, of course, dear."

"And if you'd prefer a reception at the Yacht Club, we can make that our gift," added Mary Sophia. She was warming to Rhoda and appreciated her desire for beauty. Frugality, such a Canadian virtue, grew tedious.

"Before we formally announce this engagement, do you Baldwins, have any reservations?" Thomas asked.

"No, we think your William is a fine, young man for our Rhoda. Her first husband was too old for her."

"And do you expect to have children?" Thomas asked of William, but Rhoda responded first.

"Yes, of course," Rhoda said. "We both adore children. It's why I teach school."

"And do you know our racial background, Rhoda? Do you know that it is quite possible for the two of you to have a dark-skinned child?" Thomas asked.

"What do you mean?" Rhoda's mother asked.

"I mean that we have African blood as part of our heritage, Mrs. Baldwin," stated Thomas with a smile. "Our mothers are the origin of William's darker complexion."

"You mean a Negro heritage, don't you, Mr. Hanscome," interjected Rhoda, meeting his eyes directly. "When I last saw Negro blood, it was as red as ours. And yes, I am aware of your lineage. William and I have talked about his family history. I find it to be fascinating and have no concerns. Do you, Mother?"

"Well, it is a surprise to hear, but of course not. I have no reservations," Rhoda's mother said, quickly regaining her composure from the shock. Certainly, Mr. Hanscome's admission was hardly proper, but now, she could hardly take back her consent. She felt trapped and angry with her daughter for omitting this important detail. Why did her Rhoda always challenge the proper social order? Oh well, there was no reason to be angry, not really. Mrs. Baldwin was usually an agreeable and very tactful person, much like William. But she also disliked being surprised and ill-prepared for her best response. "I had wondered if you had a Spanish, Indian or perhaps Moorish background, Mr. Hanscome. I do appreciate your addressing that question, however, make no mistake, we would welcome a grandchild of any complexion."

And with that Mary Sophia beamed, William and Rhoda beamed and Mr. Baldwin smiled. And Thomas? He frowned. His plan was foiled. Why did he dislike this Rhoda so?

On the way home, Mary Sophia challenged him. "And since you were so boldly divulging our family heritage, why didn't you tell Mrs. Baldwin that my grandmother, Lucy Moor, was a Muslim and that we all owned slaves! I think your plan is to chase away any marriage prospects. And why? Well then, you can keep all your children tethered to you, locked in our house, so you won't have to face the fact we are growing older. It is their time."

"You are being ridiculous. I am only looking out for their best interests."

"Let William be a man. Let him create the new Hanscome lineage. Let William go! If you don't, we will become extinct - not ravaged by disease as in Charleston, but because you are so selfish!"

Silence.

"Oh, I am sorry, Thomas. My words were unkind. I do know you love William and all of our children. It is simply time they became adults. Remember how we hadn't even reached our age of majority when we married, then we had Alice and Edwin and moved. We would now be penniless in Charleston, if your mother Ann hadn't pushed us from her nest. Help me help our children to leave. Please."

May 10, 1880

The wedding went off in great style. Rhoda knew exactly what she wanted and took great care with every detail.

"Do you, Rhoda Baldwin Cooper, take you, William Kissick Hanscome, to be your wedded husband?"

"I do," she replied. "Yes, I definitely do!"

The Toronto Yacht Club was ideal for the wedding reception. Rhoda, it goes without saying, definitely preferred the yacht club over the church hall. William had no preference. He was practicing, *Whatever you'd like, dear*. Thomas didn't care anymore, either; he was learning to appreciate Rhoda's directness. He was also proudly footing the bill. And Mary Sophia appreciated Rhoda's flare, especially the color and pageantry she, too, craved. Rhoda certainly wasn't drab.

The slight May breezes, warm sunshine and blue sky created the perfect wedding ambience. The music played softly on the outside patio as the guests drank champagne and waited in the reception line. And it promised to be a star-studded sky for the dance.

"What lovely bridesmaids in their fuchsia colored dresses," commented one guest.

"I found it all a bit bold," disdained another.

"A widow in a long, white gown? Bridesmaids attired in bright colors, holding multicolored flowers for bouquets? Tradition demands a virginal and demure pageant, even if the bride is not. What was that Rhoda thinking?" criticized yet another guest.

"I hear the wedding was first planned for June, but that it needed to be rushed to an earlier date. Mary Sophia may be a grandmother earlier than expected," winked an additional gossip.

"It certainly is not in good taste to flaunt the rules. There is a proper social order. Weddings are to precede pregnancies."

"Who cares? Mary Sophia is ecstatic that one of her children has actually married," excused another.

"All those girls and not one marriage, poor Mary Sophia," tsk-tsked another.

"It's interesting that none of the Hanscome sons resemble each other. I wonder if any were adopted."

"Or perhaps Mary Sophia was friskier than we thought," teased a third guest.

"And what will William do for a living? I hear he abjures the coal business."

"Well, if he chooses church music for his vocation, his wife better not stop teaching. They'll be as poor as church mice."

"If she is with child, as you suggest, she will have to end her teaching assignment. It is not proper for a pregnant woman to teach."

"Disgrace or not, the school board doesn't allow it."

"The Baldwins seem like a good family, but then they only recently moved to Toronto. Mr. Baldwin's grocery store seems to be doing well."

"I hear the young couple will live with the Baldwins."

"Oh, that's a temporary arrangement. The Hanscomes are giving them a home for their wedding gift. Not a mansion, like theirs near the water, but a nice three-bedroom house in Etobicoke, with a lovely garden, adjoining carriage house and, yes, indoor plumbing."

"How fortunate for them."

"Yes, the Gardens have expanded their business to include water closets and heated bath tubs. Their sons have become master plumbers."

"And you should see the new bathrooms in the Lee Boarding House, now the Lee Hotel. It is so modern."

"Rhoda and William are taking a honeymoon to Niagara Falls. How romantic."

"He can sing to her at the top of his lungs and no one else will hear."

July 1880

"It's a boy!" proudly announced Alice, who had assisted Rhoda's delivery.

"What do you want to name him, dear Rhoda?" William asked as he tenderly held his son.

"That I leave to you, dear husband. You can name the boys, and I will name the girls." Rhoda was high in color, spirits and energy. She could have delivered a litter.

"Thomas, after my father," suggested William.

"Hmm. How about William Thomas? First your name, then his grandfather's. Do you like that?"

"Yes, I actually do. How nice to have a son named after me."

And the Hanscomes? Were they excited?

"You have a grandson, Thomas. Now aren't you thrilled?" teased Mary Sophia. "And his name is William Thomas."

"I hope the baby's black as coal," Thomas teased back, but with a smile. Yes, he had warmed to his daughter-in-law. She was direct, true, but she also was kind, a real worker, and William was finally taking an interest in the coal business.

"You do realize, Thomas, that Rhoda is a great deal like your dear mother, Ann. She just knows what she wants and likes to spar with you."

And the rest of the family? Alice and Rhoda had become good friends. Alice had dreams of another child, but found being an aunt was a fine substitute. All the sisters vied for best aunt position. Did they lament not being married? Not really, but not ever holding a baby? Well, that was more than a disappointment. Now, they had one. Did anyone wonder if Rhoda would want to share her babe? No, they did not. They would stake their rights as aunts.

And the Baldwins? Secretly, Mrs. Baldwin was happy wee William was born fair, well, fair-enough. Time would tell whom he would really favor. Her prayers for a healthy, *normal* looking child were answered. What a relief.

And Rhoda? She managed to complete the school term, hiding her protruding belly, but the school board asked for her resignation for the fall term. Did Rhoda mind? Heaven's no. She was actually pleased.

Rhoda loved making a home. She was never without a project. First, she painted the entire house, then she painted murals of English pastoral scenes in the dining room and regal lions, wise owls and the Aesop's Fables characters in wee Will's room. Young Harry, nineteen, enthusiastically sketched the characters, and Rhoda painted them. What a team. Rhoda's mother thought the baby was born too early due to her constant activity. Rhoda laughed and just waved her mother's concerns away. She had plans to work in her garden with wee Willie tied to her back.

Yes, Rhoda enlivened their lives, and so did wee Willie.

1881

"Happy Birthday to You, Happy Birthday to You, Happy Birthday, Dear Willie, Happy Birthday to You!"

The Hanscomes and Baldwins sang the Happy Birthday Song and gathered around their child star as Harry, most professionally, snapped picture after picture with his new camera.

"Please try to get one picture that has both a smile and wide-open eyes," requested Rhoda as she orchestrated the poses. "Let's see - Willie eating cake, Willie and his parents, Willie with his grandparents, Willie with his aunts and uncles, Willie opening his presents. Do you have them all, dear Harry?"

Harry, the young man of few words, just nodded in agreement as he clicked the shutter. Rhoda felt Harry's sketches of her babe deserved to be captured in an oil painting. In spite of their opposite temperaments, or perhaps because of them, they'd developed a fine rapport. Harry was teaching Rhoda how to draw and she, in turn, became his confidante and champion. He opened his photography, design and art studio in the loft of his father's coal building. His talents in photography, signs, calligraphy and mural paintings gained recognition and clientele but, alas, his scenic oil paintings remained unsold. The truth be known, Harry was saving his photography money to study in Paris. On the day Thomas called Harry's art ambition a *pie in the sky* dream, Harry moved quietly out of the house and into his loft.

"Industry, machines, not art, are the new future, son!" his father advised, but his words fell on deaf ears.

And Mary Sophia, what did she think? She felt sorry for poor Thomas, who only wanted his sons to join him in the coal business. He wanted them to be ambitious, but then, since they gave them everything, what was their motivation? At times, her husband was his old light-hearted self, but she saw it less and less. She missed her fun Charleston dandy.

William was having more success at coal sales, but she knew his heart was not in his work. His eyes lit up on Sundays when he could sing in the choir or when he played the piano or organ in afternoon concerts. Music was in his soul, an appreciation Rhoda shared. As Mary Sophia watched the young married couple at Willie's party, she thought they were a fine match. Secretly, she hoped for more grandchildren.

"The boy will be spoiled with all these gifts," said Thomas with a satisfied smile. He was the one who had given Willie the lavish toy train set.

"He's a bit young for this train set, don't you agree, Father?" laughed fifteen-year-old Arthur. "I think we should set it up."

And not only did they set it up, they played with it, too. Then it was Mary Sophia's turn to laugh. Her old Thomas was actually making train noises, "CHOO, Choo…Choo Choo…clickety clack."

"Mother, I'd like to leave the party, if I may. Michael is here to take me to the dance at the Yacht Club," Naomi said.

"Yes, of course, but invite him in first to greet everyone."

What a nice boy, young man really, Mary Sophia thought. Harry had recently painted a new sign for Michael's father's clothing store, right next door to Thomas Inglis' barbershop. It read, *Smith and Son*. Since then, the two boys had become fast friends.

Harry vouched for Michael's good character, and his family had recently joined the yacht club, so they must be a good family. Even Thomas thought he would make a fine husband - imagine that. Mary Sophia just hoped that Michael and Naomi weren't spending too much time together, but then Harry was their chaperone.

Still, Mary Sophia worried aloud, I do hope they become engaged soon.

Naomi was as fair as Harry was dark. She was a true beauty. However, Mary Sophia secretly found Harry the most beautiful, if one could say that about a young man. He had big blue eyes set off by long black lashes and curly, black hair, but it was his white smile that dazzled against his dark skin that truly charmed her. It was a shame he was so shy, thought his mother. Girls would look at him, and Harry would simply look away. It was nice that Michael and Naomi invited him along on their outings, otherwise, he would have no social life.

"Michael proposed to me!" Naomi proudly announced to her older sisters when she returned from the dance. "Promise to keep it a secret. He wants to formally ask our father for my hand, but he gave me a ring tonight. Look, see how it shines!"

Her five sisters shrieked, hugged Naomi and appropriately ogled her diamond ring. Were they jealous? No, they were frightened. After Naomi waltzed away, the five sisters held hands and prayed:

Please, dear God, have this engagement be acceptable to our father. Take away this Hanscome curse.

The Hanscome girls' luck needed to change.

And did it? It did!

The families met, and Naomi's and Michael's wedding date was set for the following June. Good things were in store for the Hanscomes. Weddings! Babies! Wealth! What could be better?

"Mother, Father," William said. "Rhoda and I have news for you."

"Oh good," thought Mary Sophia as she sat down. "Is another baby on the way?"

"We are moving," William said.

"Moving where?" Thomas asked. "Do you need a larger house?"

"No, Father, our lovely home will be hard for us to leave. We are moving with the Baldwins to Minnesota," William answered.

"Minnesota? That is unsettled territory, uncivilized! Why?" A crest-fallen Mary Sophia asked. "It will have no music, no culture, none of the things you love."

"Well, it has been a state of the United States for almost twenty-five years," replied factual Rhoda. "My family wants to farm, and the land is inexpensive." On a softer note she added, "I am truly sorry if this hurts you. It has been a hard decision for us."

"Wasn't the coal business starting to interest you?" Thomas asked.

"Father, it isn't that I dislike the coal business. I find I am just not cut out of the same cloth as you. I am not ambitious. I have no need to strive for more, for better – to achieve. Rhoda and I have enjoyed tending our garden together. I want to try my hand at farming, with the Baldwins."

"And if you don't find farming to your liking? Then what? It is hard work, and despite your best effort, harvests hinge on the whims of nature. I know farming, son," replied Thomas. "Finding a true calling is rare and available only to the truly wealthy. This is the age of industry, son, not farming."

"Of course, we want you to be happy, but I am so sad to think we won't be part of your lives. I don't think I can bear to lose Little Willie," Mary Sophia cried. "We are your family!"

"You will always be a part of our family," consoled Rhoda. "Remember, trains are quite comfortable, and Minnesota is not that far away. My family has bought land in Saint Anthony on the Mississippi River. It is a growing milling community."

"When will you leave?"

"In a month," William replied. "The land is planted with wheat and hay. We must settle before the harvest."

"We definitely plan to return for Naomi's June wedding," added Rhoda. She was finding this discussion much more difficult than she'd anticipated. She was excited about the new opportunities, in a new place. Only now, as she looked at Mary Sophia's misery, was she aware of how much she would miss them, too.

"Yes, that would be nice," Mary Sophia sighed. What a shock! She felt like someone had died.

The month passed too quickly. The Hanscomes tried to reconcile their loss.

"We have one more child to raise, a wedding to plan, a starving artist and five wonderful girls at our beck and call. It should be more than enough," Thomas said to Mary Sophia as they watched the train pull out of the station. Yes, they had much to be thankful for.

And the rest of the summer passed way too fast, as summers always did. Naomi, Michael and Harry sailed with Thomas, and sometimes by themselves. The older girls were busy with their philanthropies through St. James Cathedral and the Toronto Public Library. Mary Sophia brightened with time, as was her nature.

"Focus on the positive," she reminded herself as she borrowed Ann Hanscome's words. Naomi's high school graduation came soon enough, and the wedding was planned. Michael would be such a welcomed addition to their family.

"I see them! I see them!" Mary Sophia cried as Rhoda, William and toddler Willie stepped from the train. Willie, a big boy, was so proud he could jump to the platform.

What a reunion! What a dinner Anna Louisa had catered from the Lee restaurant. What a full table, abuzz with gay conversation. All the Lees, Gardens and Inglis' came to the welcome home party. Mary Sophia reminded Thomas to give Little Willie some time to get used to him. After only one day, though, he became inseparable from his grandfather.

"Hmm," joked Thomas, "Perhaps Willie will like the coal business!" And all his children laughed.

"Laugh if you want to, Thomas," Rhoda said, "but I might have some interest. Minnesota could use a good coal distributor."

"William is finally interested, eh?" Thomas laughed.

"No, he is not interested," responded Rhoda. "William is content with his music, growing vegetables and flowers, with Little Will by his side. I wouldn't dare disturb him. I am interested in being your distributor."

"Well, well…Why not?" replied Thomas. "We will talk later, dear Rhoda."

Rhoda and everyone within hearing range smiled. When had their father ever called Rhoda, dear?

"What do you miss most?" Alice asked after dinner as Rhoda wistfully surveyed the Hanscome home.

"Ah, you caught me coveting, dear Alice," Rhoda said and laughed. "The water closet and the bathroom. Minnesota lacks some of Toronto's gracious living."

"Are you happy? Are you glad you moved?"

"I miss you and all your sisters, more than I had thought. I am a lone woman among too many men, except for my sweet mother. Willie gives me such delight. I like seeing my family happy in their rural setting. And William? He is in his element. Just across the River from our farm is St. Mark's Episcopal

Parish, in Minneapolis. He has become their organist and is busy arranging concerts. The ladies enjoy his polished manners and interest in books. I envy William his contentment - perhaps my nature is such that I'll never be. I do know I want something more."

"Do you want to make money?" Alice asked.

"Yes, shallow as that sounds, yes."

Later, Thomas invited Rhoda to his study.

"Well, I have been looking at the wrong gender in my family," he said and smiled. "I do know you to be industrious to a fault. What is on your mind?"

"I am interested in bringing your coal business to Minneapolis and St. Paul. Minnesota is a timber haven with many lumber mills, but whole areas of the East coast have been stripped bare. It could also happen there. And coal is better. I miss my coal-heated house, so toasty warm in the winter. I think we could make a good profit. The area is booming. The Mississippi River and the railroads make it a major crossroad to the western territories. Picture your coal barges on the river, Thomas, bringing lasting heat to all the hinterland homes and businesses. I didn't expect winters could get any colder than Toronto's, but I was incorrect. Frostbite is common, and any exposed hair turns brittle and breaks. It's deathly frigid. I welcome coal."

"And what about William?"

"We have discussed this. He learned the coal business from you, and he will teach me. Once we are established, I will run the business, while he tends to his interests and Willie. It will be a good arrangement for us. We work rather well as a team. And also, while I am here, I should talk with Uncle John about his furnaces, and water closets."

"So you will be the organizer? We must include William in this plan."

"Of course, but make no mistake, I am in charge. You and I must figure the expenses and the profits. William's charm can bring in the customers."

Business completed, it was time to focus on another Hanscome wedding.

• • •

"No! Oh no!" Naomi screamed, just two weeks before her wedding. There was no consoling her.

What happened?

Michael had drowned. He had been sailing by himself, and his boat capsized. The Hanscomes were distraught. Secretly, her sisters felt an evil omen had once again left its curse. No Hanscome female would ever marry. Naomi had been their hope! It was as though each sister had been vicariously in love with Michael, except for Alice. And Harry? He just cried and cried.

Sad as it was, Alice felt relieved, not that she wanted Michael dead. She found him charming, but she also had reservations about his marrying Naomi. Perhaps Michael's death would solve the problem of the love triangle she had discovered. Who else was in love with Michael? Was it Martha Sophia? Was it Anna Louisa? Was it Eugenia or Virginia?

No. It was Harry. On several evenings after Naomi had retired, Alice had seen the two of them in embraces that scorched her eyes. What could she do? What should she do? She confessed to her priest, a rare thing for her. The priest simply counseled her to let it be. He said that once Naomi and Michael were married and had *relations*, the boys' attraction to each other would fade. He said it was not uncommon for boys to experiment. But Harry and Michael were not boys anymore. And how could that intensity of passion she'd witnessed fade?

Alice decided to say nothing, but she felt sick inside. It felt like she was betraying Naomi. And now, after Michael's death, she also wanted to console Harry.

The Hanscome house felt sad, as though it had absorbed the grief of the family into its very plaster and wood. Even Little

William seemed puzzled. William and Rhoda considered fleeing on the next train to Chicago, but decided to stay - to simply share the sadness. Little William's presence was a tonic for them all. He had to be sung to, played with, laughed with and hugged.

"Mother, Father, I want to tell you I am leaving," announced Harry a few days after Michael's burial. "I am leaving for Paris. I was planning on telling you after Naomi's wedding, but now, there is no need for me to wait. I have made arrangements to study art."

"I know you have been saving your money for Paris," Mary Sophia said, "but can't you wait? This doesn't seem like the best time for our family to lose another person."

"Don't worry, Mother, I will return. It's a great time for me to study the new Impressionism. I want to become a serious artist, not just a photographer." Harry hoped he had been convincing. He did his best to muster a smile.

"I know about your deep affection for Michael," whispered Alice as she gave Harry an extra hug goodbye. "I am so sorry you lost such a good friend. I will also keep your secret, Harry. In my life, I have also challenged the proper social order."

And Arthur teased his older brother. "Harry, how can you abandon me to this house of sad women? I want you to set Paris on fire with your art, then come back to Toronto. Soon."

Chapter 4

Winter Kill
January 1884
St. Anthony Falls, Minnesota

Rhoda's face was hot and dripping sweat. But it was not summer. The sun hung low in a haze, and the darkness would come too early, again. Rhoda and William were waiting for the doctor to arrive during a fierce January freeze. It was not a blizzard - it was way too cold to snow. It was the kind of cold that propelled steam from the horses' nostrils, formed icicles on moustaches and eyelashes and snapped whole branches from the trees in the dead of night.

"Crack! Crack! Crack!"

"What is happening outside? What is that crashing noise?"

"The tree limbs are breaking off the trees. Winter kill, it's called," Rhoda's father said as he covered his whole face with a wool scarf before he faced the cold trek to fetch the Village doctor.

"This baby is coming. Help me, William!" Rhoda cried as she gave one final push.

"It's a girl!" William shouted, as he triumphantly held her up for Rhoda to see. "She looks perfect!"

"I always get what I want," Rhoda said with a smile. "First a boy and now a girl!"

"Do you want to name her Rhoda, after you?" William asked.

"I think not, that is way too confusing. Let's call her Muriel - Muriel the miracle."

"Muriel has a musical tone as it rolls off your tongue. I like it!"

Was little Willie pleased? He didn't know, yet. William had taken him to his Baldwin grandparents when Rhoda's birth was eminent.

And the doctor? He arrived, along with Rhoda's father, but way too late to be of service. Nonetheless, his reassurance and warm cheeriness, in spite of the cold, was welcomed.

"I was detained by my last patient, who died of consumption. His condition was so aggravated by the severe cold, I wanted to list *winter kill* as the cause of death. Then, when I was ready to leave, I had to coax my stubborn horse from the warm barn, only to find that the wheels of my buggy had frozen solid to the ground. Frozen solid, mind you. Whatever you do, don't use your outhouse," he half-joked. "BRR! It is colder than a witch's kisser outside. Please let me warm my hands before I examine you." After he had blown on his hands and rubbed them together hard, he proceeded. His prognosis? "Excellent! I pronounce you both healthy. You are rosy radiant, Rhoda, and so is your baby girl. And William, you did a good job of catching her."

How did the Hanscomes survive living in this frigid ice box called Minnesota? Like the good doctor, humor helped and, luckily, their coal furnace didn't need to be fed during the long winter nights, like a woodburning stove. Their heat was ample. The front door of their wood frame house opened to a small hall with a very necessary coat closet. While it held a gilded mirror for grooming and a bench, the hall's practical function was to keep the cold that seeped into coats, scarves and mittens and the ice and snow on boots away from the interior parlor. Only after discarding outer garments did one dare to open the other hall door to the living quarters. Even then, the cry of *Close the door!* could be heard as an almost visible trail of cold snuck in with each guest.

How smart was Rhoda Hanscome? She was smart enough to birth a baby and smart enough to know that coal and wood not only made the winters bearable, they were also the keys to Minnesota's growth. The timber mills, twenty in Minneapolis alone, supplied nation-wide markets, but it was coal that fueled the timber-laden trains and barges back to the east coast. Steam engines demanded coal.

"Trains, rivers and coal," had preached her father-in-law, Thomas. "Those who control transportation control the future. Industries' appetite for fuel is insatiable."

Minnesota was no exception. Railroad tycoon, St. Paul's J.J. Hill, ran the government from behind closed doors. Corruption abounded. Business boomed. The train tenders were refilled with coal at St. Paul's Union Station and the new Minneapolis Union Depot. The coal barges traveled west on the Ohio River and up the Mississippi to the Twin Cities. In return, hundreds of trains left those stations daily, loaded with timber, flour, livestock, fodder and other nonperishables, headed for the transportation hubs of Chicago, Omaha and New Orleans.

The new railroad trestle on the Stone Arch Bridge connected the east and west banks of the Mississippi. The River also powered Pillsbury's prosperous flour mills and served as the border between Minneapolis and the old Village of St. Anthony Falls. Minneapolis legally swallowed St. Anthony Falls, but the locals still preferred the familiar old name. It was on this rich farm land near the Village that the Hanscomes and Baldwins settled. Wheat was king.

What happened to Rhoda Hanscome's business with her father-in-law? She had been intent on helping him gain a coal stronghold in Minnesota, but that did not happen. It seemed she underestimated the amount of time her children and farm would take.

Did William pick up the financial slack? Yes and no. At times, he helped the Baldwins with their new cash crops, such as sugar beets, hops, flax and sorghum. They even experimented with tobacco, but the crop dismally failed. The Baldwin's were gradually increasing their dairy herd. Why? The new wheat fields of the Dakotas were competing for their wheat profits. Dairy might become the new king.

They counted their blessings. The coal heat, ample lamps and inside plumbing made them as snug as bugs in a rug inside, except for an occasional bout of winter cabin fever that took its toll on mind and soul. Were Minnesota springs any more glorious than anywhere else? No, but after the bone-chilling winters, one green bud was hailed as a miracle and a reason to continue living.

The customs of the English were being diluted by the influx of Germans and Scandinavians. While cordial greetings among friends in other parts of the country might include a general inquiry about one's health, in Minnesota, the favorite topic of conversation was the weather. To skip the essential conversation starter, "How's da weather?" was indeed a sign of rude impatience and poor upbringing.

And how were the Toronto Hanscomes? They were smart enough to visit in the summer. Mary Sophia and Alice were coming to greet the newest Hanscome, wee Muriel, and celebrate Willie's fourth birthday.

"I see Grandma! I see Aunt Alice!" Little Will yelled as he ran down the train platform lickety-split.

"What a bustling city this is," declared Mary Sophia as they rode the new electric street car from the Minneapolis Depot to the Nicolette Avenue Suspension Bridge, where William had safely left the carriage.

"I can see why you didn't want to bring your carriage into this morass of mud and traffic," Alice said as she noticed horses and carts haphazardly tied to streetlamp posts, saloon steps, storefronts and stables. "We could as easily be run over by bicycles as horses. Thank goodness they use their bells. There is no order to this sloppy mess of a roadway."

"We needed the rain. The streets aren't always so rutted and wet," William laughed. "This *sloppy mess*, to use your words, is called development. Lift your eyes upward to these magnificent structures. This is the only bridge that spans the Mississippi River. From here, you can see the locks and dam, the Stone Arch Bridge and the flour mills. The Village of St. Anthony Falls, where we live, lies to the north, on the other side."

William proudly showed off his new city to his family. It was summer, and everything was in luscious bloom. But he was even more proud of his little girl, Muriel. Rhoda had miscarried two children after Willie. Of course, that sadness was simply swept under the rug. Rhoda knew only strong babies could survive in this harsh land. Acceptance was hard, but she set her jaw and determined to carry on.

"Welcome! Welcome!" Rhoda said, standing on the porch. "Come in and greet our newest addition. We call her our miracle Muriel."

"She looks more like you, Rhoda, while Willie still favors his father," remarked Alice.

"Yes, one child for each of us. I am so thankful at thirty-eight to have birthed her."

"I haven't stayed on a farm since Pennsylvania," Mary Sophia wistfully said. "I hope you have some cows to milk and chickens to feed."

"Yes, we have a few, but I am truly a gentleman farmer, Mother. The Baldwins have what I call a serious farm, backbreaking and very prosperous. I supply them with fresh vegetables and flowers for their table, while they make silage to transport down river, raise livestock for the St. Paul slaughterhouses and supply milk to the German cheesemakers. I also take our summer produce to the weekly fresh market in Minneapolis. I have to take a vacation from my music to help them during the busy summer months."

"My mother and I put up all the surplus fruits and vegetables for the winter," added Rhoda. "We live on pickled everything – cucumbers, tomatoes, beets and even sweet corn. And what vegetables we can't pickle, we can. Canned carrots, peas, beans, even squash. Our potatoes keep quite well in the cellar until spring. And we make tomato sauces, apple butter and berry preserves. We are having rhubarb strawberry pie for Willie's birthday, his favorite."

"Glowing! Our William is positively glowing, which I credit to you, dear Rhoda. I never thought he would survive here, but he is," Mary Sophia exclaimed. "He is happy. He is working and still devoted to his church music. And I can see why you are too busy to mess with the coal business. I will tell Thomas you are the new frontiersmen."

What a birthday party Willie had. The Baldwins came bearing his first pair of ice skates and a sled, but Willie's favorite was the small tricycle his grandfather Hanscome had custom-made for him at the Garden machine shop and sent by rail. Bicycles of all shapes and sizes were all the rage.

Was everyone happy? No, Alice was not. Her mother thought a trip might lift her spirits.

"Why are you so despondent, dear sister?" Rhoda asked one night during an evening stroll.

"Does it show? I miss Arthur. I wrote you that after he matriculated this spring, he left for Vancouver on the railroad. Being a railroad engineer was his dream, always. His ticket was his best graduation gift. What I didn't tell you is that he is not coming back to Toronto. Not ever." Alice broke into uncontrollable sobs. "It is all my fault."

"I don't understand," Rhoda said.

"It's a secret that we even kept from Mary Ann and Elizabeth Sarah, although Elizabeth Sarah, in some way, may have guessed the truth. Oh how I miss her, too."

"You needn't tell me if you don't want to," said Rhoda. "I know that things are not always as they seem in families."

"It is time. We only kept the secret because of Arthur's welfare, but now, he has left us because of it. I promised that after he was grown, I would tell him the truth. My parents and sisters all swore to it, too. The truth is Arthur is my son, not my parents'." Alice exhaled deeply and looked better, as victims of long kept secrets are apt to, after disclosing a most heinous sin.

"Oh, Alice! I hadn't a clue."

"He hates us for it. All of us! The whole family intended to be here for Willie's birthday, but father and my sisters decided to stay in case Arthur returned. He was father's hope. His hatred for me, I can understand, but not my parents. He called us all liars, hypocrites and me names I dare not mention."

"Hate you, his mother? Surely, with time, he will see the wisdom of your decision. It is considered a shame and a sin to bear children outside of wedlock. He had a privileged life."

"I think he has always felt different, *the light caboose of the family*, our father called him. Oh, Rhoda, Arthur flew into a rage!"

"Well, young men are rageful. He should be grateful. And his real father?" Rhoda asked.

"He is irrelevant, or so I thought. He is a Charlestonian who could not marry me because of the miscegenation laws – or perhaps wouldn't have anyway. That subject is still difficult to discuss, Rhoda. I was so in love with him. But then, you know about lost love."

"If you are referring to my deceased first husband, he was no lost love. Ours was a marriage of mutual financial benefit. I wanted to have, and he wanted to provide. Do you find me terrible to admit to such a failing?" Rhoda asked and then laughed. "No, my only love has been your brother."

"We all admire you because of your honesty, brutal at times, but also so endearing. Look at the pretense of respectability I hid behind."

"With good reason, dear Alice. Don't we all want the best for our children? You sacrificed your happiness for Arthur's."

"Arthur was no sacrifice. He was the love of my life. And that is too big a burden for any child. I think that's why he is so angry with me now, why he needed to run away and why I feel so, yes, abandoned."

"And your father?"

"With the passage of time, he actually came to believe Arthur was his son. It was as though I was the only holder of the truth. And there has been no news from Harry in Paris. Father is more despondent than I am, but he exhausts his sadness by working ever harder."

"That's not a very good strategy at his age," Rhoda said.

"It's not a very good strategy at any age. I think I came here to escape my father. Every day I witnessed his sadness, I felt worse. You see, it was my error in judgment that started this whole mess. It is my fault."

"Please don't wish away Arthur. You all will adjust, and be much better for the truth. Breathe, dear sister. Stop your sobbing. Arthur will return - and return a man, free of your apron strings. Had you continued the lie, Arthur would have lived as Atlas, with the weight of the Hanscome's prosperity and happiness resting squarely on his shoulders. You can also release the burden of your secret. I, for one, believe good will come from this, for everyone."

"You see things differently, Rhoda. I knew I needed a different lens to feel better. I do hope you are right."

"So do I." Alice and Rhoda strolled back to the house, arm-in-arm, feeling closer for having had their conversation.

Later that night, Rhoda turned to William.

"William, I have a question."

"Yes, Rhoda. What is it? Pray tell me so we can both sleep. You have been tossing and turning in bed."

"Does Minnesota have miscegenation laws?"

"Ah, I see you have been discussing Arthur's origins with Alice. Do you wonder if our marriage is legal, and if our children are legitimate?"

"Yes, I have been worrying," Rhoda admitted.

"We were married in Canada, which has no such laws. We are listed as legally white in the census. And, I checked before we moved. Minnesota is one of the few states that does not have miscegenation laws. Don't worry, Rhoda, our children look as white as the driven snow, well white enough, so please don't waste your time borrowing trouble."

"My, my, you are starting to speak like a true Minnesotan, one cliché after another," Rhoda said and laughed.

"Yes, I am. I am a Minnesotan," William jested in return.

"And I forever will remain English."

"Then, all is as it should be. Good night, my dear wife. We have an early train to catch tomorrow."

"I will miss your family."

"Me, too, but I must say, I relish the freedom our move has given us. I finally feel like a man."

October 30, 1886

"It's a girl!" the doctor announced.

"And Rhoda? How is she?" a worried William asked.

"She is fine. The baby is fine. However, William, I suggest you stop having children. Mind you, I know there are fifty-year-old women who give birth to healthy babies, but you push your luck. Many children of older mothers are deficient in mind or body or both."

"Rubbish! I'm as healthy as a horse and as strong as a mule," declared Rhoda. "I will have another child."

"I can see she is your daughter by her demanding wail," the doctor said and laughed. "She is full of the spirit, appropriately born just one day shy of All Saint's Eve."

"I will listen to no silly superstitions about All Saint's Eve as belonging to the dead. She is a strong, most determined baby," countered Rhoda.

"And what do you want to name our little sprite?" William asked and laughed.

"Jane," Rhoda said.

"Oh that's way too plain for one with such a need for command performances," protested William. "Let's name her Rhoda, after her enterprising mother."

"Fine, dear husband." Rhoda laughed, but she was very pleased, yes, very pleased, indeed. "Front and center Rhoda she will be."

Was that their last child?

Oh no, Rhoda soon became pregnant again. She did not heed the doctor's caution about her advanced age. She was forty-one.

December 1887

"Look at our early Christmas present, William," Rhoda said. "I swear his birth was the easiest, and his temperament is definitely the sweetest."

"What should we name this easily-pleased babe?" William asked.

"We could name him Henry, after both our brother's," Rhoda suggested. "We could call him Harry as they both are called."

"I think that name may bring bad luck," William replied. "My brother Harry has not turned out to be a happy man, although I know you like him the best."

"Then let's name him Robert. Robert means glory."

And so it was the Hanscomes celebrated a glorious Christmas with four children. After the New Year, Robert was baptized at St. Mark's Parish and welcomed to the congregation.

"Oh no!" Rhoda cried when she found the wee precious boy delirious with fever that very same night.

"Please save him," William begged when the doctor arrived. "We bundled him up so warm on our ride to the church. Do you think he caught a cold?"

The doctor was unable to bring his fever down. Come morning little Robert was gone. "Why?! Why?!" Rhoda shouted. "He seemed so healthy."

"I cannot explain why," the doctor replied. "You know, Rhoda, it could just simply be the weather. Our Minnesota winters challenge most newborns."

But was that true? As the January days passed, and the winter landscape became bleaker and darker, Rhoda fell into despair. She hated the fierce cold snap that broke whole tree limbs from sturdy tree trunks, attached one day and gone the next. She kept the children inside when they begged to try out their new Christmas sleds. Rhoda promised that she would not lose another child to the Minnesota cold.

No. No more *winter kill*.

Chapter 5

You Can Always Go Back Home
1888
The Village of St. Anthony

"I have train tickets for us to Toronto," William announced to Rhoda, as he quickly shut the hall door, keeping the warm air inside and the cold air outside.

"I told you, William, I am not taking our children anywhere until spring. Those trains are drafty and cold," shouted an angry Rhoda.

"Rhoda, I want to see your bright smile again. The children need to see your bright smile, again. They are getting cabin fever from your fear of the outside. Wee Robert was not killed by the cold. His death was unexplainable. Think about Muriel who was born during a cold snap. She is thriving. Stop protecting them from the weather. It is not to blame. Why are you so angry?"

"I can't bear the thought of losing any of our children. Robert's death was so unfair. I am angry with God, if you want to know the truth."

Rhoda cried and cried and William just held her. When she was spent, she appeared calmer, sad, but no longer angry. William was relieved. He wanted his wife back.

"I want us to go to Anna Louisa's wedding," he said calmly. "It will be a happy occasion and good for us all."

"Toronto is no longer our home, William," Rhoda said with a sigh.

"My family loves you, Rhoda. We can always go back home, to them. I want to celebrate our family, with our family."

February 16
Toronto

"Do you, Anna Louisa Hanscome, take you, William Phillip Marston, to be your wedded husband?"

"I do."

Where was the large church wedding? Where was the big reception? There was neither. The ceremony was held in the small St. James Cathedral chapel on the coldest day of the winter. Only the Hanscome family and the groom, William Marston, and his son, Harry, attended.

Was the bride blushing? Was the groom enthralled with her beauty? The answers to both questions were no, but it was a polite affair. After his second wife died, social convention dictated that William propose to Anna Louisa. It also dictated that if Anna Louisa wanted to continue as his housekeeper, she accept his proposal. Remember, even the famed Mary Bachiller of Kittery, Maine, married the Reverend in the 1650's to keep the skin on her back, rather than be lashed to shreds by a Puritan whip, branded with the scarlet letter and called harlot. Yes, the code of propriety, even after two hundred years, still needed to be honored.

What had lured Anna Louisa from the safety of the Hanscome nest? Friendship. She had been a true friend of William's second wife. When she became ill, Anna Louisa moved in with the Marstons to better care for her, and inadvertently for him as well. But alas, she died. Mary Sophia encouraged Anna Louisa to move back home. However, Anna Louisa liked being the mistress of her own house. And why not, she was forty-two-years-old. She wanted her own kitchen, her own parlor, her own piano, her own bedroom, yes, freedom. Did she care that her groom was the same age as her father, sixty-seven? Apparently not. Her family surmised this was merely a marriage of convenience.

Nonetheless, it was a marriage, the first for a Hanscome female. Thomas was pleased. He had known William Marston to be a good gunsmith and businessman. Anna Louisa would be well provided for.

Cupid may have missed his opportunity for true love by two days, but the February 16 wedding date could not have been better for a family gathering. Mary Sophia decorated the table with bouquets of red and pink flowers. Each guest had a Valentine heart and card, in lieu of a formal place card. The Hanscomes had many reasons to celebrate, not just the wedding, but then they never needed reasons to be gay.

"What a full and festive dining room table," Rhoda exclaimed. William was right, she thought, she did feel she had come home. She felt vibrant. She felt alive. She determined to listen to her husband's wisdom more frequently.

"Yes, a full table and a full house. Everyone has come home, exactly what we love," chirped Mary Sophia.

"We thought we might sell the house a few years ago, but today, we need a larger one," commented Thomas, standing at the head of the table carving the meat.

And who, precisely, were all these people?

Seated on Thomas' right, in the guest of honor chair, was Harry, baptized Thomas Henry as a babe, if you remember. He had just returned from Paris. Had he only been gone six years? Yes, but he looked much older than his twenty-eight years. Was he well? He looked the stereotype of the Parisian starving artist. Hollow-eyed and gaunt.

On the other side of Harry sat the youngest son, Arthur. Yes, the prodigal sons had returned. Unlike the Bible parable, they had not squandered their inheritances. They both left without funds, hurt and disgusted. They wanted out of their despicable family and away from the pain it had lain at their feet. Were Arthur's and Harry's heartaches the same? Absolutely not. Were they hurt on purpose? No. They were simply a family. Normal? Well, what, pray tell, was a normal family? Arthur and Harry learned there were much worse. They discovered they loved their family and were most grateful to be home.

"I propose a toast to Anna Louisa's and William's marriage and the health and prosperity of all our children. Welcome home," Thomas said, raising his glass.

"Hear! Hear!" The crystal wine glasses clinked, much to Little Willie's and Little Muriel's delight.

"Take the extra portion of meat that Father is serving you," Arthur whispered to Harry. "His mission is to fatten you up, as he did me after I returned from the rails, thin as a rail." Arthur said and laughed.

He was quite pleased with his clever joke. Was that a Hanscome trait, to delight in one's own voice or silly jokes?

"Were you a hobo then?" Harry asked, as he pushed the food around his plate. He truly was not hungry.

"I might as well have been. After two years as a train engineer, I realized my dream had become a nightmare. Don't misunderstand, I love trains, the thrill of the power and speed, but we were treated little better than slaves. We had twenty-four-hour shifts, slept in dirty shacks by the tracks and ate on the run. In the end, our attempts to improve conditions and unionize were thwarted. Do you believe the many train accidents were blamed on us? *Engineer error* was the usual citation - not the broken rails, faulty brakes or overlapping train schedules. Furthermore, we were docked pay for any accidents. I ended my career exhausted and in debt to the train company."

"Bondage to the railroad company? It sounds like the coal miners' plight. How did you finally free yourself?" Harry asked.

"One day I just quit, walked out and hopped a train from Chicago home. I suppose if I return to the United States, I could be thrown in jail. Now, I am getting a degree in engineering from the University of Toronto, mechanical engineering. I want to design better trains, not drive them. I have also been learning from our Uncle John. He is quite the engineer of new machines. He predicts our dependency on horses will soon end. Imagine that. But I am prattling on and on, like our father. And you, Harry? What made you decide to come back, except that you were starving to death, too?"

"I sold a few paintings and booked passage on a ship to New York. I had had enough of poverty and starvation, you are correct in that," Harry said and laughed.

"Well then, stop pushing the food around on your plate. Eat!"

And Harry did take a bite. He was amused that not only did he have five sisters, a mother and father coaxing him to eat, his baby brother was no better. Would they ever let him be in charge of his stomach?

"I was, like you, waking from my dream to find a nightmare. I love art, as you love trains, but I was not as talented as I thought. I am indebted to a few masters for their instruction, room and board and other amenities. I grew skilled at the new impressionist style, but the greatness of my mentors eluded me. Luckily, so did their craziness. It seemed the longer I stayed in Paris, the more I became a stranger to myself. Paris does that to people. It seduces you. It deludes you. There is craziness in living on the edge. I left when I simply thought I would fall off."

"Fall off?"

"Yes, fall off the edge, slip into the nether world. Is hell heaven or vice versa? I could no longer distinguish between the two. I could not discern between debauchery and bliss."

"It sounds worse than my slavery to the train company. I am truly sorry, dear brother. No wonder you can't eat. Do give yourself some time. There is no rush. Can I help? What do you want right now?"

"More meat on my bones." Harry laughed. "I don't know. For now, I am content and so thankful to be the Hanscome resident artist. Father has even hung a seascape in his office. I painted it on the Mediterranean, but he says I have caught the essence of his South Carolina youth. Perhaps I'll resurrect my photography studio. I do need to make a living and interact more with other humans, now that I feel like one. I credit your mother with the return of my sanity."

"Our mother?"

"No. I mean Alice - your Connie, your mother," Harry whispered. "She and I have talked, about my youth, who I am, who I love, my love triangle with Naomi and Michael, her love for Howling Wolf and your South Carolina father and the pure wonder and destructiveness of love. I feel saner because of Alice. I want the peace she has. I am ready to paint with a tranquil mind."

Not wanting to draw undue attention to themselves, they both smiled and joined the lighter dinner table banter.

"I see Father has had success at recruiting a partner for his coal business," William whispered to Rhoda, from the other end of the table.

"Yes, that lets us both off the hook," she responded.

And who might be on the hook? None other than Thomas' brother James from Charleston. James' short visit had become permanent. His third marriage, to Emma, had soured as the first two. James seemed unable to stay away from gambling at the track. He had lost his position as a policeman and last worked as a lowly janitor. When Thomas heard about James' demise from Louisa Rebecca, he sent him fare money to Toronto. So far, James was sending money back to support his four younger children. He, like Arthur and Harry, was benefitting from Thomas' largess. Thomas liked feeding his family. His nature was to provide.

"Let us have a toast to my brother James and our father, your grandfather, Thomas Hanscome, who is responsible for our prosperity," Thomas boomed.

"Here! Here!" chimed the family as they clinked their glasses in salute to the portrait of their grandfather in the place of honor on the wall. Next to him hung the portraits of Thomas and Mary Sophia and their Uncle James. The other portraits of Thomas' siblings were, of course, hanging in their respective homes.

"And let us have a final toast to our bride and groom, before we cut the cake."

"Hear! Hear!"

Later, after the bride and groom were showered with rice and sent on their way, the family excused themselves, but separate conversations continued, late into the night.

"Connie, how do you like my friend, Sarah?" Arthur asked of his mother, Alice.

"I don't know much about her, except that she'd follow you to the end of the earth, if you asked," Alice replied. "More importantly, do you like her and do her parents like you?"

"Yes, I think she's the one I should marry, and her parents, I think, will agree. After I finish my degree, I will ask her to marry me."

"I must say I expected as much. Congratulations! Tell me, have you told her the truth - that I am your mother and about our Negro heritage?"

"Yes, I have. Sarah doesn't care. She is like Rhoda, finds our family story fascinating. But she hasn't told her parents."

"Perhaps it is premature to tell them, and perhaps you'll decide not to. That is your choice, but I think we are doing much better as a family without our secrets. And you? You seem to have forgiven me."

"I am over the shock. I believe I have learned to accept, rather than forgive. I felt my foundation crumble. I found you, my family whom I trusted and admired above all, to be hypocrites. I hated you and Mother and Father for the illusions you passed as truth."

"And now?"

"I am fine. I don't hate anyone anymore. It's a waste of time. I grew up. Your imperfections are a gift to me. I needed to leave home, test my own mettle and develop my own imperfections. I don't even judge my train debacle as bad. I like knowing how flawed all of us Hanscomes are."

"Imperfection is a questionable legacy, but I'm glad you find it liberating," Alice responded.

Arthur had made peace with his family. He had a mother, a father, too many doting sisters, two strange brothers and a special *Connie*. Did Arthur hold a hidden desire to look his blood father in the eye, to see a resemblance in face or body? No, he did not. That was a lifetime ago. He knew now why Alice had treated him with so much devotion and love, sometimes too much. Now, at times, he did call her *mother*, just to see her glow. Yes, he did love his Connie. In return, Alice worked hard at letting him go.

In the kitchen, Rhoda cornered Martha Sophia.

"I am worried about Harry. He looks like he is dying. Is he?" she asked.

"I do not know, but there are sexual diseases that have killed men from the beginning of time. I researched them at the library. You do know that Arthur loves men?"

"Yes, of that he has been quite open. What a secret he hid. I do hope he will regain his health. Perhaps it was the cold and wet in Paris that made him ill. Has he told your mother and father?"

"No, and I don't think he will. It is sufficient he has confided in us. He doesn't feel alone anymore. I just wish he and Naomi would make peace. They have not spoken to each other since Harry's return."

The next day, it was as if Harry had overheard Rhoda's and Martha Sophia's conversation.

"Naomi, would you take a walk with me to the shore?" Harry asked.

"Yes. Yes, I will. We used to walk along the water - you, Michael and I. Do you remember?"

"Yes, I remember. I was happy then."

Silence.

"I wanted to ask you if you harbor any resentment towards me," Harry asked once they had reached the promenade along the shore.

"Resentment? Is that what you call it!" Naomi was shaking with rage. "You shattered my illusion of Michael's great love for me. I didn't know whether to mourn him or hate him, or hate you. I do know his untimely death saved me from making a terrible marriage. Should I be grateful to you for your betrayal?"

"I am so sorry. I had no idea you knew about my affection for him," Harry quietly said.

"Only after he died. I saw your deep grief. I felt your guilty eyes. I started viewing our courtship in a different light. Michael was never very affectionate with me. Kind, yes, respectful, yes, but affectionate? No. Then, all of a sudden I understood. I had to admit to myself that the man I almost married used me to become close to you. How naïve I was. How gullible. By that time, you had run away to Paris, with not one concern for my welfare. First, you destroyed my dream, then, you left me to die inside with my grief - alone!"

"I want you to forgive me, dear sister. It was not just Michael, I loved. It was you, too. I loved the three of us, together. I pursued him, too, but it wasn't planned. I want you to know that. Nonetheless, I was a terrible brother to you. Selfish. I should have told you to break off that engagement. I should have told you that Michael could never be a good husband. I should have told Michael I could never be part of such a deception. But I didn't. I am so sorry."

Harry wept. Did Naomi console him? No, she did not. She turned and began to walk away.

"I don't know that I can forgive you, Harry. What you did was the cruelest act, to steal the man I loved. There were other young men, with your proclivities, you could have chosen. And you betrayed me further by not warning me."

Silence.

"I am surprised I still hold so much venom inside - toward you, brother, and also toward me. I deceived myself. I made Michael and me into the idyllic couple. Perhaps with time, I will feel less foolish, and my ire will diminish. At least we share the same sentiments toward your heinous behavior."

"You were such an innocent. And to have your sweetness replaced with your current sarcasm makes me feel quite reprehensible. Nonetheless, this conversation has helped me. I apologize if I just reopened memories better forgotten. Again, I have been selfish."

"Yes, you have."

They did not walk home together.

• • •

That night, Rhoda couldn't sleep. As she tossed and turned, William awoke.

"What's wrong, Rhoda?" he finally asked.

"I've been thinking. Do you think Alice, Martha Sophia, Eugenia, Virginia and Naomi are destined to be maiden ladies? I understand they all have suffered heartaches, but most ladies move forward and find another to marry. It just doesn't seem normal. They are attractive, musically talented, educated and full of fun mischief."

"Anna Louisa's marriage surprised us all, so anything is possible. Nonetheless, they are considered too old, no longer eligible. I don't think the twins could stand to be separated. Perhaps some man will marry them both," William said and laughed.

"I do think bigamy is against the law, but actually, in their case, I can see that such a marriage could be to everyone's advantage," reflected Rhoda.

"That's an interesting notion. Their love for each other could include a third person. Eugenia and Virginia love all of us, just

~ 65 ~

not as much. And my other sisters? I think they have given up hope, partially because of our questionable whiteness in the eyes of some."

"What is the exact law that governs color and marriage?"

"I have not caught up with all the changes in the pecking order of color. Canada has no such laws, but in practice, the races stay separate. In the U.S., each state is different. Some had thought that after the War, the whole color issue would disappear. People would marry those they knew, regardless of color. My cousin Charlotte Forten's wedding seemed to be the wave of the future. Every shade of humanity attended that Washington DC gala. But as you know, a blessed integration has not happened. White is good. Black is evil. Some states are looking at percentages of African blood. The term mulatto has been confusing, and thus, people are discontinuing its usage in favor of only two categories - black or white. Some say, *just one drop* makes a person black. How ridiculous is that? That would make everyone in South Carolina black, not just our Hanscome family."

"Well, I still think it's a shame Alice couldn't marry Arthur's father."

"It's the same reason my grandparents couldn't marry."

"How silly. This is 1888. Slavery is abolished, and Negros have equality."

"Only on paper, dear. There has been a terrible backlash following their emancipation. The southern whites need to hate someone for the ruin of their society. They are blaming the victims for their poverty. They are lynching whole families, even now. The miscegenation laws against racial intermarriage have been rewritten, even tighter."

"One day soon, the Negros will blame the whites," Rhoda added.

"We won't live to see that day. But then, the Negros would have to blame their black slave masters, too. We Hanscomes would be blamed double, both the white and black of us."

"Sometimes, I don't think you are very funny, William."

"Blaming never serves any purpose. It keeps us from moving forward."

"Well, I'd like to see your sisters move forward. I just hate to see them give up. I know your father could handsomely reward any suitor."

"Rhoda, stay out of it. You needn't be a matchmaker. My sisters seem perfectly content with their work, church guilds, card clubs, needle point and knitting groups, to name a few. And don't forget their philanthropies for the orphanage and the library."

"I just know I wouldn't be happy with such a life."

"Go to sleep now, Rhoda, please."

The morning came all too soon, and they were bustled off to the train for Chicago.

"What do you think of our children, Thomas?" Mary Sophia asked as they watched the train disappear down the tracks.

"Well, William and Rhoda bring such merriment when they visit. They also take the laughter with them when they leave," Thomas said with a sigh.

"I think it's because they have children. And our other children? What lives will they have?"

"I think they have grown up, left their youthful illusions behind," Thomas replied.

"I want them to recover from their dashed dreams. I want them to find partners they can trust. Partners who won't betray them. I ache inside."

"William and Rhoda seem to have managed, in spite of his lack of ambition, to form a solid family. And Arthur has recovered from his riding the rails fantasy. He has a budding career ahead and an eye on a fine lady," reflected Thomas. "I want you to recover your faith in their abilities to figure out their lives."

"But Harry and Naomi are too young to lose their zest for life. That awful love triangle still warps their minds and closes them to others. I think we should talk with them about it."

"We chose not to discuss it. I believe they think we are ignorant of the true circumstances. Now, I see them walking and talking. Perhaps they will help each other move beyond Michael. I don't think we should interfere."

"I hope you are right. And the other girls? I believe the die is cast. They will live with us, forever."

"Perhaps, dear, but we cannot foresee the future."

"It didn't seem like we had so many disappointments when we were young and frivolous in Charleston. We grew up together, we were best friends, and we married full of trust, and yes, even lust."

"Ah, but we had the outer dragon to slay, the perilous and tenuous nature of our freedom. It glued us even more together. Our children have not feared for their existence."

"But what is existence without love?"

"They have love. They always come back home."

Chapter 6

Assimilation
1890
Train ride

Another wedding and another train ride back to Toronto. Ten-year-old Willie could hardly contain his excitement. He was enthralled by the clickety clacks of the train, the *All Aboard!* calls of the conductors and the ringing of the shiny metal triangles that announced the dining car was open for service. He felt like a protective adult as he clutched Muriel's and Rhoda's small hands and headed toward the aroma of the sumptuous food. His parents trusted him to hang onto his little sisters.

As the train lurched this way and that over the uneven tracks and challenged steady balance, he ordered, "Don't look down. Jump!" in the treacherous open air spaces between the coupled cars. The girls, of course, looked down, shrieked and nimbly jumped to safety, while Willie mastered opening the heavy door to the next compartment. "Home free!" they shouted. Heaven opened before them as they entered the elegant red velvet-curtained dining car. Fancy meals were presented with great fanfare on white linen tablecloths, graced with rose buds in small silver vases. "Napkins in your laps," Willie parentally whispered.

After they'd cleaned their plates, yes, eaten every morsel of food, they confidently wound their way back to their compartment, flew over the wide gaping holes between the cars and, out of breath, hurriedly interrupted each other as they unloaded their dining adventure to their smiling parents, who appropriately nodded and lauded their achievements.

Even more memorable was the sleeping compartment and the immaculate, dark-faced Pullman porter, who politely catered to their every need. Willie gallantly took an upper berth so his sisters, aged six and four, wouldn't have far to fall if the train lurched in the middle of the night, sending them crashing to the floor.

"Why is your face so black?" little Rhoda asked of the porter. She had never seen a person with black skin before.

"It's the way God made me," the porter answered with a smile.

"You must not live in Minnesota," Willie said. "Everyone is white-skinned there."

"No, I live in Chicago, but I came from the south where the sun kissed my skin too much," answered the porter with a gleam in his eye. "Do you think if I lived in frigid Minnesota, my skin would turn as white as yours?"

"It could," Muriel answered. "Minnesotans are the color of snow."

"Well, maybe I should move there, then."

"Why would you do that? Don't you like your black skin?" Willie asked.

"Now that's a very good question, young man," the porter said and laughed.

"Maybe you just need to stay out of the sun. My mother is always telling us to stay out of the sun, as our skin will burn and turn dark," Muriel offered. "Maybe dark as yours."

"Children," Rhoda scolded. "Stop pestering the porter. It is not polite, and he has work to do."

"Oh, don't worry, I find their questions amusing, Missus. They're just curious."

"When I grow up, I'd like to have a coat like yours with the shiny buttons," Willie said.

In the few years they had lived there, Minnesota was becoming a true melting pot. People migrated from Europe, from the East and the South. There was a new neighborhood of Negros, just north of St. Anthony Falls, called Shingle Creek, where they lived and worked making shingles for roofs. But the best paying positions were as Pullman porters on the railroads.

Toronto

What a reunion there was at the Toronto grand depot. Of course, all the Hanscomes squeezed the children to death, tweaked their cheeks and said, "Oh, how you've grown!"

"Why do grown-ups always pinch my cheeks?" Willie asked and winced, as he tried to be polite. "I hate it! I'm not a baby anymore."

And who was getting married? One of the old maiden aunts?

"Do you Arthur Randall Hanscome take Sarah Jean Brady to be your wedded wife?"

"I do."

"I just love new beginnings," said one sentimental guest, wiping the tears from her eyes.

"What a lovely couple," said another.

"What a lavish, expensive wedding!"

"Aren't you pleased our son has married," Mary Sophia whispered to Alice.

"Yes," Alice said and smiled, enjoying her mother's recognition of the son they shared. "I was afraid Sarah's Catholic family would be set against a marriage to an Anglican. But as luck would have it, their priest consented to officiate the wedding. The Brady's have been in Toronto longer than we have. Her parents came in the 1840's to escape the potato famine in Ireland. Half a million immigrated to Ontario alone. The Irish must outnumber the English in some parts of Canada. Don't you find it ironic, Mother, how fair our Arthur is and how dark-haired and dark-eyed his Sarah is?"

"They are called the *black Irish*, quite ironic, I think. Wouldn't it be interesting if they had a truly dark baby, a throwback to the Moorish conquistadors in Ireland and your father's and my Negro grandparents?"

"They might have to move to the colored neighborhood," joked Anna Louisa. Yes, marriage had lightened her spirit, indeed. Did any of them think their jokes were offensive? No, they did not.

"Oh, that's nonsense. The term *black Irish* comes from the term *black blight*, which destroyed the potato crop," remarked Thomas. "I respect Sarah's father and grandparents. They were destitute when they emigrated. He has opened his third blacksmith shop and is quite prosperous. They have recently joined the yacht club."

"Who cares about any of this?" Martha Sophia asked. "We are finally having a real wedding."

Harry, the best man, looked every bit as handsome as he always did, albeit still too thin. However, the show was stolen by the solemn ring bearer, Willie, and the two, sunny-faced flower girls, Muriel and Rhoda, who were anything but solemn. Were Arthur's sisters in the wedding party? No, they were considered too old to meet the standards for virginal bridesmaids.

"Very nice ceremony, Father Smith," Naomi said, holding his gaze longer than was seemly. Was she flirting? Yes, she was. And did he blush? Yes, he did. None of this was lost on her brother Harry, who knowingly smiled. He was happy Naomi had moved on. To a priest? Well, he knew love came in many guises and should be honored wherever one found it. Harry was thankful the wedge between them had disappeared.

And Harry's other maiden lady sisters? Martha Sophia had been seen riding horses in the Toronto Island surf with the Irish

Catholic locksmith. He had five children and cared for his mentally ill wife. With his acute sensitivities to the vagaries of love, Harry was also happy for them. Alice seemed most content with her lot in life. It was as though she and her mother had become best friends.

And observer Harry? Had he found another love? No, he had not. He knew he was dying. His only mission was to leave landscapes of familiar Toronto scenes for his family. Today, he was adored by his nephew and two little nieces. He smiled and hoped his paintings reflected the many faces of love in his family.

"Uncle Harry," Willie said, "I have a question about our family. In Minneapolis, my friends' families have all come from different countries. Some even speak German, Norwegian or Swedish in their homes. When their parents ask where we came from, I say Toronto. Then they say, but your father doesn't look English. And I say, well my Grandfather says we're of English background and have been in the United States since the early colonial days, since the 1600's. And my mother's family came from England. Then they say, perhaps you have some Indian in you, somewhere. I laugh and say I don't know. I wondered if you know. Your skin is darker, like my father's. Are we part Indian?"

"Not that I am aware of, but anything is possible. Our darker pigment comes from our Negro background, William. Both my parents had African slave grandparents. Hasn't your father told you about my grandmother, Nancy Randall?" Harry had decided his legacy to his nieces and nephews would be a good dose of the truth. He had lived too many lies in his life.

"No, my father never said anything about being Negro. We have been studying the Civil War in school and how the Negro slaves were freed. Was Nancy Randall a slave?"

"No, she wasn't a slave, but her mother had been a slave. Nancy Randall's father owned her mother, but freed her before Nancy was born. That was one hundred years ago. Your father and I never had the chance to meet her, but all our older sisters spent time with her in Charleston before she died. She was a fine lady, a mulatto lady. She and our grandfather, a white plantation owner had six children. Your grandfather is named Thomas, after him. And my mother's Inglis family also had mixed blood."

"I thought all Negros were slaves and whipped, had terrible lives. That's what my teacher says. I never saw a Negro until we were on the train. He had black skin."

"Not all the Negros were slaves, Willie. And in many parts of the world, slaves were also fair, as well as dark, and of many nationalities. Many slaves earned their freedom or were freed by their owners way before the Civil War. Our relatives, both the light and the dark of them, were quite wealthy. My parents owned slaves themselves."

"Our family owned slaves? Grandma and Grandpa owned slaves? What a horrible thing for Negros to own other Negros! Are you certain that is correct? My teacher never said anything about that."

"Yes, I am correct. Why don't you ask your grandma and grandpa about slavery and being a great mixture of English, Scottish, Negro, maybe Indian and Moroccan?"

And Willie did.

"Grandpa! Grandpa!" Willie called in shock. "Harry told me we are part Negro. He said that's why his skin is darker. He told me to ask you why you owned slaves. I thought that slavery was terrible! My teacher says it is wrong for one person to own another and that's why we had the Civil War. How could you do such a terrible thing, Grandpa?"

Willie idolized his grandfather and was on the verge of tears with his discovery. His grandpa had owned people!

"Come here, Willie. You are a bit young to have slavery make any sense to you. And the longer I am away from Charleston, the less sense it makes to me. Slavery is wrong, but it is how I was raised. We owned slaves because our parents owned slaves. We did not question it. We accepted it. Slaves were part of our family. As children, we ate, slept and played together. Let me ask you, Willie. If I gave you one thousand dollar bills and told you it was your choice to keep them or give them away, what would you do?"

"One thousand dollars?! That's more money than I've ever seen! If my family needed the money, I would share the thousand dollars. I have food, a home and go to a good school. I have no need for money, but I sure would like a new bicycle. Maybe I would keep part of the money."

"That is very admirable. Now, if your father owned a chicken, had been feeding it, should he sell it for money or give it away?"

"Selling chickens is how farmers make money to feed their children. He should sell the chicken."

"So, it is alright for farmers to sell their animals, to make money to live?"

"Yes, it is why we raise them, for us to eat and to sell."

"And it is proper to kill animals to eat them?"

"Yes, it is. I don't like to kill animals, so I try not to think about that part."

"So, we didn't question the order of slavery. In the south, we treated slaves like animals. I know that isn't right, but we did. We bought and sold slaves, just like you take your animals to market. They were our valuable property. Many of our slaves were worth over $1000. Slaves made it possible to raise cotton and rice and sell them at market. We didn't pay them wages, but we did have to provide food, shelter, clothing and medical care."

"But slaves are people, not animals, Grandpa! Did you whip them?"

"No, I didn't, but many slave owners did. Do you have friends that are whipped if they don't mind their parents or work from dawn to dusk?"

"Yes. I've seen some bloody belt and switch marks on my classmates' legs and backs. My parents tell me to stay away from their homes, that they are not good families."

"Some men feel they own their wives, and some parents feel they own their children. To beat anyone ruins their spirit and breeds fear and hatred. It is good that slavery is gone. Your teacher is correct. People are not animals. They should not be owned. We need to feed our families in ways that do not hurt other people. I buy and sell coal. No one gets hurt.”

“Father says the coal miners are little more than slaves. He says the miners do not make enough money to feed their families.”

“At least they own themselves and are not slaves. William, the world is not always fair or kind. It is our job to live in it as best we can, to take care of our families and not hurt others.”

“That’s why you left South Carolina, isn’t it?”

“Yes. Your grandma and I needed to take care of our family. And we could have been sold as slaves if we stayed.”

“Because you are part Negro?”

“Yes, because of that.”

“But you look white! Both you and Grandma look white. You are lighter than my father.”

“Well, we are mainly white. I know this is confusing. We are about one-fourth black and three-fourths white. We used to be called mulatto, which means mixture, but we changed our status to white.”

“Why?”

“The truth is that Negros are considered inferior. The highest status is to be white. You need to remember that and call yourself white, keep the Negro a secret. Only whites can be their best, have the best and prosper. Other peoples are kept down.” Thomas sighed as the perspiration dripped from his brow. His explanation was falling short. “None of this makes much sense, does it?”

“No, it doesn’t. Slavery is wrong, and you make it seem alright.”

“So, use that as a test for your life. If you have to work too hard to make sense of something, to explain or excuse something, it probably is wrong. It is hard for me to explain because I loved my slave-owning relatives. I loved our life, created by mistreating others. And I want you to respect me and your grandmother, even though we were slave owners. I hope you can love us and not love slavery.”

"William, you need to talk to your children about their heritage," Thomas said to his son. "All of it, the English, the Scottish, the Negro, the Moroccan *Turks*, the Indian and, yes, slavery."

"I assume by your tone Willie asked you and you told him," said a disgusted William.

"Yes, to the best of my ability. I did not defend slavery, but I want him to not hate us for being slave owners."

"That's a tall order, Father, an impossible one. Rhoda and I had thought we wouldn't tell our children. We just wanted them to accept their whiteness and blend into the new Minnesota frontier."

"It's too late for that. What were you going to tell them? That you are part Indian or East Indian? Rubbish. Your skin is dark, and your nose is broad. Tell your children the truth. And tell them they are legally white. The Negro part is a proud heritage. Tell it. They can be proud of the Hanscomes, my mulatto mother and my white father. They bridged a gap that was rarely crossed in South Carolina. Tell them of their love story. Tell them how they had the courage to be different. Tell them how they took care of their family. Tell them of their honor."

"And tell them of the elite, slave-owning Brown Fellowship Society of the Inglis? How you and mother had your own slaves from birth, to cater to your every whim?" William was angry.

"Yes. They may be too young to understand the Southern way of life. But tell them the whole story, the beautiful graciousness as well as the ugliness of slavery. It is a dead society. And hold your head high when you do. Willie's questions have just begun. They will not stop."

"I fail to see the beauty in any society based on slavery."

"It's because you didn't live it or accept it as normal. How could we pluck out the evil when it permeated our every pore? It was too close to our hearts to see. History has inspiring and evil tales, but don't take your children's history away from them, please. Don't lie to them."

"It is dangerous for my children to repeat this story, Father. If you think they won't suffer the same prejudice as those who live in the *colored* section of Toronto, you are mistaken. If you think we didn't suffer because of our *differentness*, you are mistaken. Ask my sisters who couldn't find mates. The Negros may not be slaves in Minnesota, but they live in poverty, just like the Indians. It's better if my children don't claim this history."

"Your children are white, just a drop remains of our magnificent mothers. What difference can that make?"

"A world of difference, even in Minnesota, Father! We intend to be just like everyone else and assimilate. Our past heritage is unimportant."

What started as a happy visit to Toronto ended on a sour note for Rhoda and William. Thomas had opened the family can of worms. What would they now tell their children about the black, the white and the in-between? Wasn't America the new melting pot? Didn't they simply need to forget the old allegiances, differences, cruelties and blend into the new American? Other immigrants abandoned their languages, their customs and religions so their children would fit in, become successful. The Hanscomes could do the same.

1891
St. Anthony Falls

"Oh no! William, come quick! Read this letter." And without further ado, Rhoda gave him the letter.

"We knew it, didn't we, Rhoda? At Arthur's wedding, we could see Harry's weakness. I knew it would be the last time we saw him. I just felt it in my bones."

"We have missed his funeral! We have missed our chance to say goodbye!"

Rhoda cried. William cried. They wept for Harry and their whole family.

"I felt like he was saying goodbye when he gave us those canvasses, so carefully wrapped. At least we have a part of him. I think he put the remainder of his life into his art. He was so happy at Arthur's wedding. That is a final memory we can cherish. Our family will give him a good send-off, Rhoda."

"We need to get Harry's pictures framed, beautifully framed and hung," Rhoda said. "I want to look at his landscapes. I want the children to know they had a great artist for an uncle. I want them to know they could have his talents. His last paintings were so ethereal, such subtleties of texture, color and substance. They seemed to reflect the peace he'd made. When I look at them, I feel I've been to the Cathedral."

"He always appreciated your support of his early work, Rhoda. You were so kind to him - accepting."

They held a special remembrance celebration for Harry where they unveiled his newly framed oil paintings. After the prayers, William and the children planted a tree.

"We will call this oak, *Harry's tree*. It will be a good place for you to sit, read a book, contemplate or even daydream. It will be a peaceful place. In South Carolina, these oak trees live forever. It is a good way to remember Uncle Harry."

One day, Little Rhoda, who was learning to read, asked her mother, "Why do Uncle Harry's pictures have the name Thomas Henry Hanscome written on them, if his name was Harry?"

And Rhoda smiled and retold the family tale about how his older sisters had named him after their boyfriends. Little Rhoda found the tale about *Harry Howling Wolf* and her Aunt Alice to be especially romantic. Maybe she would fall in love with an Indian and have a handsome, dark baby like her Uncle Harry.

"Oh no! Oh no!" cried Rhoda again. This time the news came in a telegram. What a shock! "We must leave today for Toronto, William. Your father has died. If we catch the afternoon train to Chicago, we can make the funeral."

Rhoda's brother drove the horse carriage as fast as he could to the depot. Did they make the train? Yes, they did. Did they make the funeral? Yes, just barely. They hired a carriage that delivered them, bags and all, to the cemetery the next afternoon.

The children were confused. They gawked wide-eyed at the graveyard scene and all their weeping aunts, dressed in black. They knew death, had buried animals on their farm, but had never witnessed a funeral.

"It's good that Uncle Harry has grandpa's company in heaven," Rhoda said. "Now, he won't be lonely anymore."

"I hope Harry's happy, even though the rest of us are sad," added Muriel.

"Don't be silly," Willie replied. "Dead people are just deader than doornails. They don't have feelings."

"Oh, you're heartless, brother," Muriel said.

"And hopeless," Rhoda added. "How do you think Grandpa likes to hear you talk like that? He can hear you, right now. I can hear his voice talking to me, can't you?"

Later, when his sisters were gone, Willie said a special prayer to his grandpa.

"I will be just like you when I grow up, Grandpa!" he promised. "I will be proud of who I am." Then he added, "except for the slave-owning part. I love you, Grandpa."

The sad-faced children placed flowers on his grave, then lost all decorum as they laughed and played hide and seek amongst the granite headstones. The Hanscome plot on the cemetery knoll outside the gothic Chapel of St. James-the-Less overlooked the Don River. Lovely. But today was sad. Thomas was seventy-three, robust, the very picture of health. He had returned home from a Sunday sail and didn't get up from his study chair when dinner was served.

After the service, the family returned to a house full of mourners, food and the sounds of a party. The children were fed, then re-fed from all the guests' plates. Young William was served his first glass of wine at fourteen. It was so tasty, he drained all the half-full crystal glasses left by the departing guests. His mother was puzzled as to why he threw up before he went to bed.

They stayed two weeks. The children had a good time riding bicycles up and down Toronto's gentle hills and along the waterfront. William helped his mother sort through all his father's papers.

"Father has left you well off, Mother. You will not need to sell the house, unless you want to leave these memories behind."

"I have no need for new memories. We have been together since Thomas' father died and our mothers became inseparable friends. Your father was eleven, and I was so young that I don't remember a day without him. I will stay here. These familiar rooms will comfort me."

"Do you want me to sort through his clothes?" Rhoda asked. "We could donate them to the needy."

"No. I want them to hang in the closet. I want everything to stay the same. At least for now. I don't want to accept our chapter closing."

"Will you visit us soon?"

And she did. Mary Sophia and one of her daughters visited Minneapolis every fall, to help with the harvest, apple picking and canning. They laughed and watched Mary Sophia's red hair slowly turn silver.

Her breath was taken away on the coldest winter day on January 29, 1899. She was seventy-four-years-old.

"I don't want to go to Toronto," cried young Rhoda. "I don't want to go to Grandma's funeral. I don't want to cry, not again. I don't want to see that grave site get packed full of our relatives, all dead. Who will die next?"

"We will miss you," teased Willie, "but someone has to take care of the animals, so why don't you just stay here, Rhoda."

"You're mean, Willie. I hope that Eva Isaacson knows how mean you are!" Rhoda retaliated. "I think I'll tell her."

At thirteen, Rhoda was given to bouts of emotionalism. Muriel, at fifteen, was usually calm and proper, but she was crying, too. The children had also lost their Baldwin grandparents in the last two years. From their view, all the people they loved were dying. Their grandmother had died January 29, but of course the ground was too frozen to inter her. Now, it was late March, and her body could be moved from the cemetery crypt and properly buried in the thawed ground. Young Rhoda was correct, as much as she hated it, she would cry, again.

All five of them took the train to Chicago. They knew the route by heart. In Chicago, William booked a two-night stay for the return trip. It was time they saw the sights of a truly big city. And some levity, after the sadness and the family upheaval, would be welcomed. Rhoda and William decided this would probably be the last time their whole family would return to Toronto or perhaps take a vacation together. Willie was getting married next year, at the turn of the century. He would be twenty.

The service was held at Holy Trinity Anglican Church, officiated by the Rector John Pearman with the burial at St. James Cemetery. The Garden and Lee children attended the services along with the Hanscomes. Yes, the family plots were filling. Young Rhoda's fears were materializing, and she wasn't the only one who wondered who God would take next.

Her dear Grandmother Mary Sophia lay next to her Grandfather Thomas who lay next to Uncle Harry. The Gardens were buried in the lot next to the Hanscomes. Joel Garden, who died at forty-four, his sister Iona Butler, who died at twenty-four, lay next to their parents, Elizabeth Sarah and John Garden. And right next to them laid the Garden's infant granddaughters, Sadie and Helena Francis Garden. The cause of death, consumption, was clearly listed on their death certificates.

The children explored the St. James neighborhood, walked to the harbor, Queen's Park near the University of Toronto, the Toronto Public Library, museums, art galleries and the Cathedral. They felt their father was privileged to have grown up in such a fine city. While they walked, they told stories about their grandparents, Uncle Harry, the Gardens, Inglis' and the Lees. Willie wondered silently what his life would have been like if his parents had stayed in Toronto. It was much more refined than their farm and Minnesota. Did he truly want to be a farmer like the Baldwins?

William and his siblings settled their mother's estate and divided the family possessions. The larger lovely things were left to the sisters who would remain in Toronto. Each item was special because of the story behind it. As they reminisced, they laughed. The hardest part was selling the large family home at 10 Wood Street. Arthur and William helped move their sisters to 65 Hazelton Avenue, just a few blocks away and conveniently right next door to the public library.

Arthur finally announced he and his wife were moving to the city of his dream, Vancouver. The separation of their family was another changing of the guard, another ending, and the sadness set in, again. Of course, Arthur and Sarah thought it an enchanting beginning. They had not been blessed with children and wanted a change. He was thirty-three, had his mechanical engineering degree and wanted a new challenge. This time, he would engineer safer trains, not drive them. Growth followed the train routes, and the new frontier was the West Coast.

They invited his real mother, *Connie*, AKA Alice, to move with them, but she declined. Alice did promise to visit. What could be better than to see the scenic Canadian Rockies on the transcontinental railroad? She was now the matriarch of the family and took her duty to her younger sisters seriously. She was as strong as her grandmother, Nancy Randall. She would let go of her son.

William and Rhoda left Toronto with heavier bags than they'd brought with them. His mother had left him the candelabras from the Charleston mansion. They were of no monetary significance, but the Hanscome children of every generation loved tracing the rainbows from the crystal prisms with their fingers, trying to capture the colors. Willie, Muriel and Rhoda were as entranced by them as William had been as a child. William was also given the portraits of his parents, his Uncle James and his grandfather Thomas Hanscome. His sisters wanted their nieces and nephew to have them.

It was sad saying goodbye. It was the end of an era. It was the end of a century. William was taking his family on vacation to Chicago. He had inherited a great deal of money. William, who had scoffed at his father's *Coal is King* rhetoric, was now so grateful for his father's largesse. How could he have been so short-sighted? Their family farm barely sustained them. In truth, he had never become ambitious. After they returned to Minnesota, the William Kissick Hanscomes determined to live their lives as *WASPs*. Goodbye Toronto. Hello *White Anglo-Saxon Protestants*.

Chapter 7

In With the New!
1900
Minneapolis and St. Paul

Happy New Year! Happy New Year! Ready or not, the 20th century had begun.

Did the Hanscomes venture out on New Year's Eve to celebrate the turn of the century? No, in spite of the new electric arc lights on Washington Avenue, Minneapolis was a dark and dangerous place. Lawlessness, prostitution, gambling saloons and opium dens flourished in the Gateway district, just across the Mississippi River from the Hanscome's St. Anthony Falls neighborhood.

The cowboys, who drove herds to St. Paul's stockyards and slaughterhouses, were nightly swindled out of their profits. The poor unsuspecting farmers, who sold wheat to the mills and produce in the market, purchased whiskey in the Pig's Eye of St. Paul, only to be fleeced by confidence men with purchased police badges. Yes, false police badges, enticing dance hall girls, heavenly opium and orphaned, dirty children sold as farm workers - everything and everybody was for sale in downtown

Minneapolis. With a population of over 200,000, it was no longer a small, unassuming city. It was touted as the nineteenth largest city in the United States.

Something had to be done about the total disregard for the law. Four terms of Mayor Ames' rule had made it the land of opportunity for racketeers, crooks and robbers from across the nation. Rumors had it that Mayor Ames would soon be indicted by a grand jury. He indignantly stood by his record of progress and prosperity. And, yes, there was that, too. He cited Minnegasco, the new gas company, safer trains, paved roads, street cars, churches, schools, bicycle paths, parks and orphanages among his proud accomplishments. Politics only seemed dirty when scrutinized under a microscope.

The Hanscomes celebrated the ominous beginning of the new century on New Year's Day. During the night, the Mississippi River held its own celebration as it howled, moaned and froze solid. They wouldn't hear that sound again until the ice broke up in spring. Despite the cold, they were excited to take the new, inter-city streetcar from Minneapolis to St. Paul, a distance of eleven miles along the scenic Mississippi Riverbank. Rhoda had finally mastered her fear of the cold, and, like a true Minnesotan, never let the weather deter her from fun. She told her children that while the Mississippi might freeze, she'd never seen a smile frozen on a face. "Smile children! Smile! It's New Year's Day! In with the new!" Rhoda was enthralled, always, by the new, the better and the best.

"I've never been to St. Paul," said young Rhoda, stylish and warm in her new muskrat coat, woolen hat, scarf, mittens and fleece-lined boots. Her warm brown eyes smiled as she nestled closely into her mother's rich mink coat, also new.

Furs were not considered luxuries by the senior Rhoda. They were necessities, unless one wanted to stay inside during winter months of sub-zero temperatures and succumb to the nasty cabin fever that dulled the brain and depressed the spirit. Although the heyday of fur trapping had passed, the furrier business was brisk. Yes, the trappers were right. Minnesota winters demanded fur coats. Practical Rhoda wore hers to the barn and back as well as to the Cathedral. And today, they all sported new furs, Christmas presents from Willie.

"I thought we'd have St. Paul's finest steak dinners to celebrate this auspicious New Year before we ride the streetcar back. There is nothing more lovely than the sun glinting on the snow and ice," replied William in his stylish, dark brown beaver coat and matching hat.

"I've been wondering, Father. Don't you find it strange that people from one side of the River don't mix with the other?" Muriel asked. "We never go to St. Paul. Why is that?"

"That's because like attracts like, dear," replied her mother, answering for her husband. "We settled near St. Anthony because of the small English Community already there. St. Paul has more Catholics, Irish and Germans. The Scandinavians settled in Minneapolis."

"But some of our neighbors are German," Muriel replied.

"They are the low Germans, the Protestants, and farmers, like us," schooled her father. "The high Germans, the Catholics, settled in St. Paul. It also has an influx of southern European workers, who work in the stock yards. Catholics all. And the Jews, Hungarians and Poles have settled not far from us in north Minneapolis. Big changes are bound to happen in this new century. Some predict our north Minneapolis farmland will become city. If you get lost in all this development, Muriel, just follow the blonde hair and blue eyes to the right side of the River," William said and laughed.

"That's a terrible thing to say, dear," admonished his wife.

"Yes, it is," he replied, pleased with his witticism, "but there's always the good and bad side of the tracks and the good and bad side of the River. Minneapolis is the right side."

"What's that horrid smell?" Muriel asked as she wrinkled her nose.

"It's the smell of money," her father said and smiled. "It's the stock yards. The wind must be blowing from the west today. Give it a few minutes, and your nostrils will adjust to the pungent odors. This is why St. Paul has the best steak houses, but I wouldn't want to live here."

"Well, it smells worse than any manure pile we've had," Muriel wryly commented.

"Think hundreds of heads of cattle, Muriel. And hundreds of pigs, too. They are the proud source of farm prosperity."

"I'll never complain about our smelly chicken coop again," young Rhoda said and laughed.

"After dinner, I will rent a carriage to drive us by St. Paul's majestic Catholic Cathedral and up Summit Avenue to view the regal mansions. J.J. Hill and other tycoons have made millions on the development of our fine state. His home is fit for a king."

"I'd rather be in Toronto with our family," Muriel quipped. "Can we move there, please, dear Father? I miss my aunts. I'd like to live with them. I don't believe I ever want to marry."

"Muriel, you look quite white, if that's what's troubling you. I wish your grandpa had never divulged our history, but it is nothing to be ashamed of. Did you read in the *Minneapolis Star* about the young Negro lawyer and Congressman, John Francis Wheaton? He was named orator of his University of Minnesota law school class. His south Minneapolis district serves only white people, and they elected him to the state legislature. Think of it, both you girls. You can be anything you want to be. Mark my word, after women are allowed to vote, we'll even have a woman president. There is no reason for you to worry."

"Yes, I would marry Mr. Wheaton in a minute for his dedication to ideals, but, alas, he is already married," Muriel declared. "I have also read that those Jim Crow laws are affecting Negros' success in every area of the country. Some of the new laws make it almost impossible for them to vote, can you believe that? I don't like to think their hard won freedom will be lost, again. And the rights of women? I hardly see that. Where I work, all the women are the secretaries and the men the bosses with the offices. Fetch and carry, fetch and carry, sit on my lap and think it's a privilege for you to do so. Does that sound familiar?"

"Stop it. Stop this talk right now, dear sister," Rhoda whispered in anger. "We might be overheard. We are four generations removed from any African, and I will not identify with this heritage. You are sixteen and I, a mere fourteen. Decide to be a spinster, if you choose, but me? I am going to marry. It is the only way to have a future and avoid the female slavery you describe in your office. I will not diminish myself, to anyone."

"Well, at least I get a salary," retorted Muriel. "You'll receive an allowance, at best, from your husband and still be at his beck and call, still one person away from respect."

"Hush girls, please. This bickering is not becoming. Your father and I treat each other as equals, although I know it isn't the norm. This is the New Year, a new 20th Century era. Things will soon change for the better, regardless of color or gender. Today is for fun, not sociology. Life is to be enjoyed, regardless of one's circumstance."

"I agree, Mother. Minneapolis is an adventurous place. I see many eligible young men at Central High School. I have hope for a new 20th century life," said young Rhoda, beaming. "I've made a New Year's Resolution to be open to all great men and the comforts they can provide."

Where was young Willie on this first day of the century? He was working. Well, someone in their family needed to provide. He had decided to harvest the remainder of his mink crop, except for the ones he would breed in March, and deliver the pelts to the newly opened Schlamps' Furriers in Minneapolis. On his last delivery, he had bartered for new fur coats for his family's Christmas presents. Willie was following his Grandpa Hanscome's advice to take care of his family and do no harm. Was it wrong for him to kill the minks? The thought never crossed his mind. Minks were merely animals like the cows raised on their farm. They were an important part of the basic need for food, shelter and clothing.

What had happened to that Scandinavian Ava Issacson, Willie's girlfriend? Her family had moved west, and she went with them. They were not pleased with her choice of Willie for a husband. Why? Because he was not Lutheran. But Willie was too busy working their farm to notice her absence, or so he said. He gave nary a thought to his darker complexion.

1909

Development had come to north Minneapolis, and William and Rhoda sold their farm for a handsome price. Farming had never been in William's blood, and Willie was ready to strike out on his own. Mayor Ames had gone to jail, and south Minneapolis had become law abiding, safe and quite the cultural center. The Hanscomes bought a simple, two-story wood frame house on Lyndale Avenue near Lake Street, the end of the streetcar line. It was the very edge of town, on the right side of the river and in the best neighborhood. Rhoda loved the newly paved streets. Gone were the ruts and the dust, but the traffic had doubled, trying to accommodate the horses and buggies, the streetcars and the new automobiles. What a dangerous, yet exciting spectacle. It made Rhoda smile. Like a wild child, Minneapolis had finally blossomed into an energized and respectable adulthood.

William swore he would never own a Model T. He was quite content taking the streetcar and his bicycle. Their house was located on the very popular, cinder bicycle path where they bicycled to the country for picnics on Lake Calhoun, Lake Harriet, Fort Snelling, Minnehaha Falls and even as far as Lake Minnetonka. Bicycling was all the rage. Rhoda had a tricycle, so her skirts wouldn't get caught in the chains or spokes, but the girls opted for the faster bicycles with the low bar and the chain guard that protected their skirts. Muriel rode hers to the Minneapolis Business School where she was studying stenography and dictation so she could secure a better position.

"How do you like our new house and neighborhood?" William asked, quite pleased with himself. "We are again on the outskirts of Minneapolis, but I like this south side. I think it's noticeably warmer here." William delighted in making his girls smile. But young Rhoda was smiling for a different reason and not her father's corny joke. Young James Arthur Campbell was coming all the way from North Minneapolis to see her.

His family called him Arthur, but Rhoda called him JAC, for his initials. They met at the farmer's market when JAC stopped to admire her artfully displayed watercolor paintings, carefully placed behind her freshly cut bouquets of the same varieties. How clever she was matching real flowers with the subjects of her pictures. Rhoda loved gardening, like her father, and painting flowers and nature scenes, like her Uncle Harry. But handsome JAC quickly became her number one interest. He was a strong-faced, strong-chinned, strong-framed, tall Scot with blond hair and penetrating, bright blue eyes. Rhoda was petite with straight, warm chestnut brown hair, like her mother's and big brown eyes, like her father's that could charm in a flash. But it was Rhoda's warm laughter drifting through the market that drew JAC's attention. She had a big captivating laugh for such a little woman. She knew how to make conversations engaging, bright and light.

"Rather than simply displaying the flowers with your paintings, why don't you sell both together," JAC suggested. "My favorites are sunflowers."

"Sunflowers? Why on earth do you like sunflowers?" she asked, her eyes twinkling. "Some consider them little more than weeds."

"Because they remind me of your big, brown eyes." Truly, did this hardworking, practical, solid, stoic Scot utter such a flirtatious phrase? Apparently so, unless of course romantic Rhoda remembered their first meeting differently and put those words in his very mouth in the retelling. Rhoda loved to make conversations and parlor games of all kinds *interesting*. Truthful, always, but *interesting* was even better.

"I thank you for your kind compliment, but we grow no sunflowers in our garden," she blushed.

"Then I will bring you some."

And he did. And she painted them. And she sold them, most of them back to JAC. And this was their beginning, according to Rhoda. JAC provided, and Rhoda created beauty. Rhoda thought that made a perfect and complimentary relationship. Giving and receiving at its finest.

Soon, JAC was courting her. In the fall, they rode horses through the colorful foliage and had picnics by the River. JAC set up her easel, while Rhoda captured the bright red sumac, yellow oaks and orange maples on her canvas. At times, she would let him kiss her. In the winter, they held hands while they ice skated on the River and drank hot chocolate in the Village. At times, she would let him kiss her, again. How romantic.

"Do you think JAC wants to marry me?" she asked her parents one day. "I've been waiting, a bit impatiently. Do you think he is slow or just not interested?"

"Your JAC is quite enamored with you, but he has yet to mention his intentions to your father. Is he still thinking of working the family farm? The Campbells have quite a few acres in Camden, but he has all those brothers, and they are marrying, too. A piece of land can only support so many families."

"I have been talking to him about the barge and coal business," William said. "For a youth who quit school after the eighth grade, he can certainly do those figures in his head. I think it might be a good use of our inheritance from my parents to help him get started in his own business, if he is interested."

"Father, I certainly hope you didn't tell him that. I don't like to think he is marrying me for a dowry. That is such an outdated practice. It's like paying for a brood mare or prize cow."

"I haven't. My, you are head strong, Rhoda. And bossy, like a cow. How does your JAC like that?" her father teased.

"We complement each other, Father. He is strong and silent, and I am a strong chatterbox. I talk, and he listens. I told him he can decide how to make the money, and I will decide how to spend it. Now don't you think that is complementary? All that JAC needs is a smart wife to prod him in the right direction. I have ambitions; his family has none. JAC is curious, and we delight in each other's company."

"You sound rather flippant, Miss Rhoda," replied her father. "It's not becoming, like an over-confident man."

"Oh, don't worry, Father. We love each other to death."

"Not to death I hope," her father said and laughed. "By the way, Rhoda, what have you told him of our family history?"

"I told his mother that the Hanscomes hail from Toronto, and the Baldwins, who they also know from the markets, come originally from England. I told JAC I didn't know much more than that about our ancestors. The Campbells came from Scotland to Nova Scotia, dirt poor. Did I tell you that their ancestors capsized their boat on the Flume River and decided to claim that piece of land as home, as an omen direct from God. With no boat, they could travel no further. Isn't that interesting? They are most happy to have soil instead of rock to farm. You have met the Campbells many times, Father. What did you tell them?"

"Nothing, simply nothing. Minnesota is a land of immigrants. No one is very interested in family lineage. They want to learn English, be like everyone else and let go of the past. Their uprooting from Europe ripped families apart and left holes in their souls they are eager to fill. It's better to deny the past, so the future can take hold," her father said.

"What do you think of the Campbells, Father?"

"They are on the surface simple, dull, uneducated and hardworking farmers, but they are smart. That is one thing I like about them. You will have smart, attractive, probably blue-eyed and blonde-haired children. Oh yes, and the palest of skin, if that makes a difference to you. At the same time, they are a bit boring, dear Rhoda. I hope you will be happy being part of their family. You are vibrant, shiny and bright, like a copper penny and the new electric lights. You are not like them."

"Well, you say I am like my strong-willed mother, and she loves your family, not dull but different. JAC will do anything to please me, and I will love his family, even if they've never read a book."

"Back to the subject I was discussing. Have you told JAC about our Negro lineage?"

"No, I have not. I intend to erase that era from our family history, at least mine. It can only hold us back, as you said. I have also asked Willie and Muriel to silence their tongues, at least around JAC. I do appreciate that the Campbells do not hold prejudices against the Negro families, who settled not far from them on Shingle Creek. Hard work is the Campbell motto. They admire the Negros' persistence and tenacity."

"Secrets created pain in our family – the lies about Arthur's birth, Harry's homosexuality and our African roots. I clearly have a darker complexion. How did you explain that?"

"I said nothing, Father. I told them somewhere we might have some Indian blood."

"I must laugh. Today, as in old South Carolina, Indian blood is still better received than Negro blood."

"Well, Father, I was thinking of another kind of Indian. Do you remember the East Indian merchants who lived next door to you in Toronto? I simply planted that seed. Let them guess. You are most cultured, Father, just smile and admit to nothing. Talk about your common Scottish blood, your Kissick middle name. JAC's family is not pretentious. They love me because I make JAC laugh. Nothing else is important."

"You are too glib about this, Rhoda. How do you think JAC will feel about our family trips to Toronto? Are you going to ask your aunts to lie about our grandmother, Nancy Randall, whom they dearly honor?"

"I have thought about it, Father. I think you and mother should continue to visit Toronto, your dear sisters, but I will not be taking JAC or our children. That chapter has closed for me."

"Don't deny your family, Rhoda," her father cautioned. "Your aunts love you."

"First, you say denial of the past is good, now you say, don't forget your relatives. Isn't that exactly what your own parents did when they crossed the 49th parallel and declared themselves white? They left their family in Charleston. And I understand why. Grandpa made that quite clear. They were whitish enough. Father, you know it and I know it, no one thinks highly of Negros. They are being lynched, still, in the South. They are considered inferior in every way. I don't believe that is true or morally right, but I want my children to have every opportunity. I won't lie about our Hanscome past. I'll just say I don't know it."

"Rhoda, what is it you want from life, if not the love of your family?" her mother, who had been listening to the conversation, asked, with a frown.

"I want you and Father, Willie and Muriel to be part of my new life. I want light-hearted laughter as well as love. I intend to be a part of the new Minneapolis. I choose social position, wealth and opportunities for my children. Yes, that is the selfish, and I hope not a too despicable truth. In return, I will do my utmost to do good works and practice my calling, which is to make people happy."

"And JAC agrees?" Her mother asked.

"Yes, he does. JAC wants to test his mettle. He wants to be wealthy. He's tired of Scottish frugality."

"And you think if JAC knew the truth about your Negro heritage he would refuse to marry you?" she asked.

"I don't know, but I don't intend to find out. Wasn't that the curse of all my aunts?"

"Prejudice was part of it, but not the only reason. Oh, Rhoda, your sin of omission, your denial may return to haunt you one day, but the choice is yours. Your father and I may not agree with your decision, but we will not ruin your party. We understand that fun is the life goal of your generation, and it seems so - so shallow! You may spend your life atoning for this transgression."

"Please don't make me feel guilty for being honest about my desires. I am a good, kind, loving person, Mother."

"I know you are, but you are too direct, sometimes," her mother replied. "Blunt."

"I wonder where she gets that trait?" William said and smiled, looking directly at his wife. "I rather like knowing who a person is, with no pretense or ploys."

"Touché, dear. She has a good dose of my determination, but I think our Rhoda gets her ambitious trait from your father."

May 22, 1911

It was a beautiful spring day for an afternoon wedding. St. Mark's, now the Episcopal Cathedral, was bathed with the sunlit glow from the stained glass windows. The ushers seated the parents of the groom, Rachel and William, yes, another William, on the groom's side. Across the aisle, the mother of the bride, Rhoda, breathed deep. JAC and his Campbell brothers Wilmot, Bert, Melvin, and Edwin waited in front of the altar for the procession to begin. The music from the pipe organ resounded off the stone walls. Was William the organist today? No, he was proudly walking his radiant Rhoda, purely dressed in white lace gown and veil, slowly down the aisle. She carried a fragrant bouquet of tiny white roses, lilies of the valley and one large sunflower that made for smiles and fun conversation.

"Do you, Rhoda Hanscome, take James Arthur Campbell to be your wedded husband?"

"I do," she soundly stated, looking JAC directly in his eyes. Of course, JAC followed her lead.

The wedding, like most weddings, was too soon over.

"Those five Campbell brothers are certainly a handsome lot," remarked one guest.

"I certainly feel sorry for that solo sister growing up with all those men," said another.

"Don't feel sorry for Stella, she's the apple of her brothers' eyes and quite lively, like Rhoda."

"Didn't the church smell heavenly?" commented another.

"I don't think the altar could hold another bouquet of lilacs. It was all I can do to stifle my sneezes," complained another. "And why, pray tell, did Rhoda carry that weed of a sunflower?"

"Muriel looked quite flushed as the maid of honor - surprisingly lovely today!"

"That one will never marry. She's a suffragette, plain and a working girl."

"Oh, a working girl? That is a pity, indeed."

"I hear the bride is doing charity work for the Washburn Home Orphanage."

"I certainly hope she intends to have her own children. One must be wary of an orphan's unknown lineage."

"Well, Rhoda certainly has gumption. She is spunky like her mother, and so much fun!"

The bells of the Cathedral rang as the couple descended the steps on a beautiful, warm, May afternoon. After they had been gaily drenched with rice, the reception began in the church hall. Rhoda loved a fine party so why did they leave so soon?

"Oh, JAC, we must hurry, or we will miss the last streetcar to Excelsior!"

"Yes, dear," JAC replied, in a dutiful style that would mark many of their future conversations.

The Twin City Rapid Transit Company boasted one of the most extensive streetcar systems in the nation. Forty miles of track ran between Stillwater on the St. Croix River in the east to the Village of Excelsior on Lake Minnetonka in the west. The streetcar delivered Rhoda and JAC directly to their honeymoon suite at the elegant, four-story Tonka Bay Hotel.

"This room and the view are magnificent, JAC," Rhoda exclaimed as she threw open the windows to the lake breeze. "This panorama takes my breath away. We came at the best time of the year."

"Yes, I agree, dear. It is not too crowded with tourists from Chicago or boats. Wait a few weeks, and this old hotel will be bustling with several hundred guests."

The newlyweds ate a lamb chop dinner with mint jelly, one of Rhoda's favorite meals, before JAC hung a *DO NOT DISTURB* sign on the outside of their door and powerfully carried her across the threshold.

"Kiss me, dear JAC," Rhoda romantically cried as she flung herself upon him. And he did. And when he did even more than that, her eyes bulged out in amazement. Was she pleased? Well, the kisses were magnificent, and she didn't dislike his touch, but to her it was unimportant. Of course, she loved JAC and would do her utmost to please him. "Men will be men," she thought. What did excite her were their conversations of the fine life they would create together.

The rest of the week was not totally spent in passionate embraces in quiet seclusion. They attended the playhouse and rode the steamboat to the amusement park on Big Island. Music blared from the Big Island Casino that hosted 1500 people on the Fourth of July. They danced at night and rode the roller coaster, carousel and other rides during the day. One special day, Rhoda packed a picnic lunch, and JAC rowed a boat in and out of the many coves on Lake Minnetonka. How romantic.

"Oh, JAC, our honeymoon was perfect. Can we have our own lake cabin one day?"

"I'll see what I can do about that, Rhoda," JAC said, with a smile. "But first we need a house."

Spring 1912

"Do you, William Thomas Hanscome, take you, Ethel Dixon, to be your wedded wife?"

"I do."

And the church bells rang, but not at St. Mark's Cathedral. Willie had moved when his parents sold their farm. The Hormel Food Company in Austin offered him a lucrative position. Their slaughterhouse and fresh meat and sausage wagons distinguished them as a leader in Minnesota's meat industry. And when Hormel was able to answer the question, "How can we preserve meats better?" their business boomed. Soon, Hormel's indestructible canned hams were being shipped all over the world. An industrious young Hormel employee copied the farm women's success with canning chickens and meats and pickling vegetables. All they needed were airtight tins.

The couple met at Christ Episcopal Church's annual German sauerkraut and sausage potluck dinner. Ethel was serving her homemade pickled beets. Did Willie like beets? Not particularly, but he liked Ethel and returned for more.

The Hanscomes took the train to Austin, a few hours south of Minneapolis for the wedding.

"Thank goodness Ethel is not a Lutheran," William remarked, remembering the fate of Ava Isaacson. They were relieved that Willie at thirty-two had found a bride, just a few years younger than their Rhoda.

Out with the old century, in with the new! The Hanscomes had tossed away horses, simple farm life, candlelight and family history. And the new? They had telephones, bicycles, automobiles, electric lights, indoor plumbing and, of course, marriages. They were forward thinking and living the American dream, the WASP ideal. Prosperity was headed their way.

Chapter 8

Prosperity
1911
Minneapolis

"JAC, I think it's time we had a family. Do you agree?"

"Of course, dear." JAC said, smiling at his own standard reply, then added with a grin, "I will truly enjoy giving you your heart's desire."

1912

"It's a boy!" the doctor announced. "Both the baby and Rhoda are doing well."

JAC, his parents and the Hanscomes were waiting for the news in the Campbell's new bungalow near Minnehaha Creek.

"What will you call him?" proud grandfather, William Campbell, asked.

"We agreed that if we had a boy, he would be named James, after me, but we also wanted a solid Scottish middle name, Gordon. James Gordon. Do you like the sound of that?" JAC asked.

"We'll have to look at him first," Grandma Rhoda said and laughed. "Gordon is also an English name, a good choice." Soon, all had a chance to hold the curly, blonde-haired, blue-eyed baby.

"He's a copy of my boys, a true Scottish lad, except for the surprisingly curly hair," said his Grandma Rachel.

Was he doted on? Of course, like all firstborns, Gordon was bright, perfect and would conquer the world.

And how was JAC supporting his family? He was working for Minnegasco. Energy was his keen interest. However, he was toying with starting his own business. He wanted to be his own man, to make his own mark, and his father-in-law's coal conversations had piqued his curiosity.

1914
Austin

"It's a boy," the doctor announced to Willie Hanscome.

"What should we name our son?" Ethel asked.

"Let's call him Thomas after my grandfather from Toronto. He came from a long line of Thomas Hanscomes, and my grandpa was my hero. You can choose the middle name."

"Dixon, after my family. I like Thomas Dixon Hanscome. It's a good blend of family names, don't you think?"

And so, he was named.

"It's a girl," the doctor said, calling JAC into their bedroom.

"Isn't she sweet?" Rhoda beamed as she held her new infant. "Do you think we should call her April after this fine spring day?"

"We could also call her Sunshine, if you'd like, since this is the first time we've seen the sun in months." JAC said and laughed.

"Or, we could call her *Plenty*. I truly wanted a girl this time. Now, we have one for each of us, quite equitable, don't you agree, JAC? Perhaps we should quit, if you think she is *plenty* enough." Rhoda said and laughed.

"What a strange name, *Plenty*. Where did you get that silly idea?"

"*Plenty* is an old Hanscome family joke about how many children make *plenty*, and *plenty* is a stopping point for having children. Silly, I agree. I don't even know the origin of the *Plenty* joke."

"Well, I'm not sure I've had *plenty* enough children quite yet. How about you, Rhoda?"

"I want a whole brood. A big family. And you?"

"Let's name this daughter Rhoda, a third generation of Rhoda's," he suggested. "And then, we can decide if the next one's a *Plenty*."

"Fine," Rhoda said and smiled, "but let's add a middle name, like Jane. Rhoda Jane. It was confusing to have the exact same name as my mother."

"Little Rhoda Jane, it is. Let's show Gordy his new sister."

Wide-eyed, little three-year-old Gordy peered at the newborn. Soon his lip trembled. "Up," he demanded, holding his arms out to his mother. "Mama, put that baby away!"

"Come here, dear Gordon," his mother said as she handed the baby to JAC. Once he was settled next to her, Gordy took a second puzzled look. "Something's wrong with her, Mama. She has no hair. Baby Rhoda Jane has no hair!"

"Don't worry, her hair will grow. It will be blonde like yours. Remember, Rhoda Jane is your baby, too, Gordy. You are her big brother, a big boy, and your job as she grows bigger is to help take care of her. You must protect her from any neighborhood bullies."

And he did. As Rhoda Jane grew, Gordy corralled her like a watch dog protecting a baby lamb. And her hair grew, blonde like his, but straight as a stick. She, too, resembled a fair-skinned Scot. The strong jaw, wide-set blue eyes and sturdy, friendly face announced her Campbell clan to all.

Grandma Rachel remarked, "It's too bad Rhoda Jane didn't get Gordy's curls."

And Rhoda? She was thankful. She wanted no curls for any of her children. Her Grandmother Mary Sophia hated her curly, red hair. It was painful to brush out all the tangles before she pulled it tightly back in a bun. And Rhoda wanted no one guessing the origin of the curly hair.

1916
Austin

"It's a girl!" the doctor announced.

"Look, Tommy, do you want to kiss your baby sister?" Ethel asked. Tommy just shook his head no. He was only two and didn't quite know what to make of his sister. He decided to stay safely nestled in his father's arms and turned his head away from his mother's touch.

"It will take some time, but he'll adjust. Soon, he'll be like Gordy herding Rhoda Jane," Willie said and laughed.

"What name do you think suits her?"

"Barbara. Let's call her Barbara Jane," Ethel said. "It will be fun for the girls to share the same middle name."

"Oh, JAC! Oh, JAC!" Rhoda called from the other room. "I've been thinking, JAC."

"It is always dangerous when you think, Rhoda. Why do you always yell for me from the other room? Please don't treat me like our children. Come here, please. What is it you want?"

"I simply had an idea I wanted to discuss with you. I know it is a bad habit I have, to expect you to come when I call, like the children. My apologies, dear."

JAC smiled, in spite of his irritation at Rhoda using the identical tone of voice to summon him and their children. The positive was that he never had to guess what his wife wanted. He appreciated Rhoda's directness, bright temperament and blunt honesty. He felt sorry for other men, who had to guess their wives' true desires and ended up guessing wrong. Men wanted to please their wives, and Rhoda knew that. In return, she did her utmost to please him. It was simple.

"I'm thinking it would be good to get some help with the children, now that I am expecting again. I have been donating time at the Washburn Orphanage Home and think one of the Swedish girls would be a perfect maid and mother's helper for us. She is too old to be adopted at thirteen and is so good to the younger orphans. If I could arrange for her to live with us, she could continue her schooling at South High School. After school, she could help with the children and housekeeping. Otherwise, she will have to quit school and go to work, indeed, not a bright future for her. What do you think, JAC?"

"And if she lived with us, where would we put her? We have three bedrooms, ample room for us and another baby, but not a mother's helper."

"Take a guess, JAC. I think we need to have a bigger house, one with five bedrooms. One for a nursery, one for Rhoda Jane, one for Gordy and one for the live-in help. And I'd love for us to have more space, perhaps a separate dressing room and an upstairs veranda. And another bathroom would be essential, perhaps a sun porch, a formal dining room, a music room, a library!" Rhoda was good naturedly prattling on – and on. What a vision of gracious living. But then, she felt it was her duty as his wife to educate him on the finer things from time-to-time.

"Whoa, I see where this is going. And do you already have this mansion in mind?"

"Yes, I do. I spotted a lovely home right on Minnehaha Creek and Stephens Avenue, right near the outskirts of town. It has a wooded lot for the children, and perhaps a dog, yes, a watch dog would be nice. After all, we can't expect Gordy to do all the protecting. I don't know anything about the inside of the house, but it looks double the size of our bungalow."

"And tell me, is your father buying this for us, as he did our bungalow?"

"No, JAC. He isn't. I think his inheritance is gone. You know he has a generous heart but is not a businessman, not like you. You'll just need to make more money." She smiled.

And what did JAC do? He talked with his father-in-law about the coal business. Soon, he was financed for his first business, the Campbell Coal Company. Did the Hanscomes lend him money? No. A St. Mark's Cathedral vestryman and banker friend of William's agreed to finance JAC.

1917

"It's a girl," the doctor announced to JAC, Gordy and Little Rhoda Jane.

"Another girl?" Gordy asked, now five, with a big sigh. "I hoped and hoped and hoped for a baby brother."

"We have to take what the good Lord gives us. How about if we call her Hope, Gordy's Hope?" his father laughed as he tousled his son's curly hair.

"JAC, Hope is fine for a middle name, but let's give her a first name without a meaning attached to it. She could be teased with a first name of Hope. What other name do you like, Gordon?"

"Jean," Little Gordy answered. "Rhoda Jane and I both think Jean Hope would be a good name."

Did Gordon always speak for his sweet-natured, two-year-old sister, Rhoda Jane? Yes, but apparently she didn't mind. She had become his devoted shadow. Today, Rhoda Jane was also full of hope, not for a little brother, but hope that this baby would be taken away. It was her turn to cry. She hugged her father's leg, until he pried her off and plopped her on the bed. Soon, she took an interest in the bundle.

"Patty-cake, patty-cake, baker's man..." she said, clapping her hands with glee.

"And I have a surprise for you, Rhoda," JAC said as he handed Rhoda a little wrapped box.

"Oh, I just love presents. What could it be?"

"Shake it and guess," he said with a smile.

"A ring? It rattles when I shake it." Rhoda loved JAC's surprise gifts. "I know, a diamond ring!"

"It's a key," Gordy blurted out, unable to keep the secret.

It was a key. JAC had bought that home at 45 East Minnehaha Parkway. He was in hock to the bank, but his coal business was booming, as were many American businesses as they filled the war demands in Europe.

"Oh, I am thrilled, JAC. A big house! But I see I am not the only one who gets a present today. Do you hear something in the big box? Open it, Gordy."

And Little Gordy was all smiles as he peered in the box. He had a puppy, his very own dog, to help with the herding of his sisters. Gordon named him Jupee. And how did he choose that name? From the approximation of the word *jumping*, of course. When the puppy excitedly jumped all over Rhoda Jane, her garbled words excitedly flew out - *Jupee!*

Jupee was a mutt JAC selected from the Minneapolis Animal Rescue League, the philanthropic charity for orphaned dogs.

Minneapolis wanted to end the packs of stray dogs and cats roaming its streets. They were becoming more than a sanitary nuisance, some of the dogs had attacked people. What a novel idea the director had to have the strays adopted. And if they weren't adopted? Well, if they weren't trainable, it was better for them to be put *to sleep*. The Executive Director Myrtle Dickinson and her young son Wesley helped select Jupee.

Rhoda was all smiles, too. Her JAC never forgot her requests, even if it took time to fulfill them. She was thrilled with her five-bedroom, two-and-a-half bath home. It had a sun room, an outside veranda overlooking the Creek, a spacious parlor, formal dining room, and library, each with separate fire places. It did not have a music room, but Rhoda made do and placed the grand piano in the parlor. Rhoda was a born organizer and soon had the most efficient household, like her mother before her. Of course, she had time to see to everything as she had her live-in mother's helper, Shirley.

Shirley was ecstatic to be able to continue her studies, be a part of a real family and have her own room, her very own room with a cozy bed, study desk and bureau with a real mirror above it. The best thing was her window with a sweet view of Minnehaha Creek. Did she wonder why the Campbells hadn't adopted her? No. She had long accepted that opportunity had passed for her. She was too old for anyone to want.

Shirley remembered her own kind mother quite well. She was eight when her dear mother died, and her father dropped her and her younger sisters and brother at the orphanage steps before he left town. Did that bother Shirley? Not really. As everyone knew, men weren't meant to care for children. And he was not a kind father. When he came home drunk from grief, he would throw things around their shack. She was afraid of him.

What did bother Shirley is that her younger brother and sisters had been adopted. They were taken by separate families - just whisked away before she could even say goodbye. It was best that way, she was sternly told by the orphanage director. Shirley would sometimes wake, crying in the night for them. She prayed they were loved by their new families and not used as farm hands and kept in a cold barn with the animals – treated like slaves. She had heard that happened to some of the adopted children. But then, she'd shake herself awake and create dreams about having her own magnificent husband, family and home one day. She wanted to be just like Mrs. Campbell.

"JAC! Oh JAC!" Rhoda called. "I've been thinking, JAC."

"I'm all ears, Rhoda. What is it you want now?" he asked with a smile when she entered the room.

"I am finding myself stretched for time. It is just too much for Shirley and me to manage the children, the cooking, the cleaning and the laundry, even with the new, electric washing machine and mangle. She has her school, and I have my church guild, orphanage and suffragette work. Our dinner parties and evenings of whist are so much fun, and all those contacts are good for your business, but I am exhausted. I simply must have more help."

"Rhoda, we don't have room for more people in this house."

"I'm not suggesting a live-in-person, JAC. I am suggesting we just hire a weekly cleaning and laundry lady. I enjoy doing the cooking and planning for our parties, and Shirley enjoys helping with the serving of our guests. What do you think?"

"Yes, Rhoda. The answer is yes. As long as my business prospers, why not? I didn't want us to enter the War, but as a result, my businesses are prospering."

JAC also decided it was time he pleased himself, too. Yes, he bought a brand new Model T Ford. The talk about town was that Minneapolis was in competition with St. Paul for the location of the new Ford plant. JAC toyed with jumping into the car business himself, but he was a methodical man and too stretched for time. He was busy managing his businesses – coal, barges, construction projects and city properties.

"Move over horses," JAC said as he drove the new car slowly into his carriage house.

Were the Campbells and Hanscomes oblivious to the Great War? Like most Americans, they wanted to stay far away from Europe's affairs. Perhaps they didn't care about the difficulties of the monarchies, the political upheaval in Russia, the carving up of Mesopotamia and Arabia, the decline of the Ottoman Empire, or the killing of millions of Armenians by the Turks. Or perhaps they didn't know.

Both JAC and Willie were too old to be drafted. However, they were the correct age to financially benefit from the war. Coal might be king, but Minnesota's agricultural products, including Hormel's preserved and canned meats, were in big demand in the military. JAC added more barges to his fleet to transport goods from America's bread basket to the East coast and beyond.

And as fast as the men were making money, Rhoda and Muriel were taking in donations to help needy military families, particularly the war widows. They considered it their duty to share their prosperity. During the 1918 influenza epidemic, Rhoda and Muriel helped the ill veteran's returning to Fort Snelling. And as abhorrent as it was, they were also educating women at the Minneapolis Women's Club about venereal disease, the silent gift from the war.

1919

"Choose your signs, women!"

Stand up for Women
Women's Rights
VOTE YES FOR YOUR WIFE'S RIGHT TO VOTE!
Pass the 19th Amendment
Vote Yes for Public Education
Vote YES for the Orphans
Soldiers Need Benefits - They Fought for US!
Help the Starving War Widows

On other days, Rhoda and Shirley pushed the children in prams while they canvassed the neighborhood, gaining signatures on petitions for the amendment to enfranchise women. They already had thousands of signatures, but that was not enough. The New York branch of the Women's Suffrage Movement had obtained more than a million signatures.

"Tomorrow, I will hold a tea. Some of these women are afraid of their husbands' reactions to their right to vote. Can you imagine that?" Rhoda asked Muriel.

"You are fortunate to have JAC, who caters to your every whim. Look around you, Rhoda. Don't you see the bruises on some of these women's faces? Some of them are cowed and beaten. Yet, they come to the meetings, secretly. They want a voice. They want to vote."

Rhoda held teas, explained the benefits of the vote and how to convince husbands that they would also win if their wives could vote. In that way, men could also double their power.

"Do not needlessly challenge or disagree with your husband – men can be easily frightened if they feel they are not in control of their families. Make them feel needed, instead," Rhoda coached. "If your husband hesitates, say it will be like him having two votes. Then, of course, since the ballot is private, you can vote your conscience."

"Isn't that a dishonest manipulation?" challenged one woman.

"Yes, it is. Women have been manipulating their men for centuries, but what recourse is left for women who have no clout, no way to influence their futures? Once we gain the vote, our voice will count, and we will be free to be direct and honest. We can then, in turn, advocate for our children's welfare, stop the abuse of working children. We will no longer be dependent, like needy children. Stand tall! Demand the right to vote!"

Then Rhoda focused on her list of DO's:

Engage your husband, tactfully, in political discussions that show your knowledge.

Educate yourself on the issues of taxes, health, education and welfare. (Here Rhoda would hand out educational pamphlets on the issues.)

Enhance your knowledge of your husband's affairs.

Laugh, smile and LISTEN to him.

Then express your views, calmly, succinctly and repeatedly.

"Why not say - 'If Negro men can vote, why can't we? Aren't we smarter?" asked one suffragette.

Rhoda winced. "Why not say, equality is for all," she suggested instead. "We support the vote, education and true citizenship for all, regardless of race, religion or gender."

And what were JAC's views?

"Rhoda, I support the vote for women," he said, "but I don't want you to march anymore. You will have our next child on the street."

"Oh, don't be ridiculous, JAC, but if it will make you more comfortable, I will only hold my teas. I have been feeling more tired of late."

"You have boundless energy, Rhoda, but I want you to take better care of yourself. Rest, like the doctor ordered."

And, like in many things, JAC was correct. The baby was born the next day.

"It's a girl," the doctor said.

"Another girl!" Seven-year-old Gordy pouted and frowned.

"Come, come, little man, put on a smile," cajoled his father. "Otherwise, a little bird will come and go *doo-doo* on your lip."

Gordon hated when his father teased him, but he did pull in that bottom lip.

"My baby," said two-year-old Jean.

"I want to hold her, please," begged four-year-old Rhoda Jane.

"What should we name her?" JAC asked.

"Let's name her Muriel, after my sister," Rhoda said. "I think she will have Muriel's brown hair. It isn't curly, but it looks like it will be wavy, have a nice bend to it." Rhoda also noticed her skin also had a golden glow, but said nothing. Rhoda hoped her little baby had just a touch of the jaundice.

"I like Patricia," Gordy said. Yes, he was only feigning disinterest. He loved all his little sisters, except when they were pests.

"We can call her Pat," JAC suggested.

"I like Muriel Patricia, but I don't care for Pat. It sounds like an Irish boy's name," Rhoda said as she laughed. "Please remember, we don't live in St. Paul."

But they called her Pat, anyway. And, by some mistake, her birth certificate read Miriam Patricia.

"It's not important," Rhoda's mother said and laughed when she saw the birth certificate, "but I will call her Muriel Patricia."

The grandchildren loved it when their grandma visited. She cooked them the tastiest Sunday chicken dinners with mashed potatoes and gravy. She indulged them, played house with them, sang with them. She even allowed them to substitute cookies for their nasty lima beans. Rhoda usually stayed for several weeks following the births of her grandchildren and pampered them all.

"Rest," she commanded her daughter. "I am insisting JAC buy you a chaise lounge, where you can nurse little Muriel Patricia, nap and read. I also told JAC that you need extra help for a few months. If you rest, at least one hour every afternoon after lunch, your energy will return. The doctor said this delivery was very hard on you. Perhaps I should stay with you for a few more weeks."

"Thank you, Mother, but I think we can manage. It is good for me to move around a bit. I truly will miss your company and being treated like a queen. I asked Shirley to interview a few girls at the Washburn Home for me. She will be getting married and leaving us in a few months. That should be ample time for her to train a new girl, but I doubt anyone can measure up to Shirley. I feel as though my own daughter is getting married and abandoning me."

"Imagine how I feel, losing Muriel, after all these years?"

Losing Muriel? Yes, she was getting married, finally.

"I can imagine you have mixed feelings about her marrying that Gerald, but at thirty-six, it is a gift from God that they found each other. And she will keep more children, his children, out of the orphanage."

"Well," her mother said, "I do hope Gerald loves her as much as he needs a mother for his children."

"Don't worry, Mother. Muriel will be a good mother and a good wife. It's time for her to live."

Chapter 9

Cracks in the American Dream
March 9, 1919
Minneapolis

"Oh no! Oh no!" Rhoda cried.

JAC could not console his usually steady wife. Her mother, Rhoda, had died. No one thought of her at seventy-three, as old. Her energy was as great as her daughter's. But as distraught as Rhoda and Muriel were, their father was completely done in. How could this happen, just when their rosy world was so perfect?

"Hello, operator? Please connect me to the Hanscome residence in Austin. Wait? No, I can't wait. I know this is a party line, but this is an emergency! Can you please ask the other party to call back later? Thank you," Rhoda said.

"Oh no!" Willie cried, after answering the telephone. "Of course, we will leave as soon as possible."

Willie, Ethel and their two children, Tommy, age 6, (yes, another Thomas Hanscome) and Barbara, age 4, caught the next train north from Austin. JAC met them at the spectacular new

Great Northern Depot with his gleaming, brand new Ford. It was a sad greeting, but the children were thrilled to be riding in their Uncle's Model T. What a luxury. Tommy even got to squeeze the horn - *Ooga! Ooga!* At home, the Campbell children were waiting with anticipation. Gordy, age 8, was pleased to have another boy in the house. Soon, he and Tommy were throwing sticks for their dog, Jupee, in the snow.

"It must be Christmas," Little Jean said, clapping her hands together. "Our cousins are here!"

"Let's make a sign that says *NO BOYS ALLOWED*," suggested five-year-old Rhoda Jane, who had long suffered her older brother's pranks. It was high time to get even. She could read and write and painstakingly tried to make the letters even. Jean, now three, laughed with glee when they hung it on their bedroom door. Was it obeyed? No, the boys instantly took it as a dare and mischievously broke up their *Girl's Only Club* meeting as soon as it convened. In return, the girls shrieked and laughed. Even Jupee joined in the pandemonium.

Two days after the St. Mark's church funeral service, Rhoda Cooper Baldwin Hanscome was buried in Lakewood Cemetery. Why the wait? The gravedigger had to bury hot coals to defrost the ground sufficiently enough to dig the grave. It was a nasty cold March day. The ice skating rink on nearby Lake Calhoun was still frozen solid. Gray skies promised more snow. The graveside service was as uninviting as the bleak day. The wind whipped snow crystals into their faces and froze their quiet tears. No children were allowed to cry out loud. Did God think that was rude – crying out loud? Finally, it dawned on the older children that their Grandma was inside the casket. Inside, mind you.

"Grandma is inside the box!" Gordy whispered to Tommy, amazed. Now they knew she would not be back to tuck them in bed, say their evening prayers or serve hot cocoa while they warmed their little tootsies by the fire. Not ever again. It wasn't the biting cold that sent the shivers down their little spines. It was the sight of that coffin being lowered into the ground. If heaven were up in the sky, why was Grandma put down in that cold ground? She always told them to bundle up and stay warm. Nothing about that day made sense to them. And no one bothered to talk to them about death.

What a relief to be back at Grandma's and Grandpa's warm house. It felt like a holiday party. Ethel cooked the deluxe canned hams from Austin's Hormel factory, and the neighbors brought tuna noodle and goulash hot dishes, fresh baked buttery rolls and shimmering, molded jello salads frosted with mayonnaise and freshly whipped cream for dessert. What a feast for Grandma. She would have liked the party.

Before the Hanscomes boarded the train back to Austin, Willie said to his sister Muriel, "We will be back up for your wedding for certain. July, is that right?"

"Perhaps, Willie. Gerald and I haven't set a definite date, yet."

"Are you changing your mind, Mur? You don't look like a happy bride-to-be."

"I might reconsider. Now that mother has passed, father will need someone to look after him. She did everything for him. I don't know how he will manage without her."

"Stop that talk, this instant, Mur," scolded her sister, Rhoda. "Our father is quite capable of taking care of himself. Like all men, he enjoys being waited on like a king. And if he proves too helpless, well, he can live with us. The last thing mother would have wanted was for you to sacrifice your happiness to be the dutiful spinster caring for Father."

"Perhaps I will put Gerald off until fall. I told Father I would go with him to Toronto to see his sisters this summer. We called them last night on the telephone to tell them the sad news. They loved our mother so. It took us hours to get a clear phone line to Toronto. Father felt terrible that he missed Martha Sophia's funeral. He wants to see Alice, the twins Eugenia and Virginia, Naomi and Anna Louisa, at least one more time. Rhoda, our father is feeling like he might die next. I told him that was nonsense." Muriel paused. "No one has heard from Arthur for years, not even Alice..."

"Do you mean he has disappeared from their lives, as I have?"
Rhoda bristled.

"Don't bristle, Rhoda, I am not criticizing you. If you feel that
guilty, you could write to them from time-to-time, as I do,"
Muriel suggested.

"This is better for my family, Mur," Rhoda said and sighed. "I
must put my children's welfare first. I want them to be the best
they can be. People of color, any degree of color, in spite of
emancipation, education or refinement have limited
opportunities. Why create an albatross when there is no need? I
must hold strong. And I never told JAC. He has no idea we have
living Hanscome relatives. I am committed to my secret. Will
you and father still keep it, now that mother has passed?"

"I cannot speak for him, but I see no need to upset your
applecart. In spite of your lies, you have arranged your life very
nicely, Rhoda," Mur said with a hint of frosty irritation. "We will
tell him we are going to Toronto, if he asks. It is up to you to tell
JAC why."

And when JAC asked, Rhoda said, "We have several elderly
Hanscome aunts in Toronto, who were close to our mother. I'm
sure I mentioned them."

"You can go, too, or, if it's important, I would go with you.
I'd like to meet them. I'm just surprised this is the first you have
mentioned living Hanscome Toronto relatives. I would have
remembered. Why weren't they invited to our wedding? Were
you ever close to them?"

"No, I wasn't close to them. I was quite young the last time I
saw them. Truly, it is not important for me to go, not important
to me at all. I think Willie will accompany Mur and Father.
Willie was very fond of the aunts and visited Toronto often when
he was young. As you know, he was born there. Like Ethyl, I
think it's better to take care of our children. They are still too
young to travel."

JAC let the issue go, but he could see Rhoda was visibly upset
when she excused herself to rest. Too upset. What was the big

secret, he wondered. Well, it was her family and her business, not his.

Rhoda prayed the same prayers every night:

Forgive me Lord for betraying my family, my dear aunts. Forgive me for putting my children's future ahead of truth. And yes, I must confess, selfishly mine, too. Let me serve you Lord by doing other good works.

The prayers gave her relief, but never cleared her guilt.

Did Muriel marry? No, she did not. She stayed with her father and cared for his needs. He always felt his death was imminent. How could Mur abandon her dear father?

Willie and Ethel Hanscome moved back to Minneapolis where he became a *drummer* for that wholesome whole wheat porridge, *Cream of Wheat*. It was made from the first cut of the grain in the milling process, called farina and advertised by a smiling Negro chef named *Rastus* who promised it was *sho'nuff* good for breakfast, lunch, dinner and even desert. Yum! *Cream of Wheat Rastus* and pancake mix *Aunt Jemima* greeted their children for breakfast. They were the only images of black people the Hanscome and Campbell children ever saw. Did Willie and Rhoda ever wonder about that? Probably not. Willie's and Ethel's newest baby, John Baldwin Hanscome, affectionately known as Jack, was served *Cream of Wheat* as his first cereal.

1925

"I've lost two more babies, JAC. I think we need to be done having children," Rhoda said in her matter-of-fact voice.

"Why didn't you tell me, Rhoda?" JAC just looked at his wife with amazed irritation. "I had no idea. Are you alright?"

"I'm okay. I just didn't want to upset you. In truth, I'm just sad. I have a hard time admitting to sadness, JAC. It is just easier for me to deny it. I think it's a Hanscome trait. If I don't talk about unpleasantries, they just never happened. I am so fortunate to have you for my husband. We have such a wonderful life and four healthy children. I must focus on my blessings.”

Did Rhoda allow herself to become despondent? Absolutely not. She joined two new churches, the Unitarian Church and Christian Science Church. And she prayed fervently for the forgiveness of her sins in all three. She liked the Unitarian Church because it included all religious wisdoms, embraced the new humanism and social action. She came home from the Sunday afternoon sermons, attended by thousands in the downtown Minneapolis theatres, with renewed zeal to right society’s wrongs. And the Christian Science Church supported her *mind over matter* philosophy. She refused to take her children to doctors for simple childhood complaints. Rest, healthy eating, daily elimination, positive thinking and prayer were the keys to good health. Did she abandon her Episcopal Church? No, but they left St. Mark’s Cathedral for St. Luke’s Parish located in their neighborhood. At times, she went to three different Sunday services. She read the Bible avidly.

“It says it in the Bible, children, *Be ye perfect*. Thus, we must strive for perfection in all our endeavors.” And she left no stone unturned in her quest for the best American dream.

Did JAC agree with her spiritual beliefs? No one knew, but he dutifully accompanied his family to St. Luke’s Episcopal Parish. He just smiled, nodded and let Rhoda meet-and-greet. However, he did refuse to take the castor oil she poured down the children’s gullets. He did chuckle, though, when he discovered it was a great lubricant for his tools.

Bone Lake, Wisconsin

One fine spring day, JAC took his family on a picnic outing across the St. Croix River to Wisconsin. JAC played the musical car horn while the children sang: *The Campbells are coming, tra-la tra-la! The Campbells are coming, tra-la tra-la!*

"Surprise!" JAC yelled when he stopped the Ford outside a wood and stone lake cabin. He had successfully tricked his family. They believed they were simply going on a fun Sunday afternoon drive in the countryside.

"JAC! Oh JAC!" Rhoda laughed as she clapped her hands together with glee. "Did you buy us this lovely lake cabin?"

"Yes, I did. I promised you on our honeymoon to buy you one. However, we'll only keep it if you like it, Rhoda." To the children he boomed, "Everybody out of the car, stretch your legs. Let's explore the cabin."

It was an old, one-room field-stone house, surrounded by screened wooden verandas on every side. In the center of the massive room was a floor-to-ceiling stone fireplace with a wide, two-sided hearth. It could be used for cooking, but there was also a smaller, wood cooking stove that overlooked the lake. In the back of the big room was a door that opened to an outside ice house and a privy. "Oh no!" the children shrieked. "We can't go in there! It stinks! We need a toilet and a bathroom! Where will we take our baths? And where are our bedrooms? Where are the electric lights?"

"I think our children are spoiled," Rhoda whispered to JAC as she clapped her hands for their attention. "Children! Children! Stop your racket and come here, please. Do you see that lake? We will bathe there. And the outside pump will give us fresh spring water for drinking and cooking. The bookcases are for books we will read by kerosene lamps. And we will eat and play board games and cards at this fine, round, wood table. By night, we will sit in the comfy overstuffed chairs and roast marshmallows and sing by the fire. Now look at the porch. Do you see the swings and the swinging beds? Gordon, you can have one bed all to yourself. The rest of us will double up. Oh, JAC, these mattresses need some airing and sunlight to kill the mold," she declared, as she gave them the sniff test. "Lakey, definitely lakey. However, it will be so wonderful to lull ourselves to sleep listening to the owls and loons. Most importantly, the screens will protect us from the mosquitoes."

"Does that mean you like it?" JAC asked.

"I adore it. But on second thought, I think we'll need to buy new mattresses and pillows. These old ones are beyond salvation. And I think the children are correct. If we are going to spend more than a weekend here, we'll need a bathtub and perhaps an outside shower. And a telephone line for me. Please, JAC."

And did the children love it? Yes, they did. Soon the Campbells were spending all of their summers at their cabin on Bone Lake. The woods and the water became their playground. JAC would bring food and supplies every Friday and return, his car loaded with dirty laundry, early Monday morning to Minneapolis. The children made new friends from the other cabins.

And Rhoda? She was thrilled to take off her foundation garment and don her swimsuit. She felt like a liberated woman - goodbye girdle! Did this freeing in body and spirit also free her artistic side? One day, she bought sketchbooks, charcoal and books on painting. The next week, she purchased an easel, oil paints, canvasses and began to paint. She lamented she had put her art on hold while her children were babies. Before she began her first drawing, she silently said, "Thank you, Uncle Harry, for this gift."

The children came inside to find their mother weeping and smiling, paint dripping on the floor. How strange. They had never seen their mother's tears or such a big mess! But Rhoda's nature was an organized one. Soon, her children all had little easels for her careful art instruction. Unfortunately, their interest waned, except for Rhoda Jane. Yes, Rhoda Jane had a flair for color, texture and form. She could paint! Gordy was excused from art lessons so he could resume building a swimming raft with the neighbor boys. Jean retired to her books, crooked reading glasses smashed to her face, and Pat escaped to the sailboat with the older neighbors.

"Pat! Oh Pat!" her mother scolded. "Get out of the sun! Come inside this instant. I have told you a million times to wear a long-sleeved shirt and hat when you go outside. I'll draw water for a bath. Your skin looks positively filthy!" And Rhoda scrubbed and scrubbed her daughter's deeply tanned skin until it was raw.

"May I speak with my husband?" Rhoda asked the Campbell Coal Company operator. "JAC, I've decided we need a piano at the Lake. Patricia needs a rest from her constant activity in the mid-day sun. Her skin is turning black! Actually, they all need a reprieve. They are turning into a band of wild Indians, and their sweet noses are peeling from sunburn. Rhoda Jane has her painting, Jean her books, and Gordon, well, he can build things in the shade, under the trees. I lather them with zinc ointment, but it washes off quickly in the Lake. The girls' lovely skin will soon be as tough as shoe leather. We certainly can't have them looking like common field workers, now can we! No, that just won't do."

"I'll bring a piano in the truck this weekend," JAC said. "Anything else, dear?"

"Yes. If you can also fit two new mattresses in the truck, that would be helpful. We are having company."

Rhoda's father and Muriel were driving over for an extended stay in his new roadster, bought directly from the new Ford plant in St. Paul. By the time they arrived, JAC had added two more swinging beds on the sleeping porches. JAC was very good with his hands.

Aunt Mur read with Jean and Grandpa taught them all the latest game – bridge. Soon, they were addicts to the game, even JAC. *For interest's sake*, Rhoda gave a quarter to the winner of the rubber. And Grandpa continued the girls' piano lessons. Little six-year-old Patricia was a natural, just as he had been as a child. Laughter graced their summers. Rhoda loved games and played right along with her children.

"It is important to be a gracious winner as well as loser. Remember, proper etiquette in sports is as important as that dinner napkin in your lap," she taught them.

In the meadow, they set up badminton and croquet courts and held archery matches with the neighbor children. On rainy days, they solved crossword puzzles from old, yellowed newspapers, played chess and checkers, hearts, poker and gin rummy. But if four people were available, their favorite game was bridge.

Minneapolis

When they returned in the fall, their lessons in civility and deportment quickly repaired the summer damage. After school hours were taken up with lessons that taught refinement, good sportsmanship, as well as mastery of tennis, golf, sailing and English riding. In the winter, after ice skating or chilly sled rides Rhoda would serve hot chocolate from the delicate pink and blue china set her mother had done before her. The children were expected to slowly sip from their cups – no gulping allowed. And on special occasions, marshmallows were added. Their mother always had a way of making food scrumptious and learning proper table manners fun.

"Sit up straight, slide your napkin in your lap, wait for the hostess to lift her fork before you begin, eat small bites, chew your food thirty-two times and rest your fork and knife on your plate at an angle to signal you have completed your meal. Then the *girl* will know she can remove your plate. If you need to leave the table, you must ask to be excused. It is polite to sit until everyone has finished. Be still, listen to the grown-ups, and answer questions we may ask you. Remember to not monopolize the conversation and use your magic words of *please* and *thank you*. It is a privilege to be able to listen to adult conversation. Also, remember to always mind and respect your elders. You are here to serve them, to make them most comfortable. And, Gordon, be a gentleman and pull out your sisters' chairs before you seat yourself."

Did Gordon mind? Yes and no. When no one was looking and with a wicked gleam in his eye, he would pull out a chair so far that his sister plopped onto the floor. If he was caught, he would be sternly excused from the table to go hungry until breakfast. Or sometimes, when he seated them, he would quickly push their chairs in so close to the table that they could not breathe and their eyes bulged out of their sockets.

"Gordon! You may be excused from the table," his mother said. And Gordon would compliantly leave the table, also quickly. Yes, he didn't want to have to cut a switch for his father's cruel punishment when he didn't mind his mother. No pranks were worth those stripes. However, missing a meal was no problem. He could sneak down in the middle of the night and raid the icebox for leftovers.

As little ships sail out to sea, I push my spoon away from me. Soup spoons were a particular challenge for their little hands. *Tip and sip, don't slurp from the spoon. Practice, it is impolite to make unrefined noises at the dinner table. Now, left hand in your lap, always.* They learned to identify the proper spoon, fork or knife by *working from the outside in. Mable, Mable, strong and able, keep your elbows off the table. This is not a riding stable, this is Campbell's dining table!* And it went without saying that they needed to wash their grimy hands, comb their hair and put on a clean shirt or dress, even at the Lake. *No wet swimsuits in the house! Ever!*

Rules, rules, rules!

Why were the children so eager to abide by them? Because no little messy children were ever allowed to eat in the dining room. It was a privilege to be allowed to eat in the dining room. Only babies had to eat in the kitchen with the help. Once they learned the rules, they graduated. And, if they forgot their manners, they would be excused from the table, post haste. No more dinner. No more food until breakfast.

Lessons, lessons, lessons!

"I refuse to take ballroom dancing, again," Gordon said. "I don't want to be pushing miss goo-goo eyes around the dance floor. I want golf lessons, instead."

"You must take them one more year, Gordon. Dance with your sisters if you don't like the other girls. But you may also take golf."

"I am having nightmares about riding a horse named Thunderbolt, Mother. In my dreams, I am practicing my *one, two, three, post, one, two, three, post*, but my insides fall out, and he runs away with me," complained Rhoda Jane. "Please, may I skip the riding lessons? Horses are smelly and mean. I want to take driving lessons, instead."

"I'll talk to your father about teaching you to drive, but one more year of English riding lessons for you, young lady."

"I want to take tennis lessons," begged Pat.

"I want to quit swimming lessons and take jumping lessons," Jean said. "I love horses."

1927

"JAC, you are too strict with Gordon and critical of his every effort. He needs encouragement, not punishment. He can barely sit down today. You need to stop switching him! I abhor it."

"He is not responsible. He thinks money grows on trees. The last time he took the car he dented the front fender and snuck off to his room, as though I would not see the damage. But last night, he came home drunk! Drunk, Rhoda! He's been frequenting those beer joints and speakeasies downtown, then dragging Lake Street. Racing my car! I will not tolerate his insolence."

"Gordon is only doing what all the young people are doing today. I don't agree with his bon vivant lifestyle, but inside, he is a good boy. My father never punished us. The Hanscomes did not believe in the old adage of *spare the rod, spoil the child*. My Grandpa Hanscome in Toronto said he'd seen too many beatings in his lifetime, and they ruined people."

"Well, I learned from my whippings. I even had to cut my own switch and hand it to my father. A switching is not a beating. It is a reminder. We worked hard, and we learned respect."

"Did you learn respect or fear?" Rhoda challenged.

"Probably both. Rhoda, at fifteen, Gordon is hardly a child. Is he studying? No, he is not. He challenges me. He says, 'You quit after grammar school. Why can't I? I want to work.' Look at the opportunities he has. We have given him everything, but he wastes it. And that accident that Rhoda Jane had. Do you really think she fell off that wall? Or do you think she had Gordy's *help?* By the way, I think she broke that collar bone. I want you to take her to the doctor - enough of this Christian Science self-healing."

"JAC, this is precisely what I am talking about. You blame Gordy for every accident, disagreement and mischief that involves the girls. Do not blame him for Rhoda Jane's fall. She took a dare from the neighborhood children. It was a silly game – children's horse play."

"Shenanigans, I call it. And Gordy is the instigator of those games. He goads, teases and sometimes even hits his sisters. I told Gordon that hitting girls is not permissible."

"I know, JAC. Have you considered that if you stopped picking at him, he would, in turn, be kinder to his sisters? He believes we favor the girls. At the same time, he stands up for them, at every turn. However, I agree with you, his drinking at those dens of iniquities, carousing and driving like a maniac all need to stop. I've been thinking, JAC…"

"Yes, there you go thinking again. What plan do you have in mind for our son?"

"Gordon needs new influences and studious friends. What do you think of sending him to Shattuck, the Episcopal Academy? We can talk to the priest at St. Luke's. I think he could help us get Gordon enrolled."

"A boarding school? How are we to keep tabs on his activities in Faribault?"

"That's just the point, JAC. Gordon will have to abide by the strict school rules. He will have no car, no money for alcohol and no baggy girls to impress. Shattuck is similar to a military academy. He will learn discipline and become a young man of good character."

And how did Gordon like the idea of a boarding school?

"No! You can't make me, Father. I will not go to Shattuck!" Gordon shouted, fire coming out of his eyes.

But he did go, and soon. His sisters cried. They did not want to see their big brother, their protector, leave.

"Dad is selling me down the River!" Gordy whispered to them before he got in the waiting car. "I may not ever see you again," Gordon said, with fright.

Was he teasing them, they wondered, or was he truly scared?

Did Gordon live to see his family again? Yes, of course, he came home for holidays. Did Gordon shape up? His mother appreciated his erect posture, fine manners and improved grades. JAC and Gordy stopped fighting, or perhaps it was a truce, but a bitter coldness filled the air between them. Rhoda prayed, but no answer came. She noticed that Gordon was kinder to his sisters, had stopped his incessant teasing, but where was his laughter? She wanted the spark back in her son's eyes. She missed his mischievous glint. Resentment was not healthy. She wished JAC was not so critical of his son. Gordon hated Shattuck, or so he said, but by the time he graduated, he had a whole cadre of fun friends.

And Rhoda Jane? Yes, the doctor confirmed her clavicle was fractured, but it was too late to do anything about it. He recommended Rhoda Jane continue her ice treatment and wear a sling. The doctor also chastised Rhoda for her self-healing beliefs. "For heaven's sake, Mrs. Campbell, give Rhoda Jane aspirin for the pain and swelling."

But when friends asked how Rhoda's life was unfolding, she gaily laughed and remarked, "It couldn't be better!" The mirror in her mind allowed no cracks in her American dream. How would she react to the next downward turn of events?

Anna Louisa Hanscome 1848-1943 became the third wife of William Phillip Marston 1821-1901 on February 16, 1888. William's son and granddaughter are also pictured. He emigrated from Deal, England to New York in1832, then to Toronto in 1851. Anna Louisa became his housekeeper. He was a Toronto gunsmith. Synopsis and photograph courtesy of family genealogist Robert Hanscom.

Rhoda Hanscome Campbell 10/30/1886-9/30/1982
Photograph: Lake Minnetonka honeymoon? 5/22/1911 or other outing

James Arthur Campbell 1884-1954
Photograph: Wedding? 5-22-1911
Courtesy of Penny Herrmann Eden

Rhoda Hanscome Campbell 10/30/1886-9/30/1982
Photograph: Wedding? 5/22/1911
Courtesy of Penny Herrmann Eden

The Campbell sisters: 1930? Jean (right),
Rhoda Jane (center), and Pat (left)

Campbell family circa 1930s: Parents William and Rachel,
Bert, Melvin, James Arthur, Wilmot, Edwin, Eva (Stella)

Rhoda Jane Campbell Dickinson wedding 6/23/1939
The Minneapolis Women's Club

Rhoda Hanscome Campbell circa 1930's

James Arthur Campbell circa 1930's

Chapter 10

Perseverance
October 30, 1929
Minneapolis

"Mother, why are the McCarthys so upset?" Rhoda Jane asked, quite upset herself. "I went to see Carolyn, but they wouldn't answer the doorbell. I could hear her crying!"

"Something terrible has happened, dear. Bring your sisters to the kitchen, and I will tell you."

"Girls, please sit down. I have some very sad news. Our neighbor Mr. McCarthy has died."

"Oh no!" Rhoda Jane said. "No wonder they didn't answer the door. But Mother, Mr. McCarthy had not been ill."

"I don't know how to explain his death to you, girls, but you will find out at school. He was not ill, unless you consider an insult to his psyche an illness. Mr. McCarthy committed suicide."

"Why would he do that? I just talked to him last week, and he was his jovial self," pondered Rhoda Jane. "I really don't understand, Mother."

"The stock market crashed. He had all his money in stocks that are now utterly worthless. Worthless! It is hard to be wealthy one day and wiped clean the next. It is so unfortunate. Tomorrow, we can bring some hot dishes for them, but today, they need their privacy."

"Isn't it a sin to kill yourself?" Jean asked. "That's what Carolyn told us. Won't Mr. McCarthy go to hell?"

"I know Catholics believe that, but I don't. I believe God will forgive him. Please, girls, do not be concerned about poor Mr. McCarthy's salvation."

"How did Mr. McCarthy kill himself?" curious ten-year-old Patricia wondered.

"Oh, girls, this is too terrible to speak out loud. He shot himself, with his hunting rifle!"

Silence.

"What can I do to help Carolyn?" Rhoda Jane asked, wiping tears from her eyes.

"Pray, Rhoda Jane. Pray for their whole family. Pray God will guide them. They will have quite a cross to bear."

"If they don't have any money, how will they eat?" Jean asked.

"Charity, Jean. I will go to the Women's Club today and see if I can raise some money. In the meantime, your father can help them."

Rhoda suddenly wondered if she had spoken out of turn. It dawned on her that they might also be destitute. Luckily, the girls had not asked about that. Rhoda waited anxiously for JAC to come home that evening. When he arrived early, she was even more worried.

"JAC, dear, please talk to me. I know you invested a great deal of money in the stock market. Are we going to survive your losses?" Rhoda asked.

JAC said nothing while he mixed them both a cocktail, a rare occurrence since the beginning of Prohibition in 1920. JAC's Scottish family had been temperance folk, and JAC supported the Volstead Act. Prohibition was the law, and his family would abide by it, well, except for special occasions. And this was a very special day, indeed.

"Rhoda, I have lost all our investments, but we still have our company. We will be fine as long as people pay their accounts. But if everyone has lost their money, soon my accounts will be in arrears. Then, I will have to let employees go. And when people lose their jobs, they have no money to spend. And with no one purchasing goods, the financial crisis will spread to every business and every family. This stock market crash could trigger a downward spiral, for our whole country. We could be ruined."

"Oh, JAC! What will we do?"

"We are not going to panic, but we are going to be frugal. I have already made a list of expenses we can cut. I believe Gordon can remain at Shattuck as we have already paid his tuition and expenses for the year. Hopefully, he will graduate next spring."

"Are you feeling we can survive this crash? I don't want you feeling hopeless, like Mr. McCarthy."

"Don't worry, Rhoda. I like a good challenge, and this will definitely be one. We will persevere."

"And the cabin? Do we need to sell the cabin?"

"Not now. Actually, no one has money to buy it, so it's a worthless piece of property, like all of our properties. I will do my best to keep the bank from seizing them. The good news is that we will be warm this winter," he said and laughed, "but I wonder about our neighbors. I hope they will be able to pay their coal bill."

"I wanted to ask you, can we help the McCarthy's?"

"Not with money, but I can see that their coal bins are full this winter."

"How will they be able to keep their house with no money?"

"They won't be able to pay their bills, but it will take some time before any eviction occurs. The whole city may come to a standstill. My guess is that they'll be fine in their house until spring. Who knows, by then, the economy may have bounced back."

"And what do you want me to do?"

"I want you to let go of the help, curb your Women's Club philanthropies, stop the shopping sprees with the girls and cease your fancy parties. It will actually be good for the girls to help you with the cooking and cleaning. One more thing. Only drive your car in emergencies. The girls will have to take the streetcars. We must economize."

"I must let this sink in, JAC," Rhoda said with a deep sigh.

"Don't take too long, Rhoda. I will drive down to Faribault tomorrow to talk with Gordon. It's time to have a good talk with him about his future."

And how were the other Hanscome's faring this financial debacle?

"How are you and Muriel going to live, Father?" Rhoda asked. "You are welcome to move in with us. We have plenty of room, now that I let our girl go."

"Do not worry, dear. Yes, the bad news is that I have lost my investments, and Muriel has been let go from her secretarial position. The good news is that we own our house, and I have gained employment, old as I am."

William actually smiled. He had never worked for someone else, other than playing the pipe organ at the Cathedral.

"That is a delightful surprise. You seem so pleased."

"I am. My banker friend had to cut back on his expensive personnel. I talked him into hiring me for a pittance. My title is *Floor Walker*. I told him I would assist in any fashion - calm his customers, relieve the tellers, and be a sentinel of security. I have my first salaried job at seventy-two."

"Well, greeting people is what you're good at. I must say I am most amazed at your resourcefulness. I hope you don't feel it is beneath your dignity."

"I am reminded of the old Proverbs lesson that *pride goeth before destruction and an haughty spirit before a fall*. We have taken our prosperity for granted. And I am grateful to be able to stock our larder. I could hardly stand being a burden on you and JAC."

"You would be no burden, Father. We are your family. JAC said he plans to supply you with coal this winter, as usual."

"Let's just see how this crash ends. What breaks, sometimes, can be mended."

Ethel and Willie also faced challenges.

"Ethel, I was given my walking papers today," Willie announced. "This is not going to be a pleasant Christmas for us," he said and sighed.

Yes, the effects of the stock market crash had trickled down to even big companies like Hormel. Employees had to be let go.

"What will we do, dear?"

"I'm afraid we have to move to Minneapolis. JAC has offered me work for a mere pittance, but he has let go of employees, so I am thankful. Any wage is better than nothing."

Ethel went back to work as a nurse, Barbara, thirteen, helped care for her six-month-old brother, Billy, formally named William Dixon Hanscome, and Tommy and Jack contributed their money from selling newspapers. And they moved in with the Campbells, temporarily. The children didn't seem to mind the pandemonium, and Rhoda loved the excitement.

Summer 1930
Bone Lake

Bone Lake was empty of cars that summer. The few families that arrived for the season opener, Memorial Day Weekend, stayed for the whole summer, as did the Campbells. JAC and Gordon did not drive up every weekend. They were busy working, side-by-side, making up for the employees JAC had to let go. Keeping the Campbell Coal Company afloat was a challenge, but Rhoda noticed the lack of tension between the two of them. Good had come from the *for worse* part of the economy. Adversity made them lean on each other and heal their wounds.

Aunt Mur moved to the Lake for the summer and helped Rhoda and the girls with their extensive garden. Every fertile spot of soil had some green sprout blooming by June. It turned out to be an idyllic summer. The Campbells had returned to their farming roots, indeed. Gordon, JAC and Grandpa Hanscome rigged up an irrigation system from the Lake to the gardens. Composts fertilized the crops. Nothing went to waste. On the weekends, the men harvested while the women preserved, canned and pickled. And their corn was knee high by the 4th of July. They laughed as they worked. Rhoda even let go of her fears of sunburned and tanned skin.

"Do you want to have a farm again, JAC?" Rhoda asked one night as they listened to the calls of the loons from their bed that gently swung in the breeze.

"I've thought about it. This simple work agrees with me. I look forward to the weekends. And Willie has opened up a simple grocery in his parlor. Luckily, they got a bargain price for their house. They are selling all we bring back."

"I think it agrees with us all, JAC. Perhaps the dear Lord felt we needed our hands in the soil and a little humility."

Minneapolis

In the fall, when they returned for school, their truck was laden with fresh and canned produce. The next day, Rhoda and Rhoda Jane delivered canned beets, corn, beans, peas, crab apple jelly and apple butter to the McCarthys, who no longer lived next door. The bank had claimed their house, and they were living in a shabby apartment building in downtown Minneapolis, not far from the still flourishing speakeasies. When Carolyn saw Rhoda Jane she hugged her and cried.

"I'd invite you in, Rhoda Jane, but we are living with our grandparents, and they are resting. My mother is at work."

"Work?" Rhoda Jane was shocked. Not Mrs. McCarthy! How awful that a decent, married woman had to work.

"Yes, she is working at Pillsbury's mill, sewing flour sacks."

"I am sorry to hear that, Carolyn."

"Oh, don't feel sorry for us, Rhoda Jane. She is happy to have found a job. She has been looking all summer. When there is an opening, I will join her."

"Aren't you going back to Washburn High with me tomorrow?"

"No, Rhoda Jane. I will go to Central High, if I go at all. But right now, I am caring for my grandparents."

"Oh, I am sorry. I will miss you. How disappointing. You love school so."

"Yes, I do, but it won't be the same, Rhoda Jane. We don't have any money anymore and – well, it's embarrassing. I have gotten tired of saying I can't afford to do this or that. And I can't stand that look of pity. What's even worse is when people give me their old clothes!" Carolyn began to cry again. "I don't want to accept charity. We must make our own way. And you must stay with your social set and not lower yourself to my plight. You know the rules."

Silence.

"We grew our own food this summer, had a regular farm and canning factory at the Lake. And my Uncle Willie is selling it. It was actually fun. But now, I feel embarrassed to give you this food. I don't want you to feel like you're accepting charity. I am your friend. Will you take it, please?"

"Yes, of course, I will take it. It is thoughtful of you to think of us. I must learn to graciously accept help. I have found that receiving is more difficult than giving. How is your family managing?"

"We still have our house, but money is tight. My father lost his investments and properties, too. We are thankful he still has the coal business, but people can't pay their bills."

That was the last conversation Rhoda Jane ever had with her friend Carolyn. When Rhoda Jane returned with fresh apples a few weeks later, a neighbor said the McCarthy's had moved to a relative's farm in southern Minnesota.

"I feel guilty, Mother. We have so much more than others. My friends at school - well, they look hungry! They would work, but there are no jobs to be had. Their parents tell them they might as well go to school."

Rhoda noticed her girls were looking thin, too thin she thought. Then it dawned on her that they were giving their nutritious lunches to their classmates. It was time she mobilized her friends to see what could be done to feed some of these children.

"Girls, please do not share your lunches anymore. I had no idea how hungry people are. I have joined with some of my Women's Club friends, and we will be delivering soups, sandwiches, apples and milk to your school. We cannot have this hunger. I will not allow it. We shall persevere, together."

Chapter 11

What a Scare!
1930
Minneapolis

"Great news, Rhoda," JAC said as he poured another cocktail for his wife. Two was her absolute limit.

"This must, indeed, be a special occasion."

"I can finally see a way out of our financial dilemma. I have opened another business. It's called *Ready Mix Concrete*."

"I am puzzled, JAC. Where did you get the money for such a venture?"

"I made a bid to do the walkways at the University of Minnesota. And they awarded me the contract. We will be laying all the concrete for the new Northrop Hall Mall. I have a special concrete truck that mixes batches of concrete as we drive to the work site. We pick up gravel and sand from the pits, add water, bags of the cement formula and off we drive, the truck cylinder spinning and mixing as we go. What a time saver, what a labor saver, and, yes, back saver! It is ready to be poured it into the walkway or foundation forms by the time we arrive."

"And where did you purchase this recipe for fast cement?"

"Exactly! It is a recipe, Rhoda. I bought it from a company in Erie, Pennsylvania. Two bags of cement mix, water, sand and gravel and stir well. Sort of like this cocktail."

"I am truly pleased and relieved. I thought God was punishing me for my gluttonous desires, but I prayed you would figure this out, JAC. What a scare! However, no more cocktails, our dinner is ready."

"Rhoda, this is a new financial beginning for us. The government is spending money on improvements, as a way to employ people. I anticipate we will have more work than we can handle. I never thought I'd see the day I blessed the government. These work projects have been our salvation. If they continue, I will buy more cement mixer trucks, but I don't want to get too far ahead of myself. First, I must get the contracts. I trust you have not forgotten how to spend!" Yes, JAC was positively effusive, for JAC.

"No, indeed, I haven't. The girls have outgrown their clothes. Jean wears Rhoda Jane's, and Patricia now wears Jean's hand-me-downs. And poor Rhoda Jane, well she's always so sunny and never complains."

The girls resumed all their previous lessons. However, Rhoda Jane refused to take ballet as those toe shoes pinched her feet. Tap dance became her new joy.

Ta-da, Rhoda Jane and Jean took bows after they practiced their dance recital pieces. Pat played the piano, while Rhoda Jane danced a *Time Step* and a *Shuffle off to Buffalo* to an old vaudeville number.

"Rhoda Jane, wipe that black paint off your face, immediately. I don't like your imitation of those poor Negro steamboat dancers."

"Oh, Mother, don't be silly. It's part of our recital. No harm is intended."

"I think it is an unladylike dance for young girls. And harm is done by continuing these stereotypes that denigrate a people. I'd rather you take other lessons if that will be the caliber of your dance instruction." She was truly in a huff. "Your recital practice is over."

Rhoda Jane and Jean exchanged puzzled looks. What had rubbed their mother the wrong way? It was only a dance.

"Why don't you take riding lessons with me?" Jean asked, seizing the opportunity to be with her older sister, whom she idolized. "I love jumping hurdles."

"Or tennis lessons with me?" piped up Patricia, who didn't want to be left out.

"Well, I'd like to take golf lessons at Interlachen Country Club," Rhoda Jane said. Both her sisters smiled their knowing smiles. They knew that Wesley Dickinson would be there. Later, they would extract some advantage from Rhoda Jane for their continued silence.

What a relief. Rhoda was thankful she had married her persevering JAC. They weren't considered rich, rich like the Pillsburys, but the scare was over. They were comfortable and on their way, again. At the end of 1930, the census recorded the Campbell's worth at $30,000, the equivalent of $409,555.81 in 2015. That winter, they all received new fur coats from Schlamps. Certainly, that necessity was not gluttony.

But all was not roses with her growing daughters.

"Rhoda Jane! Come here, this instant! Do I smell smoke on your clothes, again?" her furious mother asked. "I told you before, ladies do not smoke cigarettes! You will not be going to any of those Washburn High parties, not ever again. You have way too much interest in Gordon's friends. And that Wesley Dickinson? I will have to tell Gordy to keep a better eye on you. No drinking and no smoking! A nice girl must always be careful of her reputation."

"JAC, we need to send Rhoda Jane to Holy Angels to complete her high school. It has a fine academic reputation, and the nuns' watchful eyes will guard her innocence. I'm also considering it for Jean."

"Isn't that the Catholic Academy for girls on 66th Street and Nicolette Avenue? It's the last stop on the streetcar line. We have a contract to finish the walkways. However, I am surprised you suggest it. It is a Roman Catholic School, Rhoda, and we are Protestant."

"I know that is a drawback, but I don't want to send her to St. Mary's, the Episcopal School in Faribault. She'd be at risk for the advances of the Shattuck young men, like Gordon's friends. Why didn't we know that only troubled boys from wealthy homes are sent there? We should have sent Gordy to Blake, but his grades did not meet their high standards. Northrop Collegiate is another option for Rhoda Jane, as her grades are exceptional, but it is farther away. I would have to drive her daily. I have heard wonderful things about the nuns at Holy Angels. She doesn't have to be Catholic to be accepted, and she can hop the streetcar to school."

"I think you want to have Rhoda Jane cloistered. Soon, you will be suggesting a convent," JAC teased.

"You see right through me, JAC," Rhoda said and laughed. "Really, I want her to live at home. I could not stand to send her away, even to an Episcopal school. We must learn our lesson from Gordon. We can't force her, but that Washburn High School is wild, just wild, JAC. She is smoking cigarettes and riding in cars with boys! I just won't have it! I even found a letter, a love letter she wrote to that rascal Wesley Dickinson."

"Who is Wesley Dickinson? And where did she meet him?" JAC asked, smiling at his wife's zeal. She was definitely on a mission.

"You have met his widowed mother, the Executive Director of the Animal Rescue League. Remember, we found our Jupee there? Gordon and Wesley met through friends, but Wesley goes to West High. I did some research. I hear Mrs. Dickinson is a fine lady from a good Hastings family. She graduated from St. Mary's in Faribault. Her father was a doctor and died just shortly before her husband. It is indeed a shame. She had a wonderful future with Robert Dickinson, who graduated from the University, and was selling the new Cadillacs. He became ill shortly after they married and slowly wasted away. Diabetes, they say. I have to admire Mrs. Dickinson for her perseverance. The Dickinsons, those wealthy timber people, disinherited her after Robert died, left her penniless, with a five-year-old son to raise. They simply abandoned her and moved back to Pennsylvania. Can you imagine that? Luckily, she had good social connections and was able to secure her position. She commands a decent salary, for a woman."

"I find that admirable. Why are you concerned?"

"She never remarried, although she is an attractive, educated woman."

"And that damns her Rhoda? Your own sister is unmarried. This attitude doesn't seem like your charitable self. I have never heard you - well, be so judgmental."

"It is because there are rumors that Myrtle is hopelessly in love with that playboy, her husband's best friend, Charles Odekirk. She is a fool. He hunts. He gambles. He is handsome and squires around loose women, I'm told. But when he goes to proper social functions, he escorts Mrs. Dickinson. I had to learn more about her once I knew our Rhoda Jane was infatuated with Wesley."

"Really? I know Charles Odekirk, from the Automobile Club. OD they call him. He lives at the Minneapolis Athletic Club, is quite a sporting fellow and invites many to his hunting shack near Willmar. He is well-liked and well-respected. And yes, women do fall all over him. Myrtle Dickinson, eh? Well now, I like her even better. You should invite them to our couple's bridge club."

"Oh, JAC! Sometimes, you are not funny, at all."

• • •

"Wesley," whispered Rhoda Jane softly as she answered the phone. She didn't want to be overheard. "I'm glad you called.

My mother is withdrawing me from Washburn. Tomorrow, I start at Holy Angels."

"That Catholic School? But why?"

"She thinks I am subjected to bad influences at Washburn. Bad influences like you," she flirted.

"But I go to West High. We are the gentlemen from West, not like those cocky Washburn scoundrels. Are you going to take your vows?" he teased.

"No, but I will be wearing one of those unstylish uniforms and *Buster Brown* shoes - almost as bad as a nun's habit. She has taken away my make-up and worse."

"What's worse?" Wesley asked.

"She will not allow me to go out with boys, not even in a group. She says I must finish high school first."

"That seems very strict. Why the change?"

"She caught me smoking. Darn. She is afraid I might become a baggy girl."

"And here I was going to ask you to go to a party with me this weekend."

"I'm sorry, Wesley. I really would like to - perhaps we can see each other after some time passes. I could have Gordon arrange it. He's going to the University this fall and will have freedom. Oh, I am so jealous! My mother watches me like a hawk."

And Gordon did arrange their meeting. What a good, protective brother. Parents should know better than to stop young lovers.

"Rhoda Jane, would you like to dance?" Wesley asked. Hoagy Carmichael's tune *Star Dust* wafted across the crisp fall air at the Lake Harriet Band Shell.

"Yes, Wesley." Rhoda Jane felt her heart flutter as he masterfully foxtrotted her around the dance floor.

There goes old Twinkle Toes, stealing my sister's heart, thought Gordon. *Hmm. Perhaps I should have taken my dance classes more seriously. That Wesley is really in demand.*

Soon, they were known as a couple. Rhoda Jane and Wesley biked to the tennis courts, rowed, canoed and sailed in the summer. In the winter, they skated, sleighed and sled. She loved to watch Wes play ice hockey, his favorite team sport at West High School. The chain of lakes - from Lake of the Isles to Lake Calhoun to Lake Harriet – was their playground.

The Interlachen Country Club, at the farthest end of the streetcar line in the small Village of Edina, courted young members, even women, and their whole group of friends joined. The membership fee was very affordable for the young, *smart set*.

"It's not fair that you are so good, and I am so miserable." Rhoda Jane laughed as her drive bounced only fifty feet beyond the tee.

"You are a good sport, even more important," Wes said and smiled. "But you are going to have to shout *Fore* much louder. If you can't keep up, just pick up your ball. You're still learning."

And tennis?

"You are also a good sport at this game, Rhoda Jane," Wesley said and smiled. The truth be known, he loved her for her gentle, self-deprecating and deferring ways. Kind. Rhoda Jane was a genuinely kind girl. All that sweetness was, of course, helped by her lovely blonde hair and blue eyes. And she was as bright as she was beautiful. Did Wesley care that she was a terrible golf and tennis player? Absolutely not. He could not tolerate competitive, accomplished or bossy girls.

"Good sport? - that term is only reserved for the inept." Rhoda Jane laughed. "You just stand behind the base line and run me ragged with your strategically placed balls."

But that was not all. Soon Rhoda Jane was sneaking to Alpha Delta Phi parties at the University of Minnesota with Gordon. Had she added drinking alcohol to her smoking vice? Yes, she had.

Pray tell, where were Rhoda Jane's concerned parents? Why, minding their own social life at The Minnekahda Club. High on its hilltop, the white pillared clubhouse grandly overlooked Lake

Calhoun. It's name in Sioux aptly meant *by the side of the water*. At night, the lights of Downtown Minneapolis could be seen, as couples danced to big band orchestras on its wide porches. And by day, one could sip iced tea by the swimming pool and tennis courts or watch the sailing regattas on the Lake below. It resembled a Southern mansion, complete with white-gloved, black-faced doormen who graciously opened the doors unto the sparkling, crystal chandeliers in the impressive foyer. Ah, gracious living at its best.

"Hello, Hello, Hello," Rhoda said, as she gaily nodded at her friends when they left the dining room on their way to the card room. It was considered essential etiquette to greet everyone, but long, meaningful or unpleasant conversations were out of place. Recognition was all that was required.

"How nice to see you."

"How nice to see you!"

"Yes, we'll have to get together soon."

"Yes, very soon."

"And how are you? Fine?"

"We're fine, thank you for asking."

Rhoda could really swish through a room. The audible swish was from her girdled thighs rubbing together. Swish, swish, swish. Nod, nod, nod. Laugh, laugh laugh.

"See you soon!"

"Ah, here we are, JAC. What a lovely dessert table."

Rhoda had found their name cards among the many card tables. How she loved to play cards and win. And JAC adored her – competitive, ambitious, bossy nature and all. If the truth be known, he credited much of his success to her faith, encouragement and knowledge of people. All he had to do was run the numbers. He was a lucky man, indeed. That stock market crash, however, had given him a nasty scare.

And surprise, surprise, Rhoda could really drive that golf ball. She won awards for several *hole-in-ones*. She loved their new club. Her distinctive laugh endeared her to all. Rhoda Campbell had finally arrived.

"Jean, you will be going to Holy Angels. I don't like how those nuns took the class presidency away from Rhoda Jane, but it is still better than Washburn High."

Rhoda Jane was voted her senior class president, but the nuns would not allow her to serve. Why? Because that distinct honor needed to be awarded to a girl from a good Catholic family, one with money to fund the academy. Was Rhoda Jane disappointed? No, she understood their point of view. Rhoda Jane always listened to others and put their needs first.

"I'd like to go to Washburn High, Mother. All my friends will be there," Jean said.

"Absolutely not, Jean. You will go to Holy Angels. Girls study better when there are no boys to distract them. I will hear no more about it."

Dutifully, Jean donned the plaid uniform and *Buster Brown* shoes of Holy Angels. The best thing was that she found many horse enthusiasts and joined the *horsey set*.

"Neigh, neigh, neigh... Jean eats fine hay," rhymed her brother Gordon.

His sisters had learned to ignore his taunts. Would Gordon ever outgrow his teasing? Probably not. And where was Gordon? After one year at the University of Minnesota, he quit. He convinced, or perhaps it was his poor grades that convinced his parents he was not a scholar. After an argument over his low salary working for his father, Gordy finally started out on his own. Freedom had its merits.

And guess who the Alpha Delts elected fraternity president? Wes Dickinson. As a junior, he welcomed freshman Rhoda Jane to the University of Minnesota campus personally. Wes was two years older than Rhoda Jane and one year younger than Gordon.

"Oh Oh Kappa Kappa Kappa Gamma, I am so happy that I am a Kappa... Nobody knows how happy I am!"

Rhoda was rushed by all the women's fraternities, but she found the Kappas most welcoming. Any sister of Gordy Campbells must be fun. She also had a great scholastic record, was a member of Interlachen Country Club and her parents The Minnekahda Club. What a blue-eyed, blonde-haired beauty. Charming, but not arrogant. What an added bonus. She was considered the WASP ideal.

"What do you want to major in?" asked a Kappa.

"Elementary education or perhaps art," Rhoda Jane responded.

"Education is a popular major in our house. Most of our members either major in education or nursing, although few ever teach or nurse."

"And why is that?" Rhoda Jane asked, puzzled.

"Most marry within months of graduation. We call it getting our MRS. Degree." The upper classman rushing her laughed. "However, your degree is like an insurance policy. If something would happen to your husband, you have a career to fall back on. And it is so important to be educated, just for the sake of being educated."

The Kappas pledged Rhoda Jane immediately. What a great fit. Unfortunately, her mother insisted she live at home until her sophomore year. Rhoda Jane loved her new friends, her classes and the weekend fraternity parties. Most of all, she loved that Wesley Dickinson.

"Ladies, listen! Look outside! The Alpha Delts are serenading us!"

As the Kappas ran out onto their porch, there were at least forty handsome young men holding candles lined up in front of the house, singing their sweetheart song. Who would be the lucky girl?

"Rhoda Jane – it's Wesley!" whispered a sorority sister. "You are about to be made an Alpha Delt Sweetheart!"

Wesley held out his hand to Rhoda Jane. Did she take it? Yes, she stepped forward to meet his gaze. Then, he pinned his gold fraternity badge on her sweater, right below her gold Kappa Key.

And when he hugged and kissed her, the crowd cheered. How exciting. How romantic. Rhoda Jane was in love and pinned. The next thing would be an engagement ring. What could be better?

She was in love with her life. She sang and danced to Shirley Temple's *The Good Ship Lollipop* in a fall rush skit. Thank goodness for those tap dance lessons. The whole house was decorated as a fantasy candy land, and lollipops were handed out as favors. The fall Rushees had such a good time that the Kappas won the best pledges.

"Mother, I think I won't go back to the 'U' next fall," Rhoda Jane said after her sophomore year.

"And why is that, Rhoda Jane? I thought you loved school. And Jean will be attending."

"Wesley has graduated. I think we will be getting married."

"Oh, Rhoda Jane," her mother said. "That Wesley is a decent young man, great fun, well-mannered, but he'll never amount to much."

"What a terrible thing to say, Mother," Rhoda Jane replied, deeply hurt.

"Perhaps it's because he never had a father to guide him in the ways of the world. Wesley is an idealist, a dreamer, not practical like your father. That's what it takes to succeed in business, solid common sense. Marry someone who will be a good, solid provider, not just a charming dancer."

"Grandpa Hanscome is a talented musician. He and Aunt Mur live quite nicely. You could say he is a dreamer. Where did they get their money? Surely not from his bank job."

"Your grandfather inherited money from his family in Toronto."

"And what business was that?"

"Coal. The fuel business."

"Do we have any relatives in Toronto?"

"Not that I am aware of, dear. Anyway, the past is not important."

"That's where the crystal pendant candelabras come from, isn't it? Toronto."

"Yes, that's correct. One day, you will have them, as my oldest daughter. But we have come far afield from our discussion of Wesley Dickinson. Has he asked you to marry him?"

"No, he hasn't."

"Well then, the subject of marriage is a bit premature. I suggest that you date other young men. You have had eyes only for him for years."

Did Rhoda Jane quit the University? Yes, she did. She moved home, as proper girls did until they were married. And did Wesley propose?

"Rhoda Jane, I love you with all my heart, but I have nothing to offer you," Wesley said. Rhoda Jane was crestfallen. "But I do have a plan," he added. "A master plan." Her eyes brightened.

"What is your plan?"

"I want to have my own business. More than that, I am not certain. I do know that I do not want to live in Minneapolis or any big city. I am going to canvas the state, see where I might want to open my own business, be a big part of a growing community. I have no legacy other than my own wits. After I am successful, we can discuss marriage, but I don't want you to wait for me. Please."

And he left town, just like that! He really left his Rhoda Jane flat. Heart-broken, she sought a job as a secretary. That was the best occupation open to women. And who knows, if they proved themselves indispensible, their boss might marry them. She could have returned to the University, but she didn't. Jean, also a Kappa Kappa Gamma, tried to re-engage Rhoda Jane in campus activities, but memories of Wesley haunted her. It was better to start anew, as her wise mother counseled. Oh yes, Rhoda was relieved. What a nasty scare that Wesley Dickinson was.

Chapter 12

Wedding Bells
1939
Minneapolis

"Do you, Jean Hope Campbell, take William Gage Donald to be your wedded husband?"

"I do! I do!"

St. Luke's Episcopal Church was bursting at the seams with guests. Of course, Jean's maids of honor were her two lovely sisters, Rhoda Jane and Patricia. The bride and groom exited the Church posthaste. They wanted to arrive at the reception at The Minneapolis Women's Club before their guests.

"Usually, the oldest daughter is supposed to get married first," whispered one guest.

"Well, Rhoda Jane's engagement came later, and Rhoda wanted to be fair. Jean spent most of her life following Rhoda Jane. This is her time to be special," added another.

"It's too bad neither of the girls graduated from the University."

"Jean opted to leave the 'U' and finish her normal school education at Miss Woods School," commented another guest.

"How smart of Jean to finish her teaching certificate."

"Well, she'll never use it. Women's education is a waste. Her husband will provide for her."

"I didn't know Jean's middle name was Hope. What a pretty name."

"Jean hates it. She was given the name because JAC and Rhoda had *hoped* for a son."

"No, you have that wrong. It was Gordon who had *hoped* for a brother."

"Who is this William Donald? Jean must not have known him very long," commented another. "I don't know his family, but he is so much fun, always the life of the party."

"I hope he's not a drinker – you know those Irish."

"If you ask me, all these young people drink and smoke way too much – like there's no tomorrow."

"He's not Catholic, is he? That would be most unfortunate."

"Did you hear Rhoda and JAC bought them a bungalow in Minneapolis for their wedding gift?"

"What a lucky couple, indeed!"

"Look at Rhoda's father, Mr. Hanscome. I've seen him at St. Marks before, quite well-spoken and gifted on the organ, but in this light, he looks, well - almost Negroid."

"Oh, Rhoda says he's part East Indian on his mother's side, from Toronto. He had the most delightful English wife, also named Rhoda, but she died years ago. She was ten years older than her husband, a most uncommon practice."

"That is strange. The husband, as the head of the family, is supposed to be older."

"Do you see Patricia's escort? He attends Oberlin Music Conservatory with her."

"He's quite handsome and musically gifted, like Pat."

"He's Jewish, you know."

"Oh, that is most interesting. Finding a socially acceptable mate for her daughters is simply one challenge after another for poor Rhoda."

June 23, 1939

"May I present Mr. and Mrs. Wesley Dickinson!" the priest shouted at the end of the ceremony.

The bells at St. Luke's Episcopal Church announced another Campbell wedding. Two in one year. The reception, like Jean's, was held at The Minneapolis Woman's Club on Groveland Place. The pictures flashed as Rhoda Jane posed near a Grecian column in her floor-length, lace dress, trailing ornate veil and white rose bouquet. She struck a regal pose with an elegant hint of a smile – the ethereal picture of refinement.

"Rhoda and JAC are so thrilled with this match," remarked one guest.

"Do you really think so? Rhoda was so relieved when Rhoda Jane broke off her relationship with that Armenian businessman. I think Wesley Dickinson just looks wonderful by comparison," gossiped another. "Rhoda sent Rhoda Jane to Holy Angels because Wesley was courting her in high school."

"Rhoda Jane's Armenian love interest seemed to have caught Wesley's attention, just in the nick of time."

"Oh, those two have been in love forever. Wesley is a successful businessman, has five locker plants in Kandyohi County. They will live in Willmar."

"I hope Rhoda Jane likes that small town of backward Lutherans."

"I believe Wesley is the only dark-haired, dark-eyed man in that town."

"Speaking of hair, do you notice how his once thick, wavy hair has thinned? Soon, he will be bald."

"I'm told they speak Swedish on the streets of Willmar."

"What a terrible place to live. It's out on the windswept prairie and that whole Kandiyohi County is as dry as a bone. And I'm not referring to the water," tsk-tsked another.

"Wes and Rhoda Jane will have to live at their golf club or drink at home," laughed another.

"Look over there. His mother, Myrtle, has brought that handsome Charles Odekirk as her escort."

"They have been together for at least twenty years, since her husband, Robert, died. As his best friend, I think Odey felt obligated to look after her."

"Is that what you call it?" remarked a friend, rolling her eyes. "I wonder if Odey will ever make an honest woman of her."

"I think Myrtle likes running the Humane Society. Perhaps she doesn't want to marry."

"Really? What woman in her right mind would want to work?"

"Well, I give her credit, she's done a great job raising Wesley and working. Dr. Adsit's second wife ran off with all the Adsit funds, even the silver, and left Myrtle nothing. To top it off, the wealthy Dickinson's took their timber fortune back to Philadelphia and disinherited her. She lost her husband and her money. Perhaps she has lost trust in everybody but herself."

"I don't think so. She'd marry Odey in a flash."

"Where is Pat's Oberlin boyfriend, the one she brought to Jean's wedding?"

"He's not present today. I hear Rhoda was quite displeased with that match, was afraid she would leave Minnesota and convert to Judaism."

"What do they expect? They sent her to Oberlin, that hot bed of liberal thought, full of Jews from the East Coast. Pat should have gone to the 'U' like her sisters. Proper girls need to be protected by their families. What were JAC and Rhoda thinking?"

"The lucky couple is taking the Campbell's cabin cruiser on the St. Croix River for their honeymoon. Then off to Willmar."

"Wesley's rented a cottage on Eagle Lake – until their new home on 1035 Hill Road is finished."

"I hope that cottage has indoor plumbing."

"Did Rhoda and JAC give them a home as a wedding present, like Jean?"

"Yes, they did. Rhoda will do anything for her girls."

"And JAC will do anything to please his Rhoda."

December 29, 1939

"Do you Margaret Fuge take James Gordon Campbell to be your wedded husband?"

"I do."

It was a small wedding, held at the home of friends. Mrs. Fuge, Margaret's widowed mother, could not afford a lavish affair.

"Who in their right mind would get married in the dead of winter?" commented one guest, still shivering from the sub-zero degree temperature.

"I think Gordon could not wait another day to claim his bride. He was entranced when he met Margaret – just by chance on the street. He fell so hard, I hear he almost fell on his face. Later, his sisters set up an appropriate introduction."

"What a beauty that Margaret is, flashing eyes and ever so clever. Do you know the bridesmaids, her two sisters?"

"No, I don't. I do know Margaret's mother to be a most admirable woman. She had to raise her three daughters by herself after her husband died."

"Three Campbell weddings in one year. What an adjustment for Rhoda and JAC. I hear they plan to sell their home on Minnehaha Parkway and their Bone Lake cabin."

"And how generous of them to give each a home. Lucky children!"

"Lucky Gordon and Margaret. They are escaping this cold for awhile – honeymooning in Stuart, Florida, I'm told."

"Only Patricia is left to be married. I hear she has no current love prospects."

"She plans to graduate from Oberlin first. Perhaps her piano is her true love."

1940
Bloomington Ferry Hill

"Oh, JAC, we were right to sell our home in the city. I was becoming despondent from its echoing halls and empty rooms. New homes for the children, and a new home for us. Thank you, dear. Do you know how much I love you?"

JAC smiled at Rhoda's uncommon statement of affection. Yes, he knew. They never spoke of love much, it just wasn't done, but both knew they had their perfect match. JAC was so proud of his accomplishments, and he knew he couldn't have done it without her encouraging him to be his best.

You can do it, JAC, rang constantly in his head. *You are not a starving, near dead Scottish farmer flailing on the Flume River in an overturned boat in Nova Scotia. You are not a simple Camden farmer, you are a successful businessman.* And he was. He loved her spark and how she sparked him. He loved the family she created, much kinder than his own. He loved listening to them all laugh, spoiled rotten, every child. He loved spoiling her. This was the measure of a man lived well. For him, his life was a miracle, all owed to Rhoda. Oh yes, that was love.

"I do know you do love a new challenge, Rhoda. This house is magnificent, but not as small as I'd hoped. Now, we will rattle around in here."

"One can never tell what the future holds, JAC. All of our children will visit with their children, and I want them to feel welcome. I needed to start anew. Memories are fine, but the past offers us nothing. I think we will adjust quite nicely to this country life. I love the majestic panorama from this bluff. It's too bad the ferry service across the Minnesota River was discontinued when they built the road. Do you remember how romantic it was when we took our horses to Shakopee on the ferry?"

"I don't remember it as romantic, Rhoda, but I do wish they had built the roadbed higher, as it floods every spring with the snow melt. One of these years, they'll build a tall bridge across the whole flood plain."

"Your head never stops thinking of improvements, JAC. In that way, we are alike, dear. I've also been thinking I'd like to add..."

"What, dear?' JAC asked and smiled, as usual.

"A garden. Do you see that sunny area? I'd love for you to till it for me."

"Of course. What else do you like about this bluff?"

"The Automobile Club is just down the road, if we want to dine out and socialize. I am inspired to paint this splendid view of the Minnesota River Valley. That charming Shady Valley farmhouse you see below, right below, will be my first painting. I'll definitely have to improve on my drawings of chickens and horses. You know, JAC, I had an Uncle Harry in Toronto, deceased now, who studied art in Paris. He was quite gifted..."

"You have just drifted off with another mysterious Toronto Hanscome, Rhoda. Every day, I expect another relative to wistfully appear in your conversation. I'd enjoy taking you to Toronto. Just name the time."

Silence.

"I can add a few yellow blobs of paint to that farmhouse scene, if you'd like me to," he teased, bringing her back to the present. "I would name the painting *Chickens From a Distance*."

"Oh, JAC, sometimes you are so silly, you remind me of Gordon or vice versa. I am not a chicken. I am not afraid of anything."

But Rhoda didn't mind his teasing. She was a good sport. And JAC was insightful enough to not push into her private world. Perhaps, one day, she would divulge her Toronto secrets to him. She trusted him, but not enough. She knew the rules of the society they belonged to. And while JAC didn't care, she really knew that she did. Not today, she thought. Today, I will listen to Uncle Harry's voice as I paint. I love JAC for not intruding. We are good together.

"One day, this whole river valley will be part of Minneapolis, Rhoda," JAC said as he put his arms around his wife, bringing her out of her silence.

Silently, they appreciated the rumble of thunder and the darkening storm front as it rolled swiftly down the green valley. Lightening blazes zigzagged across the sky. Their skin shivered with the sudden drop in temperature, and they nestled into each others' warmth. The fury of storms was so beautiful, so powerful, so beyond their control. It was good to feel so small sometimes. Sharing this was love, and words could only diminish it. They felt safe together.

Would Rhoda ever be able to capture this command performance of nature on canvas? She never became discouraged with her efforts. No, Rhoda loved a challenge. *Watch me, Uncle Harry.*

What bothered the Campbells, other than their children's choices in mates? Were they worried about the war storms in Europe, China or Japan? Apparently not, but it put a crimp in Rhoda's desire to travel abroad. At least they were safe on another continent, far away from the fray. After all, this was not America's war.

Rhoda had bigger issues on her mind, like the birth of Margaret's baby. She hoped it would not arrive early as it might appear she was pregnant before her wedding night. No, no, that disgrace would never do. Secretly, Rhoda also wished it would be born on her birthday, October 30. What a special present that would be. Her first grandchild!

While tradition dictated the first child of the first born should be a boy, she hoped Margaret would have a girl - so much easier to raise. She also didn't hold the view that boys were the natural leaders. Did she stop to consider what Gordon and Margaret wanted? They were, after all, the parents. Luckily, they had no preference.

It is evident they are enthralled with the whole process of making their child. Gordon is even gentler - almost sweet, Rhoda observed with a pleased smile. *My son is sweet.*

October 19, 1940
Minneapolis

"It's a girl!" Margaret's mother announced to Gordon.

"And how is Margaret?"

"She is doing fine, and the baby is healthy."

Gordon gingerly entered the room, kissed his wife and patted his baby girl. He may have been the glib, charming salesman, but now, he was at a loss for words.

"She won't bite you Gordy." His wife laughed. "She looks like you. I think she will have your blonde hair and blue eyes."

"I can't tell who she resembles, but I'll take your word for it. She has only fuzz for hair and a round baby face. Honestly, I don't really care, Margaret, as long as she has your good looks," he said and grinned in return. "What do you want to name her?"

"Take my word for it, Gordy, she's going to be blonde. We should give her a Scottish first name, like Heather, to match the Campbell."

Thus, Heather Campbell became the first of the first. Grandmother Campbell was most pleased.

"It's a girl!" the nurse announced to Wesley Dickinson at Kandiyohi County Hospital. "Rhoda Jane is doing well and wants to see you."

Wesley peaked his head into the room and presented her with a bouquet of roses. "Flowers for your labor!" He bent to kiss his flushed but smiling wife.

"She has your dark hair, Wesley. It's too soon to tell her eye color, but they look dark," Rhoda Jane said, gently transferring the babe to him for his purview.

"What should we name her?" he tenderly asked.

"Since she is the oldest girl, I'd like to name her Rhoda, after my grandmother, mother and me," Rhoda Jane answered.

"Then, I get to choose her middle name," Wes teased as he awkwardly held his baby in his arms.

"Let's hear what you choose first." Rhoda Jane laughed.

"Susan, after my Irish grandmother. My mother says we get our wavy, thick, dark hair from her. I certainly hope she doesn't go bald." He laughed as he characteristically rubbed his hand on his bald spot. Did he think such gestures might encourage his strands of hair to multiply?

"Don't be silly, Wes. Girls usually don't go bald. Yes, Rhoda Susan. I like the sound of that. Are you certain your mother's feelings won't be hurt?"

"I don't think so. Mother hates her name, Myrtle, and loved her dear mother. It's too bad I never knew my grandmother. My grandfather married his nurse after Susan's death. She is the reason my mother was sent to boarding school, St. Mary's Episcopal Academy, in Faribault. But my step-grandmother, not much older than my mother, was kind to me when I lived with them while my father was dying."

"It is so sad for me to think of you being shuttled between your Grandfather Adsit in Hastings and Myrtle in Minneapolis.

Then, both your father and grandfather died within a year of each other. And your poor mother was left almost penniless. It was a true shame that his second wife ran off to California with the silver and the rest of his money."

"Don't worry, I have no intention of dying young and leaving you in such dire circumstances," Wes said and laughed. "And Rhoda Susan will have playmates – no only child syndrome for her. I hated being an only child."

"Are you subtly telling me you want more children? Fine with me. The nurse said I'm a pro at having babies. Now, you must stay healthy. I'll be no young widow."

Rhoda and JAC arrived in Willmar before Rhoda Jane was released from the hospital. Rhoda was armed with presents.

"There is nothing too good for Little Rhoda Susan," Rhoda chirped. "I am thrilled that you honored me with a namesake."

"Oh, Mother, how thoughtful," Rhoda Jane replied as she opened lacey, wee gowns and caps, embroidered receiving blankets and hand-me-downs from Heather, Gordon and Margaret's baby. "Your lace tatting is lovely. You have thought of everything - even the obligatory engraved silver spoon, bowl and cup. She'll have these dented in no time." Rhoda Jane laughed. Was there something wrong with Rhoda Jane? Certainly no human being could be so cheery. But she was, always. She had learned from the best to deny those things she didn't like.

"I have also arranged for a three-month diaper service for you. If you wear yourself out, you will not be fit when the next child arrives. Your father will return to Minneapolis tomorrow, but I intend to wait on you for the next two weeks."

The new family was pampered. Rhoda had boundless energy. She also talked Wesley into hiring a washerwoman and cleaning lady. He didn't mind, as his mother-in-law was an excellent cook and organizer. But Wesley wondered why she never taught her daughters to cook, sew or clean. Images of burned pork chops and Rhoda Jane's tears during their honeymoon floated through his mind. He did smile at the image of her flying to the outhouse in her flimsy white peignoir. What was his mother-in-law thinking? This was practical Willmar where pretenses weren't welcomed, which is why he liked it.

Wes was even happier when his mother Myrtle arrived.

"Please call me *Mother*," Myrtle stated to Rhoda Jane, who felt she had no choice but to comply, albeit awkwardly. "I am so pleased to have a little girl named after my mother. If I had had a girl, her name would be Susan. She even resembles her."

Just like that, the Rhoda was deleted from her granddaughter's name. Susan seemed the best fit, at least in Myrtle's eyes. And Rhoda Jane did not want to challenge her mother-in-law. It wouldn't be polite. But she felt her stomach churning. What would her mother say? Rhoda had never liked Myrtle. She called her a *bold woman*. Then Rhoda Jane laughed. Who was the bold one? She was happy she was in Willmar, away from the competing grandmothers.

1942

War! This was not a happy new year. Pearl Harbor, less than a month ago, surprised the Hanscomes, Campbells, their children and the nation. The war effort was in full swing. Thomas Hanscome left his teaching position at the University and went off to the War Department to perfect atomic bombs. Wesley was in the food industry and exempt from the draft. Gordon was also exempt, as he was a government purchasing agent, but Bill Donald was not. Off to the army Bill went, leaving his pregnant wife, Jean.

"Oh, JAC! We need to make room in our house for the children. Gordon and Margaret can have the blue room, Jean and Pat can share the yellow room and the pink room will be the nursery for Little Heather and Jean's and Margaret's babies, soon to arrive."

"What would happen if we didn't have such a large home? Or if Patricia were pregnant, too," JAC teased.

"Don't be ridiculous, Patricia is not even married. But I worry about her. She is planning to marry that John Herrmann, only to send him off to war. I had hoped she would return to finish her senior year at Oberlin and that John would finish his law degree at Harvard."

"Please don't worry, Rhoda. War changes everything. Pat has made a good choice in John Herrmann. It's Jean's marriage that concerns me. Bill Donald is a drunkard and not responsible. But I told Jean not to divorce him until after the war - perhaps military service would shape him up."

"I doubt that, JAC. He is leaving her with a baby. Why not divorce him now – for her peace of mind? She is not happy." For Rhoda, happiness was the ultimate in life goals.

"One practical reason. If her husband dies in the war, Jean and the baby will receive benefits."

"That's most callous, JAC."

"Yes it is, but it is a reality."

"Then I don't believe we should allow Pat to marry – to be made an early widow. Please be more positive!"

"I am positive. Practically positive. Being a widow has a better ring to it than divorcee with child. Don't you agree?"

"Oh, JAC!" Rhoda was disgusted with his smugness. Still, she knew his judgment had merit.

August 25, 1942

The bells rang at St. Luke's Episcopal, again, for the last Campbell wedding. The bride, unlike her sisters' vibrant blue eyes and blonde hair, had beguiling, iridescent green eyes and warm, chestnut brown hair. She was dressed in a simple, floor-length, white satin dress that clung to her envious frame, while John stood erect in military whites, befitting a naval officer. What a handsome couple.

"I do," promised Miriam Patricia.

"I do," replied John Herrmann.

It was a warm summer day, and The Minneapolis Women's Club patio was filled with vibrant, patriotic, red, white and blue flowers – perfect for an outdoor reception. Who would ever guess that this city of sparkling blue lakes and parkway gardens was a bleak frozen tundra half the year? Champagne flowed as the guests gaily waited in the receiving line to congratulate the newly married couple.

"That John Herrmann is from St. Paul. I certainly hope he doesn't expect Patricia to live on that side of the River," gossiped one guest – from Minneapolis, of course.

"Well, that won't happen any time soon. I hear John has his orders, and Pat will be accompanying him, at least for his training. He is going to be a paymaster in the Sea Bees," informed another.

"Will Rhoda allow that?"

"It's not her choice," laughed another. "Remember, she's just Pat's mother."

"Patricia is so independent, wild horses couldn't keep her from following John."

"Still, Rhoda is like a pied piper with her girls. They adore her and jump to do her bidding. And why not? Rhoda is so much fun and gives them everything."

"Certainly, Rhoda and JAC have no more room in their home on Ferry Hill. Look at the rounded bellies on Margaret and Jean. I can see why they weren't bride's maids. They look like beached whales."

"I think they're advertising for fertility rites," caustically remarked another.

"And isn't that why men get married?"

"That nursery on Ferry Hill is going to overflow."

"I don't think so. Rhoda will find room for her precious grandchildren, even if it means JAC has to build an addition."

"First, the wedding bells, then the babies. Rhoda is lucky, as war sometimes reverses the proper order. They will have a big happy family. I'm a bit jealous of how she rules the roost," remarked another.

Chapter 13

A Big Happy Family
1942
Minneapolis

There was always room for more children on Ferry Hill. Rhoda clucked like a proud, protective mother hen.

September 8

"It's a girl!" Patricia Donald was added to the nursery. And did her father hand out cigars? No, Bill was doing his duty, serving his country. Rhoda was pleased Jean had named her baby after her sister Pat. And secretly, she was glad Jean had a girl, in case she had to raise her alone.

October 17

"It's a boy!"

"What do you want to name your son?" Margaret asked.

"That's your department. I leave the naming to you," Gordon said.

"I think it would be nice to name him after you, as you were named after your father. Let's name him James Gordon Campbell, Jr."

Later, they presented the baby brother to Heather. "He's your birthday present," Gordon teased. "When you get bigger, you'll get to take care of him." And Heather? Since she was just two-years-old, she didn't know what to think, except that she had to share her mother's lap with wee Jimmy. But when she was older, she took her job of herding her brother quite seriously.

After John completed his Sea Bee training, newlywed Patricia moved back to the Ferry Hill house of crying babies. Did JAC complain that his home was taken over by his married children and their babies? No, he simply excused himself to the porch overlooking the Valley and smoked his pipe in peace.

"Musical beds!" Rhoda laughed, swishing from room to room. She was in her element having such a full, fun house.

Willmar

But not all were as happy as Rhoda Campbell. When Rhoda Jane and Wesley came to town, his mother, Myrtle, was only too happy to accommodate them. Myrtle fawned over her little brown-eyed Susan. Secretly, Rhoda Jane wished she could stay with her family, but she wouldn't want to hurt her mother-in-law's feelings. She missed her sisters, brother and parents more than she had anticipated. Did she feel lonely?

"Your mother needs to stop meddling," Wesley shouted, after a gala weekend spent in Minneapolis. "We live in Willmar, not Minneapolis. We have plenty of friends here. I'd like to spend just one holiday at home. Your sisters and brother are moochers, nothing but freeloaders with expensive tastes."

This was a predictable argument, with the same predictable ending. Rhoda Jane was left in tears as he slammed the door and zoomed off in their car. Was she happy? She was never one to complain. She had surmised that underneath his anger, her sometimes charming Wesley was jealous of her close-knit family. She found it ironic that he wanted to recreate her family, except that he wanted to be the one in charge, not his mother-in-law. Oh well, tomorrow Wes would be back to normal and the fight would be swept under the carpet, again. Besides, she had other things to concern herself with. She was pregnant again. All totaled, she loved being a mother. Now, if this next babe was less colicky than Susan, everyone would sleep better. Thank God the doctor finally discovered Susan had a milk allergy and prescribed that tasty, mashed banana diet.

August 23, 1943

"It's a girl," the nurse said to Wesley. Was he disappointed it was not a son? If so, he never said anything. He leaned over to kiss Rhoda Jane and examine his sleeping, fair-haired little girl.

"What should we call her?" Rhoda Jane asked.

"Nancy. I've always liked the name Nancy," Wes said.

"I like it, too - as long as it isn't the name of some long-lost girlfriend."

"No, you know better than to think that, Rhoda Jane. I've never had any other girlfriends – just you," Wesley teased.

"I don't believe that, but Nancy fits her. And how about Jean for a middle name, for my sister? Nancy Jean."

"Fine. And I'll make sure my mother doesn't change her name to Jean. Let's simply call her Nancy. I think she'll have your blonde hair."

This time when Rhoda visited her daughter, she also brought hand-me-down baby clothes from Jean's daughter Patty.

"I wanted to bring you a new washing machine, Rhoda Jane, but Maytag has converted its factory to make military equipment. There are none to be had in Minneapolis. None!"

"It's not important, Mother. I am the envy of the neighborhood to have all the fine appliances I have. What I do need is your help with Susan – she is a bit jealous of her baby sister."

"It is only natural. She feels dethroned. Let's give her some special attention and ways to be helpful. Soon, Rhoda Susan and Nancy Jean will be best friends."

"Mother, what's the war news from Bill Donald and John Herrmann?"

"There is no end in sight to this war," she said and sighed. "John and Pat had a good time on his leave, but Jean told Bill she is divorcing him on his last visit. I don't believe she will wait until the war is over to file the papers, much to your father's consternation. She is too disgusted with his drinking. Poor little Patty. She will be raised father-less. I told Jean we will help her every way we can. She needs to put the past behind her and hold her head high."

"I know you adore Patty and want to help Jean, but please remember to take care of yourself, Mother. Don't feel sorry for them. Jean is most resourceful. After this war is over, I hope you can travel, paint, entertain your friends or do whatever suits your fancy. You have been running a boarding house."

What Rhoda Jane tactfully meant was that her mother was doing harm by taking charge of Jean's life – her child, her divorce. She even had little Patty calling JAC, Papa. And now, all the grandchildren were following suit. *Papa! Papa! Papa!*

"Of course, Rhoda Jane. Of course. But we are one family, and I want to help Jean. After the war, we will just rattle around that big house. Gordon said he would not be sad to be departing the *Babies on the Bluff Manor*. Really, Rhoda Jane, sometimes I don't know what to make of Gordon's humor. He also had the audacity to say he would give me a reference for running an orphanage."

Rhoda Jane smiled. Her mother was not to be dissuaded from her mission. She loved orchestrating her big happy family. And Gordon? Well, Rhoda Jane wondered how he'd lived there as long as he had. Her mother was the matriarch, and her son and sons-in-law were itching to run their own patriarchies. She smiled, again. Willmar did have its good points.

March 3, 1944
Minneapolis

"It's a healthy boy!" the nurse exclaimed to Rhoda and JAC who were standing in for John at the hospital. Patricia knew John would be pleased when he saw his son – soon, she hoped. She and John had agreed to name him John Heck Herrmann, after his side of the family, but they would call him Jack, after her father.

Finally on leave, John was able to hold little Jackie. Yes, his son already had a nickname, similar to most his cousins. Fine, but John hated the commotion at the Campbell household. Before he left again for duty, he spanked little Patty for knocking over his son. Rhoda frowned, surely that was unnecessary. Now, they had three crying children – Jimmy and Patty, both two, and wee Jackie. Four-year-old Heather tried to comfort them all. She accepted her duty as big sister and that pleased her Grandma Rhoda.

And Margaret? She was grateful for Gordon's military deferment and a nice place to live. She could put up with her mother-in-law for a while longer. She pitched right in and was accepted as family.

The more the merrier! was Rhoda's motto.

"It's a girl," the nurse announced to smiling Wesley Dickinson.

"And Happy *Suden da Mai*," she said to Rhoda Jane. "It is good luck to have a baby born on our Norwegian Independence Day! Ya!"

"Thank you," Rhoda Jane said.

"And is it still good luck if she isn't Norwegian?" Wesley piped up.

"She sure don't look Norwegian, with that head of dark curls, but she will be lucky," exclaimed the nurse.

"What should we name number three daughter, Rhoda Jane? How about *Number Three*?"

"I know you were hoping for a boy and wanted to call him John Adsit - John for your ancestor John Dickinson and Adsit, for your Grandfather Adsit. How about Joan instead? Joan Adsit, unless you want to save Adsit for a boy."

"And how many more children do you want to have?" Wes asked. "Three kids are enough for me. Joan Adsit is a strong name, albeit not Norwegian! YA!"

"Susan, Nancy and Joan – I like those names. I do hope she won't hate the name Adsit."

"It's distinctive. Adsit is my middle name, my mother's middle name and my Grandfather's surname."

"It's a bit different, but it is fine with me. It will please your mother. I think I'll call her Joan bug, she is so tiny. All our babies are so small compared to these plump Scandinavians," smiled Rhoda Jane, who could hardly wait to smoke a cigarette.

"Joan bug? She will hate that name. How about Joanie?" Wes asked.

"Yes, that is more feminine."

"I just wish the upstairs house addition was completed, Rhoda Jane. Your mother was fit to be tied when she saw all the sawdust. She thought it was a good idea for me to abandon the downstairs to all you ladies and move upstairs to live in the dust."

"And did you agree?" Rhoda Jane asked and smiled.

"No. I did not," Wes replied in a pretend huff. "My home is *my* castle, not your mother's!"

November 12, 1945
Minneapolis

"Oh no!" Rhoda cried as she hugged her sister Muriel. "I thought he would live forever."

"It is hard for me to imagine my life without him. He was my daily companion," Muriel lamented. "As long as he lived, it seemed as though mother was also with us."

"I'm not sure I want to live as long as he has. His eyes lost their luster years ago. All his friends had passed before him," Rhoda said.

"We need to decide on the headstone," their brother Will said, looking at the death certificate. "His birth certificate says *white*, as do all of ours."

"Why do you need to bring this up now, Will?" Rhoda prickly remarked. "He lived his whole life as a white person, as did our grandparents in Toronto. He is three generations removed from an African."

"I am bringing this up now so we can decide if we want to maintain our silence. We have kept our pact, but we could reconsider it. All of our children are married and have families of their own. Why keep the secret? What purpose does it serve? The African influence has disappeared from our lineage, albeit my young Tom is quite dark-skinned, like me. Let's be courageous. Let's own our history. Let's be honest that father's money came from slave ownership."

"Can't you see the repercussions of such a disclosure, Will?" Rhoda cried out, not wanting an answer. "It would ruin our social standing. It could ruin our children's marriages. Listen to the awful names Negros are called. Prejudice is alive and well, even among our children. Gordon and our sons-in-law think little of spewing their racial slurs and negative attributions, sometimes for shock value and sometimes with delight. It is not clever to denigrate people. How unseemly. How unkind! Gordon is lucky his curly hair is blonde and not black. And you should have seen our sweet father just last month holding his great granddaughter, little Joanie, with her jet black, curly hair. Our children know not whence they came! Yes, it is a shame, but the reality is that prejudice is worse now than when we were born. I work hard with the Unitarians to raise consciousness that we are one, more similar than different. Disclosing our secret could even ruin our marriages. You know, I never told JAC. Did you tell Ethel?"

"Not directly, but everyone knew our father had a background of color. Look at him. Even in death, he has a glow, more than his own father.

"I'm certain the artist whitened up those faces in their portraits," Rhoda said. "No one wanted black blood, not even in Charleston."

"I remember Toronto. I cherish those memories, but I am unable to speak of them, our relatives, because you refuse to recognize them."

"Do you think we dishonor father by keeping the lie?" Muriel asked. "He hid his origin because we asked him. He gave up his Toronto family for our future. His own dear wife never asked for such a sacrifice from him."

"Yes, we dishonor him," Will replied. "In a way, we dishonor all Americans. We are not the only white Americans with African roots. What if we all came forward? What if the mulatto census choice was revived and had a positive connotation? Would prejudices more easily disappear? There is so much white in every Negro I meet. They are no longer African. They are golden, not black in color. The racial lines in America are blurred, but everyone pretends it isn't so. I don't think I know anyone with pure white skin! Check the blank – Caucasian or

Negro, White, Black or Indian. How ridiculous! What a joke! What a myth! And our *white silence* perpetuates the prejudice. I am not allowed at work to even consider a talented person of color for a position. The war is finally over. We need a new society, an honest one."

"Please settle down, Willie, I do see your point," Muriel said. "But our dear father clearly understood the social and economic ramifications of racial honesty. His father made the same choice when he crossed the 49th parallel. Father knew we loved him, honored him. I really see no point in changing our story at this late date."

"Our story is not a lie, Will. It may be a sin of omission. We just let people guess. Let's just continue the parlor game – Chippewa? East Indian? Argentinean?" Rhoda suggested. "Please, Will. If you let the black cat out of the bag, my life as I know it will be over. And do you really think you would keep your job?"

"Fine, but I think you are being a bit melodramatic, Rhoda. I will keep the secret, but I feel like a hypocrite. I just lied to my sweetest grandchild, who asked why his father and I were so dark-skinned. Lied!"

"You simply need to tell your son, Tom, to shave that awful black Van Dyke beard he grew in the military. He actually resembles that portrait of our Grandfather Thomas," Rhoda remarked.

"How can you be so callous, so self-centered, Rhoda? Our father has just died!"

His sisters ignored his tirade, as they always had.

"Please, Will, we all loved our father," Rhoda replied. "I do understand why you are angry with me, but that decision of whiteness was decided by our grandparents, Thomas and Mary Sophia. Remember, Grandpa was your hero. I think they would applaud how we have assimilated. Please don't mistake your anger for your grief. And I don't want to be your punching bag. Can't we share some fond remembrances of them all?"

By the time Ethel found her husband and his sisters, they had reconciled and were dissolved in tears over their dear father's passing. She was touched by their grief. She would miss her dapper gentleman father-in-law.

William Kissick Hanscome, 89, was kindly remembered at his funeral at St. Mark's Cathedral where he played the organ for years. He was laid to rest next to his dear wife, Rhoda, in Lakewood Cemetery, overlooking their beloved Lake Calhoun. Muriel tried not to notice the plot next to her parents, her final resting place. As Aunt Mur greeted her nieces and nephews at the service, she thought her parents would be smiling. The Hanscomes had not become extinct.

At the wake back at their house, Rhoda kept saying how lucky they all were to have such a good family, a happy family. Of course, no one bothered to disagree with her. The War was over, the men were home, gasoline, clothes, sugar, butter and cheese, bacon and other meats, lard, cereals and all canned goods were no longer rationed. Scarcity was past; prosperity was returning. The assimilation of ethnic differences was considered the American way. Speak English. Secret your pasts. Homogeneity is good. Be the top of the heap, like the Hanscomes and Campbells. Be WASPs.

Chapter 14

Be Fruitful and Multiply
1946
Minneapolis

"Isn't it nice, JAC, our children are following the biblical dictate: *Be Fruitful and Multiply*."

"Do you mean multiplying like jack rabbits, Rhoda? I think they mistake our home for a rabbit warren and soon will convert our bedroom into another nursery. The whole country is making babies instead of war." JAC hummed the old Gershwin tune, *It's Nice Work if You Can Get It… And You Can Get It If You Try*.

"Oh, JAC, sometimes I know where Gordon gets his silly humor. Still, it's nice to see you smiling more."

"I think the whole country is smiling again, Rhoda. It is time to celebrate. Would you like a cocktail, Mrs. Campbell?"

"It's a boy!" the doctor announced to John Herrmann. "What a homecoming present! The war is over, and you have another son."

"Another crying son," John protested, though truly thrilled. "I mistakenly dreamt of peace and quiet when I returned home."

"Oh, I think thou doest protest too much," Pat quipped, known for her dry wit. "What do you think of Judd for a name?"

"I like it. And yes, I am very happy to come home to you, two fine sons and soon a home of our own."

"Thanks to my parents. And please remember, you said if I didn't like St. Paul, we could move across the River."

"You can almost see the River from our new house. Surely, that should do. You Minneapolis people think that's the only place to live. St. Paul people are quite civilized."

"I actually like St. Paul, and the privacy the River provides us. Close enough, but not too close to family."

"And my mother and my sister? Are they too close, interfering in your interests?"

"We get along well. I enjoy their company, and they are not intrusive."

Slowly, the Campbell big happy family dispersed to their separate homes. They were not being pushed from Rhoda's nest; they were jumping! Gordon and Margaret had quickly settled in their new home in Morningside, just in the nick of time.

"It's a boy!" The doctor announced to Gordon.

"What should we call him?" he asked.

"I'd like to call him Scott," Margaret said.

"I can't think of a better name for a Scot than the name Scott." Gordon laughed. "He does look like a little Scot with his round face."

"He looks a lot like Heather and you – whereas Jimmy looks more like me and my family."

"Would you like to even it up? The boys and the girls?" Gordon teased.

"It is way too soon to discuss more children. I am so happy we finally have our own place, not that I didn't appreciate your parents' help. Your mother was so positive, welcoming and made the whole group-living experience a fun adventure. I didn't expect to love your family as much as I do."

"My father is talking about my working for him again. I might consider it, if we can get along."

"I don't need more and better, Gordon - not if working with him makes you miserable." Margaret always had Gordon's back, even though he was quite capable of defending himself.

Were Rhoda and JAC sad to see the children leave their nest, again? No, not in the slightest. They were relieved, but then Ferry Hill was not empty. Jean and her daughter were still safely ensconced.

"JAC, I've been thinking."

"Oh, not thinking! Please don't think, Rhoda. I simply want to relax, in my own house, without the sound of crying babies."

"I agree it's a good idea for both of us to catch our breath, but then I'd like for us to travel, now that the War is over."

"Europe has not recovered from the devastation. I think it is way too soon."

"What if we toured the British Isles? We could see England, Scotland and Ireland. Don't you want to see where your people came from?"

"I know where the Campbells came from – Nova Scotia," JAC replied. "We could go there."

"Oh, JAC, you know I have no desire to see bleak Nova Scotia. And my mother came from England. I hear London is recovering from the bombing."

"Let's give it a few years. Right now, my businesses are booming. And I still haven't given up on Gordon joining me."

"Gordon likes his independence. He wants to be his own boss, just like you. And if we're not going to travel for awhile, Jean wants to teach school, and I can take care of Patty."

"She needs to find another husband," JAC said. "We need to bow out of her life."

"Well, she won't find one out here in rural Bloomington. Perhaps we should move closer to the city so she can have a social life and at least see her girlfriends. Now that Margaret and Pat are gone, she's lonely – and Patty misses her cousins."

"Let it rest, Rhoda. We have had enough change for a while."

Rest was not in Rhoda's vocabulary, but she managed to paint, read and play bridge when she was not entertaining Patty.

Jean secured a teaching position at Northrop Collegiate. Her mood and social life improved. On the weekends, she attended polo matches with her *horsey set* Wayzata friends. Had a divorce ruined Jean's life? Apparently not. Little Patty settled into a routine with her mother, Grandmother and a world of adults.

For Christmas, JAC bought Jean a car so she could get around and a new mink coat for Rhoda to stay fashionably warm. In return, Rhoda surprised JAC with an authentic Campbell family crest, complete with wild boar insignia, from the highlands of Breadalbane, Scotland.

"Those long tusks will scare off both guests and intruders," JAC remarked, most pleased. "This is a ferocious looking boar, if I ever saw one."

After he nailed the wooden crest above the door of their tutor home, Rhoda and JAC celebrated with a champagne toast: "To Breadalbane!"

JAC thought the toast was a bit ridiculous, but he loved his fun wife and hoped the crest was a sign that Rhoda had settled for good. Was that too much to ask? Yes, it was.

1949
Edina

The Campbells moved from Ferry Hill in Bloomington to Sunny Slope in Edina. Their brand-new home was again on Minnehaha

Creek. Rhoda convinced JAC that Jean, teaching at the prestigious private school, could not be expected to drive daily into the city in the snow and ice. And certainly Patty, age seven, needed a proper education, too.

Did JAC mind? Apparently not. He accepted that regardless of Rhoda's rationale, the truth was that her other children had departed, once again, for their own homes, and she was lonely for her old friends and the new excitement of the post-war city. He also knew that once she made up her mind, she would persevere. He happily agreed and raked weeds from the Minnehaha Creek bed while his grandchildren chased the crawdads that scurried back to the water.

"My dear, Jean, you must start attending the galas at The Minnekahda Club. And please don't groan. If you don't meet an eligible male, at least people will know you are back in circulation," her mother suggested.

And did Rhoda's strategy to have Jean married again bear fruit? Yes, it did.

1950
The Sunny Slope wedding

"Do you Jean Hope Donald take Clifford Gardner Johnson to be your lawfully wedded husband?"

"I do," she said.

From the music loft above, the cousins watched their Aunt Jean get married in the cathedral ceilinged living room, decorated for the occasion and catered. However, Rhoda arranged all the aromatic bouquets of flowers herself. The loft balustrade was lined in cousin pecking order: Heather (ten), Susan (nine), Jimmy (eight), Nancy (seven), Jackie (six), Joanie (five), Juddy (four) and Scottie (four).

"Don't put your head through the railing, or you'll get stuck again," whispered Nancy, poking her younger sister Joanie, who always had a hard time keeping still.

"Shh!" Susan silenced her younger sisters with a chastising finger to her lips and an angry glare.

None of them wanted to be sent to their rooms and miss the show, as the adults had threatened. Patty, the only child permitted downstairs, was looking up at them making faces and crossing her eyes, until she caught her grandmother's stern look. It was all the children could do not to break into giggles.

"Clifford?" Susan asked. "I didn't know that was Gardner's real name."

"It's just like you, Susan. You don't use your first name, Rhoda," replied knowledgeable Heather, the oldest cousin.

"Oh, I see. What else do you know about our new uncle?"

"He grew up in Minneapolis - his mother Susan lives just down the hill from The Minnekahda Club on Lake Calhoun. It's just a short walk. And he is rich. He went to Blake, the private school, and is part of the *horsey set*."

"Rich?" Jimmy asked.

"Shh," Nancy said. "You'll get us all kicked out of here, and we'll miss the fun."

"Yes, rich," Heather whispered. "He is heir to the Johnson Nut Company, and he rides polo ponies. They're going to live in Sherwood Forest."

"Will Patty see Robin Hood?" Joanie asked.

"Don't be stupid," Nancy said. "Robin Hood is just a story, not real."

"Lucky Patty. She'll have all the horses she can ride," Jackie chimed in.

"But not in Sherwood Forest. They have all these rules. No animals, except dogs, and no colored people," Heather said.

"How do you know that?" Jimmy asked.

"I heard them talking. Gardner said that it was a good idea to keep the riff-raff out, but he had hoped to keep a few horses, rather than board them," Heather replied.

"Have you eaten some of Gardner's Johnson Nuts? They're delicious," Susan said.

"What if Patty goes nuts!" Juddy laughed, elbowing his cousin Scottie. "Get it? Johnson's nuts!"

"Does Patty like her new dad?" Nancy asked.

"You mean her step-dad? She doesn't even know him," Heather whispered. "I hear he won't let Patty use his last name. Weird, Patty will be Donald, and Aunt Jean will be Johnson. I'm glad my parents aren't divorced."

"Perhaps Patty's taken a step-up, get it?" Jackie laughed.

"My dad says Gardner can play the guitar and sing," Joanie said.

"My dad says Gardner was in the war in Africa," Jackie said.

"Look at them kiss!" Susan said, her eyes popping out of her head.

"Smooch, smooch, smooch!" All the cousins puckered up and imitated kissing noises, which the adults downstairs chose to ignore.

Congratulations!

Jean was aglow. Gardner enamored. Rhoda beamed. JAC eagerly anticipated an empty house, again. Rhoda Jane was uncomfortable. She was soon to have baby number four. And the cousins ate the softest, yummiest, white wedding cake in the loft before they were tucked into bed by their parents.

February 6, 1950
Willmar

"It's a boy!" the Kandiyohi County Hospital nurse exclaimed.

"Well, I'll be!" Wes was dumbfounded as he rubbed the top of his bald head.

"I thought you'd be pleased," Rhoda said.

"I am surprised. This time, we hadn't even bothered to discuss boys' names."

"Well, he must have a name. Do you want to call him Wesley?"

"No, I've never liked my name, even though my mother named me after her twin brother Wesley, who died a few weeks after their births. It's too effeminate. Only Shirley, Carol, Marion or Sue could be a worse boy's name. Let's name him Robert, after my father. It's a hearty, manly name."

"You don't think that is a curse, since he died of diabetes so young?"

"No, I don't. I believe in science, not curses, and it would be nice to remember him, don't you agree?"

"It's a nice gesture, Wesley. And since he will be our last child, let's give him the middle name of Campbell, after my family."

"That's a solid name - Robert Campbell Dickinson. I like it."

"And also - no *Bob* nickname, please. We will call him Robert, agreed?" Rhoda Jane asked. "It seems like everyone we know is a Bob."

"Agreed."

And how did Rhoda Jane manage four children? She drank coffee, smoked cigarettes and ignored the chaos. She was tired. But no one thought she was ill, least of all Rhoda Jane. She was raised with the old adage: *Stiff upper lip and carry on!*

"Rhoda Jane, you need help," her mother said, when she arrived after Robert's birth. "You look exhausted."

Wesley agreed to have a farm girl live with them. Rhoda Jane catered to her children's every whim but was a terrible housekeeper. It didn't help that the neighborhood children all flocked to the fun Dickinson house so their mothers could cook and clean. She didn't mind, except when these same friends wondered why her home was always a mess. Didn't they know that when they shooed their children outside to play, they made a beeline to the Dickinson's back door?

"Mrs. Dickinson, Joanie's stuck in the clothes shut. We tried pulling her back up, then pushing her back down, but she's stuck good. Can you help us?" Once freed, Rhoda Jane sent them outside to play cops and robbers, cowboys and Indians or Red Rover, Red Rover. And on rainy days, the sisters dressed up in their mom's old gowns and satin shoes and made and burned cookies. What a mess, but she served them anyway for dessert. Actually, she loved the commotion. Wesley declared them nice and crunchy and thought they should bring a blue ribbon at the county fair.

Rhoda Jane also appreciated the yummy, homemade Swedish rolls that her friends brought to the afternoon *kaffe klutches*. Soon, she was making those yummy, melt-in-your-mouth caramel, cinnamon yeast rolls. It was an all day labor of love:

Mix the yeast cakes with water and set aside. Cream the butter, sugar, shortening, add the scalded milk and slightly beaten eggs, the yeast, salt, the 4 cups of sifted flour, a little at a time. Cover and raise in warm place until it doubles in size or looks ready. Flour the cutting board, pat out the dough in a rectangle shape, smooth the brown sugar on top, dot with butter, sprinkle the cinnamon, cut the rolls and place in the prepared angel food cake pans, lined with more brown sugar and butter. Raise again until doubled in size. Bake at 350-375 for 20-25 minutes or until they look done. (This was as exact as the recipe was.)

And their help? The farm girls liked going to the high school in town and cleaned, washed clothes and watched the children after school and on the weekends. Wesley liked having his golf partner and companion back, but having maids was not without complications…

Karen:

"Help!" Karen, their maid, screamed in a blood-curdling voice.

Wes ran to the kitchen, wondering if someone had died, to find her fallen to the floor, eyes rolling back in their sockets, as she tightly grasped her almost detached, bloody fingertip. The new, electric mixer's beaters had caught her finger and sprayed blood everywhere - the cake batter, the counter, the floor and the ceiling.

"Hold her fingertip to her finger, Rhoda Jane, as I bandage them, and hold tight! We are taking her to the hospital!"

"Lucky, you are a butcher, Wes, and not afraid of blood," the surgeon complimented. "Your quick thinking might save her finger. We'll see if it reattaches."

Eldora:

"I smell smoke," Susan told her mother. "It's coming from Eldora's room." And it was. In turn, Rhoda Jane told Wesley when he came home from work.

"Rhoda Jane, I just let Eldora go. Our house could have gone up in flames. She stole our Lucky Strikes and snuffed out the embers under her bedroom rug."

Susan was quite happy. She now had a bedroom to herself and was elevated in status to her *mother's big helper*.

• • •

Soon, they traded their South Side home for a larger, old tutor home on the North Side. The North Side was across the railroad tracks in the older, now *bad side* of Willmar, but Rhoda Jane fell in love with the ambience created by the flowering bushes and blooming trees. The stately elms formed a canopy over Ella Avenue for as far as you could see. She felt she had left the prairie behind. Aah, green, lush elegance.

Behind the spacious home was a woods and beyond that a city park where the children could play. Kitty corner was the new edition for the Lafayette Elementary School. Rhoda Jane bought a massive, lion-clawed mahogany dining room table and buffet from an estate sale. The perfectly round table comfortably sat ten men on Wes' poker club night, and with the leaf extensions, twenty-five for holiday dinners. It was the favorite spot for Susan's sewing projects, gin rummy and the marathon Monopoly games that Jackie and Juddy loved to play during their summer visits.

On Saturday nights, the family would roll up the rugs, listen to Lawrence Welk and dance in the living room. Boy, could their dad ever waltz, polka and foxtrot. He taught all the girls how to dance the *schottische: one two three hop, one two three hop, step hop, step hop, hop hop hop!* Their parents loved to dance as they drank their Four Roses whiskey and waters - the whiskey bought in a *wet* county.

Winter 1953

"Susan, Nancy, Joanie. Come downstairs," their dad called. The girls sat in a row on the couch, their legs dangling over the edge and stared at the strange woman sitting in a wing chair by the fireplace. "Your mother is going back to Minneapolis to live with your grandparents for awhile. She needs an operation and then rest until the baby comes."

"I will miss you, my dear children, but there's no need to worry. We have arranged for Mrs. Johnson to take care of you every day. And you, Susan, will have to help your dad when Mrs. Johnson's not here, especially with Robert. I will need to rest after the operation, so your new sister or brother will be healthy. Girls, please say hello to Mrs. Johnson."

"Hello, Mrs. Johnson," the girls said politely, but warily.

"When will you leave, Mother?" twelve-year-old Susan asked.

"Tomorrow," her mother answered.

"And when will you come back?" She asked.

"As soon as I can, but I will talk to you every week on the telephone."

Stunned and silent, the girls went upstairs to bed. They were not peaceful for long. Nancy clobbered Joanie when she rolled over onto Nancy's half of their double bed.

"Stay on your own side, or I'll belt you again and stop talking to yourself," Nancy threatened.

"You better watch out, yourself, or I'll clobber you with my baton," Joanie replied.

Silence.

"Did you know Mom was sick?" Joanie asked.

"No," Nancy replied. "She never complains, but she has been taking long naps with Robert."

"People die when they have operations. Do you think she'll die?" Joanie asked.

"I don't know."

The two girls cried themselves to sleep. That night, it snowed, but then that was nothing new.

"Now, no fighting girls," their mother warned as she hugged Nancy and Joanie goodbye.

The girls stood by Mrs. Johnson as their parents drove out of the driveway. Life settled down after that. Mrs. Johnson was organized.

"Mrs. Johnson seems nice," Nancy said.

"She smells a little, but not as bad as Emma," Susan said. Emma was the strong cleaning lady who spoke German.

"Why can't we all go live with Grandma Campbell?" Joanie asked.

The months passed.

"What's that noise?" their mom asked during a weekly telephone call. Her voice had lost some of its hoarseness. Rhoda Jane was on the mend from her thyroidectomy.

"Chirpie," Nancy said, "our pet chicken. She's pink, well, she used to be pink. We think she's a girl. The blue and green chicks died."

"Put your father on the line, please."

What a commotion Rhoda Jane heard. Fluffy, their Great Pyrenees dog, was barking, the children were squealing and Chirpie was chirping.

"It sounds like you are having fun without me, but a chicken? Wesley, I need less, not more work. And you called me a soft touch? It sounds like chaos!"

"I bet you miss it. Yes, Rhoda Jane, I know. The children wanted some of those colored Easter chicks. I couldn't see why not. Fluffy is herding Chirpie like a sheep!"

"I am thinking of coming home tomorrow. Mother wants me to stay until I deliver the baby, but I want to be with you all for Easter. I actually miss the commotion. Will you come pick me up?"

April 3

"It's a girl!" the doctor said. "You were lucky to get Rhoda Jane here in time, Wes. What a spring blizzard we're having! Rhoda Jane is fine – she barely broke a sweat. One push was all it took."

"And the baby? Is she healthy?" Wes asked.

"She looks robust to me." The doctor smiled.

"What's her name to be?" Rhoda Jane asked.

"If you agree, her name is Mary, Mary Jane," Wes replied, a bit sheepishly. "The girls had a naming contest."

"That's a very nice name," the doctor said. "May I speak with you privately?" When they were in the hall, the doctor continued, "Promise me, Wes, no more babies. Rhoda Jane will not survive another child. She is thirty-eight and almost died in Minneapolis. You might try another farm girl to help her."

And Wes did. Sally, a senior at Willmar High School, soon moved into Susan's bedroom, but the peace didn't last long. Wesley discovered a young man in her room, chased him down the stairs and yelled at him to never come back. Sally dissolved in tears. The girls quietly closed their bedroom door, and in the morning, Susan got her room back, along with her *mother's helper* role.

But all was not peaceful. The truth was Wesley didn't know how they would afford to raise the five children they had. In addition to Rhoda's medical bills, his booming business failed. While many businesses thrived after the War, the advent of home refrigerators and freezers made his locker plants obsolete. Still, Wes was optimistic and resourceful. He sold his plants in Bird Island, Svea and Olivia and bought a turkey barn. He became a Supersweet Feeds salesman and hoped they could cut expenses until his first poultry could be sold.

"Turkeys are the future of Willmar, Rhoda Jane. Don't worry. We will be fine. A new baby and a new business!"

Wes presented the picture of confidence. Underneath, he hoped his friend, Earl Olsen, who had just started *Jennie-O Turkey*, was right.

His mother-in-law Rhoda was excited to see his newest business on her next visit. She had come to help.

"What a nice Easter service, Father Butts," Rhoda Campbell said to the minister of the small Episcopal Church in Willmar. "And thank you for the blessing of little Mary Jane."

"Babies are the spirit of hope and a sign of spring," the rotund reverend said and smiled. "And I also blessed Wes' newly-hatched turkeys."

Wesley opened the door to the barn and quickly ushered his family inside. It was spring, but nippy and wet from the melting snow.

"Young turkeys are susceptible to all kinds of diseases and do not appreciate cold drafts."

The children scampered up the slippery stairs to the loft. "Be careful of the dung," Wes warned, but too late. Susan had slipped and slid into her grandmother who was following behind. Down they went.

"Shit!" Susan exclaimed, shooting daggers at her father. "Shit! My Easter dress is ruined. And look at my new crinolines!"

Susan's five crinolines, carefully starched stiff the night before, were covered in dung. Susan was a pro at profanity and had been since kindergarten. Her much chagrined mother attributed her swearing to the neighbor boys' bad influence.

"Swearing is not appropriate any time, my dear Susan, but I believe you are quite correct." Her grandmother laughed.

"I am so sorry, Susan and Rhoda," a sheepish Wes said. "Let me help you up."

"Please don't fret. Minks in their natural habitat are used to dirt. I'll have the furrier clean it when I go home. If you'll help me up these treacherous stairs, Wes, I'd still like to see those dirty birds."

Rhoda was impressed with the hundreds of chirping birds, albeit did not care for the stinky odor that shocked her nasal passages.

Susan had left in a huff for the car. She was determined never to enter another turkey barn.

"How embarrassing, Mother!" she wailed.

Calm Rhoda Jane simply listened to the lament of her oldest daughter, then washed the crinolines until they looked as good as new. Turkey dung, how disgusting, she thought with a sigh. She had not bargained to be a turkey farmer's wife or a mother of five children. At least her mother was her champion. Before Rhoda left, a new chaise lounge was delivered.

"You must rest, Rhoda Jane – at least an hour after lunch." Interesting, her mother had never mentioned the falling down the stairs in turkey dung episode. But then, she always took things in stride. Rhoda Campbell was a good sport.

Wes Dickinson's new venture was not the only one in the family. Gordon had joined his father JAC in a tool and die business, the Satterlee Company, and was prospering. John Herrmann ran a tape company, but it was unclear how much John's mother contributed to the Herrmann's affluent lifestyle, the summers on Madeline Island, the winters in Florida. And surprise, surprise, both Pat and Jean were pregnant again. That was fine with Nancy and Joanie. It meant Patty, Jackie and Juddy might come for a fun summer visit. *The more the merrier!*

September 23
Minneapolis

"It's a boy," the doctor announced.

Gardner Johnson was ready with a box of Cuban cigars for the doctor. And Jean? She was happy, as Gardner had wanted a son. Gardner had definitely had it with twelve-year-old Patty, who spent more and more time at her grandmother's. Jean felt like a chicken in the middle, tugged one way then pulled the other. She hoped Gardner would be satisfied. But he wasn't.

They called the baby James, James Richards Johnson. Was he also named after JAC? Perhaps, but no one called him that. His initials were JJ, and the nickname stuck. JJ was soon shortened to one J or Jay.

"Patty is spoiled, Jean," Gardner shouted as he made himself another drink. "The only thing your mother and I agree on is that Patty needs to go to a boarding school. I will not have her insolence in my home."

"You've already had too much to drink, Gardner. Please, let's eat dinner," Jean begged.

No, the Johnson marriage was not going well.

"Gardner is like a child himself," Jean complained to her sisters. "Patty and Gardner both demand my undivided attention – and Mother continually sides with Patty, which infuriates Gardner more. I never should have gotten married again," Jean lamented.

Her sisters silently agreed. But then it seemed as if marital bliss had eluded them all.

"I have never seen our father drunk, but the men I marry prefer that state." Jean sighed. "And I may become a drunkard out of self-defense."

Her sisters all empathized. They had all married drinkers. What was all the rage in the thirties, no longer brought joy. The wives blamed alcohol for their rageful husbands. And, of course, their husbands blamed their wives. And the wives promised to be more understanding. It was, after all, their job to make a marriage work.

Of course, nothing appeared to be wrong. They were one big happy family.

Where were the Campbell grandparents? Busy traveling and busy buying. They had been to South and Central America and were now exploring Spain. Postcards of flamenco dancers, paintings from the Prado and rolling, countryside hills arrived regularly.

> *Having a wonderful time. We have traded Madrid*
> *for a villa in the countryside where I am painting*
> *and JAC is walking. Next stop will be in Majorca.*
> *Wish you were here! Back before Christmas!*
>
> *Love, Mother*

Christmas 1953
Edina

"Why does Grandma always have two Christmas trees?" Joanie asked.

"Grandma loves the holidays and decorates to the hilt," Rhoda Jane explained. "When we were children, we had real candles on our Christmas tree, but your Papa put a stop to that. 'It's a ready mix for a fire,' he called it. I rarely heard my dad ever tell my mother she couldn't have something, but he really put his foot down when he saw all those lit candles."

"Every year, the upstairs tree is different. This year it looks like blue cotton candy. What do you call that?"

"Flocking, Joanie. It's all the rage."

"Everything matches, the blue shimmering birds and silver bells. But I like the multi-colored tree downstairs best. It has all the presents under it."

"That's a good reason. Now go play with your cousins. It is adult time, cocktail hour. It will soon be time for us to open our Christmas gifts."

And play the cousins did. Or was it mischief?

"Jump in," Juddy said as he scrambled into the dumbwaiter.

"Your legs are too long. There's no room for me," Nancy lamented.

"Just push the button for me then, and you can ride next time."

After Judd's ride up to the kitchen from the downstairs library, Nancy and Patty opened the dumbwaiter door to let him out. Then, Nancy got in and rode it back downstairs. Before Nancy could climb out, Grandma came up from behind and caught them in the act.

"I thought I was hearing voices." She laughed. "I didn't think that dumbwaiter could talk. But it will break if you children keep riding it, then we'll have to carry the food downstairs and the dishes back upstairs. Now please go down to the library, your Uncle John has some gifts for you, unless you want me to tell him you're too busy."

Uncle John solemnly and officially convened the first secret meeting of the Campbell Cousins in the unfinished, spooky basement room. Then, he gave each a little present wrapped in green and red tissue paper.

"Look what Uncle John gave me for Christmas," Nancy said, holding up her bright silver badge. "It's like a real Sheriff's badge."

"And here is your very own badge, Joanie," Uncle John said. "It's engraved. See? It says *Secret C. C. Society* right here on the front, and on the back is a sharp pin. Do you want me to pin it on your dress?"

"Yes," Joanie nodded. She liked her Uncle John. He was fun.

"The initials stand for Campbell Cousins. Only you cousins can belong to it. Now, you can't wear your badge all the time, just when we get together. And don't tell your friends what the Secret C.C. stands for," John said with a merry smile. "I hear your grandma ringing the bell. It's time to open the Christmas gifts," he said. "Now swear not to tell anyone."

The cousins all held up their right hands and swore to the secret pact.

What a Christmas. Now for the gifts! Papa had the boy cousins - Jimmy, Jackie, Juddy and Scottie – be Santa's helpers and distribute the gifts.

"This one's for Aunt Rhoda Jane," Jackie said.

Rhoda Jane gave baby Robert to his sister Susan and opened the huge silver box with the big red bow.

"Oh my! Mother, you shouldn't spoil me so," Rhoda Jane exclaimed as she tried on the long, silver, curly haired coat. "This lamb's wool coat is just what I need this winter."

"I'm happy you like it, Rhoda Jane. A fur coat is practical. It should protect you from those Willmar prairie blizzards this winter," Grandma said. She had bought fur coats for all her girls.

"Ooh," Pat said as she lifted up her brown sable coat.

"Aah," Jean said as she tried on her white fox coat.

"Ooh!" Margaret remarked as she tried on her black mink coat.

The men, including Uncle Gordon, all got new shirts, ties and slacks. It was apparent Rhoda was always more extravagant with *her girls*. For that, she made no apology.

Next, the cousins opened their boxes - new taffeta dresses for the girls with tie sashes in the back, matching wool skirts and cashmere sweaters for the *mature young ladies*, Susan and Heather, and more shirts and trousers for the boys.

Presents and more presents.

"Thank you, Papa!" and "Thank you, Grandma!"

Rhoda beamed. "We have such a nice big happy family, JAC!"

Wesley fixed himself another bourbon and water.

"I don't think he likes Mom's new coat," Joanie whispered.

"He doesn't like Grandma buying us all these expensive things. He says we don't need them," Susan said.

Was Grandma too demanding? Too commanding? Too spoiling? Her daughter's didn't think so.

"Your mother is nothing but a half-breed and so are you," Wesley yelled after they arrived back home in Willmar in record time. Did the speedometer truly reach 100 MPH?

The girls heard more arguing, then the inevitable bang of the kitchen door and their mother's tears. They heard the car screech out of the driveway. Nancy and Joanie hugged each other as they cried behind their closed bedroom door.

January, 1954

*Having a wonderful time in Scotland. Buying
Campbell plaids for everyone! Next stop London.
Wish you were here. Will be home soon!*

Love, Grandma and Papa.

All sounded well, but it was not. Their trip was cut short as JAC collapsed one day in London.

"We must move, JAC. I cannot care for you in this big house. You have had one too many strokes."

"What difference does it make where the nurse visits me?"

"Oh, JAC, don't be despondent, please. The doctor says your hardening of the arteries is just part of growing older. It doesn't have to be a death sentence."

"And can I drive? I have lost my freedom," he said.

"That's precisely why I have rented an apartment for us right downtown, at 510 Groveland. It is closer to the doctor's office and the hospital, if you need care. We can take taxis everywhere.

You can go into work when you're up to it. And we haven't lived downtown. It will be a new experience for us. There are fine restaurants, theatre, St. Mark's Cathedral across the street, the Woman's Club in the next block and parks within walking distance. Let's at least give it a try. We don't have to sell our house until we give this a chance."

May 16, 1954
St. Paul

"It's a girl!" the nurse announced to John. He was happy to have a girl. His two sons, Jack and Judd, were always bickering. Perhaps a girl would be easier.

"Let's call her Penny," Jackie and Juddy said, for once in agreement. "She'll be our lucky Penny." And the name stuck. Penny Lou Herrmann was the last of the Campbell grandchildren and the baby's baby. What a sweet addition to their big happy family.

Chapter 15

Nothing Stays the Same
1954
Summer

"Happy Birthday to You… Happy Birthday, Dear Papa, Happy Birthday to You!"

"How old is Papa?" six-year-old Robert asked.

"He is seventy-years-old. Do you want to help him blow out the candles on his cake?" Grandma offered.

"Next year, I'll have seven candles on my cake, just like you, Papa," Robert said as he blew out all seven candles. When he licked the frosting off the candles then ate the candles, too, everyone laughed, except his father.

Papa, dressed in his fine suit and tie, was sitting as usual at the head of the table at The Minnekahda Club. His family commented on how well he looked, but he didn't feel well, at all. He continually massaged a ball in his right hand and walked with a cane, but it would have been impolite to comment.

"How are you enjoying 510 Groveland?" Gordon's wife, Margaret, asked.

"I miss Minnehaha Creek, but every day my nurse rolls me over to Loring Park. I read my newspaper, feed the ducks and find I actually like taking taxis. Gordon is actually doing a good job managing our affairs."

"Why don't you tell Gordy that?" Margaret suggested, as kindly as she could. She knew how starved Gordon was for one kind word from his father. A true frugal Scot to the bone, that JAC.

"Oh, he knows."

"No, he really doesn't know, JAC. A genuine compliment from you would mean more than a bonus." JAC, of course, said nothing to Gordon, but Margaret did. Why was giving well-deserved praise so hard for JAC?

"I do miss work. I have seen more plays in the last two months than I have seen in my whole life," JAC said, changing the subject.

"Now that's an exaggeration, JAC," Rhoda replied, patting his hand. Her JAC was definitely on the mend. "When you are better, we can take another trip. In the meantime, stop flirting with that nurse!" She had a unique way of lightening the conversation and putting everyone at ease.

July 13, 1954
Willmar

"Rhoda Jane," Gordon said on the telephone, "I think you'd better bring your brood to Minneapolis – today."

"What happened, Gordon? Is it Dad?"

"Yes. He died this morning. He got out of bed, got dressed, sat down in his chair and never got up."

"Oh no!" Rhoda Jane cried.

"Oh yes," Gordon replied.

What did his father's death mean to Gordon? Freedom to run the company his way? Yes. A new burden of taking care of his mother, his sisters, his mother-in-law and his own family? Yes. The recognition that, in spite of all that rage he stored for his father, he had never loved anyone more. Aah, also very true… and very painful for him, although, he didn't discuss his feelings, even though he was aware of them. No one else discussed their feelings, either.

And did the Dickinsons bring their brood to Minneapolis?

"A funeral is no place for children," Wesley said.

"Please Dad!" Susan, Nancy and Joanie begged. "We want to go."

"Shh, girls, please. Your dad has such bad memories from his father's and grandfather's funerals, he wants to spare you such sadness," Rhoda Jane whispered to her girls. "He was only six, and he didn't understand death."

"Dad's mean," Nancy said as she slammed her bedroom door and broke into tears. She wanted to say goodbye to her Papa.

Privately, Rhoda Jane asked again, but was unable to get Wesley to reconsider his decision to leave the girls at home.

They were a big unhappy family. However, none of the other cousins, except for Patty, were allowed to attend… and that was due to Rhoda's sway with Jean. Rhoda didn't share her children's beliefs that death should be hidden away from children.

My dears, death doesn't have to be a painful experience for them. It is a natural part of life. Let them play and sing on his gravesite. Let them ask questions. Let them talk about their Papa. It will help them.

Sometimes, Rhoda didn't understand the younger, modern generation. But then, had she talked to any of her own children about death when their grandparents died? No, she hadn't. And did she ever talk about her Toronto relatives, dead or alive? That thought made her feel most uncomfortable. Best her children made their own decisions.

Rhoda's grief was real, but she held it private. She knew that with the passage of time, she would adjust, because life was kind in that way. Past pains of lost babies, lost parents, lost grandparents, yes, even those in Toronto, were born with fond remembrances instead of stabbing pain. She reflected that perhaps the older she became, the less death was an unwelcomed, fearful thing. She knew JAC wanted to live only as long as he could take care of himself and that had become more difficult. Yes, she cried and knew her life without him would be different. Would it be difficult? She told herself that she was up to the task. She intended to enjoy her final chapter.

Summer 1955

"What does it mean to *never have grass grow under your feet*, Grandma?" Nancy asked.

"Some people passively react to life events, accept things as they occur and let their destiny unfold, willy-nilly. Others, like me, plan, take charge of events and control their destiny. Thus, if you have grass growing under your feet, you may be a more relaxed spirit, but accomplish less. If you have no grass, you are a mover, a shaker and a doer! Now, let me ask you, where did you hear that expression?"

"My dad said you never let much grass grow under your feet. He was talking about your new house, so soon after Papa's death."

"Well, I think your dad is correct," Rhoda said and smiled. "I think that is the way I am, a doer. I don't want to waste any of my precious life dwelling on the past or waiting for other people. Life always moves forward. Nothing ever stays the same forever. And do you know who else is a doer?"

"My dad," Joanie replied. "He tells me to stop dreaming and use my good noggin. Be a leader, not a follower, he says."

"Exactly! Now, it's time for me to show you around my new house. I wanted a new place to showcase my new life." Then, she laughed, her most distinctive and joyful feature.

Grandma's new house was a dusty pink - all of it. Who knew there were so many soft subtleties of pink! The outside siding, the inside wall-to-wall soft, spongy carpet, the walls, the floral brocaded love seats, damask pillows, drapes, down bedspreads, bathroom tiles – all pink. It created a serene, calm environment. The only riot of color was her garden. Everything was new. She loved new. The only familiar piece of furniture was the old grandfather clock that chimed every half hour. Of course, her children were more than pleased to divide all her discarded, fine furniture.

Nancy and Joan put away their clothes in the guest bedroom. It even had its own bathroom. Then, they joined their grandma on the screened porch that overlooked her terraced, backyard garden.

"Drink your lemonade and tell me about your adventure on the Greyhound bus from Willmar to Minneapolis, girls."

"It was scary, Grandma," Joanie said.

"Scary?"

"Yes, an old man came over to us and started waving his smelly red bandana over our faces while we were napping. He kept spitting into it. We weren't really sleeping, but we kept pretending, and finally, he went away."

"How unfortunate, girls. I think your parents better fetch you – no more bus trips. I don't like the idea you were pestered by an unsavory sort."

"Oh, he wasn't any worse than the bums we pass in Bum's Alley, near the train tracks. We walk by there every time we walk to town to visit Dad's locker plant or go the movies," Nancy offered. "He didn't hurt us. He was just a bit strange, like the people in the mental hospital in Willmar."

"And how do you know about that?"

"Our friends' mother, they live across the street from us, is a nurse at the mental hospital. Genie's and Todd's father lives there, so their mother gets to take care of him."

"Really? So much for the benefits of small town life. I do wish your parents would consider moving back to Minneapolis.

You must remember you come from a good family and must only associate with others who do. But that is not important today. I am going to spoil you while you are here."

They rode the elevator to the very top of the Foshay Tower to see the breath-taking view of the City, the Mississippi locks, Pillsbury's mills at St. Anthony Falls and the tree-lined River bluffs as far away as St. Paul. They rode the escalators in Dayton's Department Store, bought new fall clothes and had clubhouse sandwiches held together with fancy toothpicks in the tearoom. "Take small, dainty bites, girls." And most afternoons, they stopped by The Minnekahda Club for a swim and fresh lemonade. Grandma hosted all the girl cousins for a fancy luncheon at The Club. A kind, black-faced man in white gloves always smiled as he opened the door for them.

"Walk as though you have a diamond on your chest girls," Grandma instructed. "Good posture is the hallmark of a well-bred, lovely lady." Patty looked like a peacock in full feathers as she exaggerated Grandma's strut behind her back, and they all giggled. After the luncheon, the girls played hearts in the card room.

"This quarter goes to the winner," Grandma said with a gleam in her eye, as she placed a quarter on the table.

When they returned home, Grandma arranged flowers in vases while Nancy and Joanie played their favorite 78 records on the phonograph. First, they listened to *Porgy and Bess*, then they listened to *South Pacific*. Soon, they were all singing along. Nancy had the prettiest voice, but Joanie could sing the loudest. Grandma's voice was wobbly, but she knew all the words by heart.

You've got to be taught to be afraid
Of people whose eyes are oddly made,
And people whose skin is a diff'rent shade,
You've got to be carefully taught.

You've got to be taught before it's too late,

"Remember the lessons in these tunes, girls. All people are worthy of respect, regardless of their color. Do you like these lyrics?"

"They're so sad," Nancy said. "I'd like *South Pacific* better if the handsome American didn't die, and he took the Island girl back home with him. I wanted them to get married."

"It's a Romeo and Juliet story, girls - a tragedy," Rhoda said. "Many love stories end like that. They just weren't meant to be."

"Why not?" Joanie asked. "They loved each other so much."

"After the last war, many soldiers brought home wives from different cultures, and the wives were not accepted by their families. These great loves created misery in the end – for them, for their children."

"But why, Grandma?"

"The sad truth is that they are too different. Catholics are better off marrying Catholics, Lutherans marrying Lutherans and white people marrying white people. We don't like people who are different from us. We belittle them. We call them names. We are afraid of any change in the social order. And it's called prejudice. One day that will change."

"Oh. I see. It's like the Swedes who don't like their children marrying a Norwegian. They are all Lutheran, but they go to different churches. I think it's silly. We had a nice Negro camp counselor this summer. He is Episcopalian, like us, but I suppose he'll have to marry a Negro lady. Do you know any colored people, Grandma?"

"No dear, I don't. Now, take these flower vases to the bathrooms, please."

"Why do we need flowers in the bathrooms, Grandma?"

"To make them worth visiting," she said and laughed. That Joanie was inquisitive. "They smell so fragrant, that's why. Go ahead, smell them."

"And these flowers we will take to my friends, the other Campbells, who have invited us for dinner tonight. We cannot go to someone's house empty-handed, now can we?" Grandma excused herself to get ready – swish, swish, swish.

"Why does Grandma make that noise when she walks?" Joanie asked.

"Patty says it's her legs rubbing together in her corset," Nancy said and laughed.

"I think it's stupid to wear corsets. Mom can hardly wait to take hers off. She says she can't breathe."

"Women are supposed to wear them, to hide their bodies, less they entice men. Grandma says nice ladies need to be modest."

"I don't know that I want to be a lady. I'd rather play football with the boys. Girls and boys are really the same."

"No, they're not. But you're just a stupid tomboy."

The visit went by too fast and so did the drive back to Willmar. Nancy, Joanie and their grandma sang all the lyrics from the musicals. *I Loves You Porgy* and *Bloody Mary is the Girl I Love* were their favorites

Summer 1955
Willmar

The telephone call came during Sunday dinner at the big, round, mahogany table. The sacred Dickinson family rule was never to take a telephone call during dinner. It was the height of rudeness - an insult to Rhoda Jane who cooked the meal, to Wesley who provided the meal, to the institution of family tradition and to the digestive process.

Wesley always stood at the head of the table to carve the chicken and fill his children's plates with servings of chicken, mashed potatoes with a well in the center so the gravy would not run all over the plate, lima beans and wiggly, black cherry Jello with Rhoda Jane's home-canned, juicy, Bing cherries. Six-year-old Robert, privileged to be included at the dinner table since he had mastered his silverware, his napkin in his lap and other fine manners, received the wings. Robert was always given the wings. Baby Mary was fed in the kitchen before dinner. The children were expected to say *thank you* when they were handed their plates and to eat everything on their plates. Oh no, Joanie thought. She hated lima beans. They made her gag.

When the phone kept ringing, and her father excused himself to the kitchen and angrily answered it, she had her big chance to stash her slimy lima beans into her napkin. *Whew!* She so wanted the apple pie for dessert, but desert was only reserved for those who cleaned their plates.

"No! Oh no!" Wes shouted.

Rhoda Jane, concerned with his unusual outburst, excused herself from the table. The children sat still, trying to catch snippets of their parents' conversation behind the closed kitchen door.

Black duck disease? They were puzzled by the phrase, but their Dad's fearful tone of voice was new to them. Their Dad got angry, but never afraid. Now, they were afraid. Then, they heard the outside door slam with a bang and the car screech out of the driveway. Their mother, as white as a sheet, reappeared in the dining room.

"Finish your dinners, please" is all she said.

And they did, quickly and in silence.

"Children, I want to tell you what happened. All the turkeys are dead or dying. They have caught a dreaded disease, called *black duck disease*. Your father has gone to the barn."

"Not our turkeys! We just helped Dad debeak them last weekend. They all looked so plump and healthy!" Nancy cried.

What a nasty, dirty process that debeaking had been. Susan luckily had a better job, a paying job, corn detasseling. That left Nancy and Joan to catch the turkeys and hand them to their father, who sat at a machine and lowered a hot iron on the end of the top beak. Sizzle and plop - off it fell.

"It's just like trimming your toe nails," their Dad said, assuring the girls that the turkeys weren't hurt. "I do my best not to cut the beaks too short, but if we don't clip them, they will peck each other to death."

"What a stupid thing to do," Nancy said.

"Turkeys are good to eat, but they're not the smartest birds. They need proper temperature, food, water and to be calmed during thunderstorms or they panic, stampede and smother each other to death. It looks like we should have a bumper crop this year."

Their dad never mentioned *black duck disease*. And now, they were dead. All dead! That was the last the children heard about it.

Thanksgiving 1955

"Beep! Beep!"

"Look! Look!" Susan shouted, eyes glued to the dining room picture window. "Here come Gordon and Grandma in a new station wagon. It's really sharp, two-toned – black and white!"

Everyone ran outside to greet them. They had expected the Campbells for Thanksgiving.

"Surprise!" Grandma said as she came up the walk. "And an early Merry Christmas to you Dickinsons!"

"Oh, Mother, is this car for us?" Rhoda Jane asked.

"Yes, dear. You needed a new one. That old Pontiac is a road hazard."

"That old Pontiac is fine," Wes countered.

"If it is so wonderful, why did Rhoda Jane almost kill your whole family when the brakes went out in Delano?" Rhoda challenged.

"Enough sparing, you two." Rhoda Jane laughed, hugging them all. "Thank you, Mother. Thank you, Gordon."

Margaret and their cousins, Heather, Jimmy and Scottie piled out of their car, not far behind the shiny new station wagon. Wes and Gordon shook hands, and Gordon handed him the keys.

"Thanks!" Wes couldn't believe Rhoda's generosity. He smiled and rubbed the top of his bald head.

"Let's take it for a spin. Everybody pile in," their dad said. It was a three-seater, 1956 Ford Station Wagon, plenty of room for a family of seven.

"Look at these red vinyl seats. Cool," Susan said. "Another year and I can drive it!"

Later, after the children were in bed, Wes and Gordon had a serious talk. The children knew the talk was serious, hush-hush. Nonetheless, the next day they had a happy Thanksgiving. The day after that came the announcement that they were moving to Minneapolis, but no one explained why. Children had no business in their parents' concerns.

"You'll like being closer to your cousins," Grandma chirped.

Why? Their home was Willmar.

January 1956
Bloomington

"I'm lost!" Joanie cried at the end of her first day in her new school in Bloomington. She hated admitting defeat, but she had to stop at a strange house and ask to use a phone. Luckily, the woman was kind and did not pry. How embarrassing! Lost! I'm in sixth grade, and I'm lost!

"What happened, Joanie?" her mother asked as she climbed in the front seat of the station wagon.

"This was the worst day of my life, Mom." And with that, the floodgate opened, and she cried like a baby, a big cry baby!

"Tell me all about it," her mother encouraged.

"First, I had to sit in the office until someone could take me to my new classroom. Then, my new teacher asked me to wait until she finished her lesson. I had to stand at the front of the class with my coat on while everyone stared at me. Finally, she asked me to join a reading group. Mom, it was a slow reading group. She put me in with the dunces! Then, I didn't know how to get my lunch in the cafeteria. I was a total dunce."

"I'll have to talk with your teacher about your academic level. Don't feel bad, Joanie. Lafayette in Willmar was a small school, and you always walked home for lunch."

"But that's not all. My teacher said I was to ride the number one bus to get home. There must have been twenty-five school buses, all lined up. I looked and looked, but I didn't see any numbers, so I finally got on the first bus. I got off at the last stop, but, of course, it wasn't anywhere near our house." And she broke into uncontrollable sobs. "Why did we have to move, Mom? I was Captain of the School Patrol. I was the best student in the whole sixth grade. We were all happy. I loved our house. I loved my friends. We could walk to the movies. I miss our dog, Fluffy! Why did Dad give her away? Everything is all messed up. Nancy and Susan are still in Willmar until the new school term. I miss them. I hate it here!"

"Didn't you meet any new friends?"

"Yes, two girls were really nice to me. Cheryl is a twin, but her sister Carol is in another sixth-grade class. There are four classes. And the other girl is Diane."

After the children were sleeping, and she could hear Wesley snoring, Rhoda Jane got out of bed. She sat smoking in the dark at their small kitchen table. The grand mahogany table, matching buffet and other furniture were crammed in the basement of their Marv Anderson tract home on a treeless lot, unless you called the sticks with three leaves, trees. Yes, it had four bedrooms and a bath and a half, but it was small.

I should be grateful for this house that the Satterlee Company, really Gordon, bought for us, but what has happened to my life?

She rested her head on her arms and wept. Hers was a rhetorical question. Rhoda Jane knew what happened. The black duck disease killed their turkey business. Wesley could not find a job with a livable wage in Willmar. His friend wanted him to join him in his new turkey business, Jennie-O Turkeys, but Wes had a family of seven to provide for. No more risk-taking. They had gone from being wealthy pillars of the community to being broke in a few short years. She knew, more than anything else, that Wesley hated that her family was helping. Wes was supposed to be the provider. Inside, did he feel like a failure? He was outwardly grateful, but inside he seethed with anger. Gordon had offered him a job, but he was too proud to take it. Instead, he took a job selling clothes in a *tall man* shop – temporarily. Wes always had a gift for sales, and, to Rhoda Jane's surprise, he actually liked it, or so he said.

Sometimes, she still loved him, but only sometimes. He was emptying those Four Roses whiskey bottles faster than ever, but it was a good sign that he could still laugh and tell those silly *tall men* stories to his children.

Myrtle, his sixty-nine-year-old mother, had been diagnosed with uterine cancer, but he didn't speak of it much. She had to resign her thirty-five-year position as Executive Secretary of the Minneapolis Humane Society. The last Christmas with her was a sad one, but they decided not to tell the children, who, instead, thought it was because they had to move. It was only a matter of time until the uterine cancer claimed her. The good thing is that Odey had been extremely attentive to Myrtle and the children. He had made their Christmas a festive occasion. Children are resilient, Rhoda Jane reflected, with a heavy sigh.

I'll tell them about Myrtle when Nancy and Susan start their second term here. The high school and junior high are on split shifts. What a mess. Susan will be starting school at 7:00 and Nancy at noon. I think tomorrow I will tell Wesley I am going to sew designer baby clothes for our new neighbor, Diane Ford. Lord and Taylor want her new line. Poor Diane's rheumatoid arthritis has crippled her hands. I can't see how she can even make the patterns. I am going to save the money I make for a family vacation. We need one. Maybe it's a blessing Nancy and Susan have split shifts - they can help take care of Robert and

Mary while I sew. What a day Joanie had at her new school, a real fish out of water. I hope Susan and Nancy are being helpful at the Luthers. I do miss our old Willmar friends. Yes, children are resilient, now can I be?

She cried, blew her nose and went to bed. There was no denying the truth, they were not a big happy family. If only she could turn back the clock, but she also knew nothing would ever be the same.

February, 1956

Myrtle Adsit Dickinson died. All the Campbells attended the funeral at St. Luke's Parish, except for Aunt Jean who took care of Robert, Mary and Jay during the service. The next day, only the adults attended the burial at Lakeside Cemetery in Hastings, MN. Myrtle was laid to rest next to her twin, Wesley, who died when he was a mere three-weeks-old and her parents, Susan Francis Maneely Adsit and Dr. Alfred Merrill Adsit, the physician for the Minnesota Insane Asylum. Why wasn't she buried next to her husband Robert at Lakewood Cemetery in Minneapolis? The wealthy Dickinson's had made no provision for Myrtle.

Perhaps young Wesley had sensed at his father's funeral he was being discarded along with his mother. Did he promise himself on that day to never take help from anyone, ever in his life? His grandfather, with whom he lived in Hastings, died a short time later. Yet, here he was, a charity case taking help from the Campbells.

What was the children's reaction? Susan and Nancy were so disappointed they could not go to the burial, but at least they were allowed to attend her church service. Each of their grandmother's was special, but oh how the girls loved the undivided attention of their Grandma Dickinson when they'd visit without their parents. She would play her baby grand piano while she listened most carefully to their clear, young singing voices, take them to work at the Humane Society where they'd play with all the animals in the pound, and of course to the Minneapolis Athletic Club for dinners with Odey. Yes, they were front and center special in her eyes. And, in truth, they liked not having to share her with any cousins.

When Joanie heard the 23rd Psalm, *Yea, though I walk through the valley of the shadow of death*...and saw the casket rolling down the church aisle, she lurched for the bathroom, locked the door and let no one in while she cried and cried. Was her grandma really inside that box?

Chapter 16

Gracious Living
1957
Edina

Dear Ones,
Having a wonderful time in Hawaii! Luau last
night, pineapple plantation tour this morning,
golfing this afternoon and whale watching
tomorrow! Wish you were here! See you soon!

Love, Grandma

"Aloha!"

Rhoda greeted each family member with a lei and a pineapple cocktail, complete with a little colored paper parasol, as they arrived at her Hawaiian-themed dinner party. She wore a soft pink, flowing muumuu with dark pink hibiscus trim and a matching pink hibiscus flower behind one ear. Hawaiian music played softly in the background.

"If you think I look ridiculous, wait until you all change your clothes. I have outfits for everyone," Rhoda said with her infectious laugh.

She had been preparing all day. Soon, Rhoda Jane, Margaret, Pat and Jean were decked out in identically styled, spaghetti strap dresses, each of a different color with matching hibiscus flowers for their hair. The granddaughters sported grass skirts and modest tops.

No, Rhoda had informed the sales clerk, *those coconut cups are just too risqué for my girls.*

For the boys and men, she had aloha shirts, multi-colored with a variety of flowers, pineapples, parrots and palm trees. She had considered having the couple's outfits match, but decided that was just too cutesy, even for her. And to everyone's relief, she did not push the hula dance lessons.

"Pictures, everybody!"

Rhoda served another cocktail while the cameras flashed picture after picture. This time, the men opted for a standard scotch or bourbon – no more sweet, syrupy drinks, please. Following her Hawaiian theme dinner of pork roast, baked apples, sweet potatoes and pineapple upside down cake, Wesley strummed his ukulele and Gardner his guitar. As parting party favors, Grandma passed out carved coconuts with painted faces and shell earrings for her thrilled grandchildren, thirteen in all. The men, in spite of having no choice in participation, bid adieu with broad smiling faces that belied their complaints about enduring yet another of Rhoda's theme parties. They were actually looking forward to what she would dream up following her trip to Italy. The wine would definitely be more to their taste than the pineapple drinks.

In the meantime, Rhoda held Saturday luncheons for her girls and granddaughters at The Minnekahda Club and attended educational lectures at The Woman's Club. She definitely was enjoying her life as a widow.

"I'm only taking flying lessons, Gordy, so I can be your trusty co-pilot," Margaret said. "If we're going to be flying all over the country, I want us to be safe. You're such a thrill seeker."

"The instructor says you have great ability," Gordon said, extremely proud of his courageous wife. "Are you sure you don't want to get your instrument rating?"

"I'll think about it. I see flying as a means to an end, but you're the boss. I have no need to be an Amelia Earhart. You can commute to Minneapolis, and we can enjoy our yacht in Sarasota. Now that boat I love. Let's invite all your sisters to Florida this winter, Gordy."

"Maybe we need a bigger boat, so they can all come at the same time," he said and laughed.

"Absolutely not. I will not be a slave to any boat," she said and laughed back. "But we do need a calendar, or we'll get everyone's visit confused."

Gordon enjoyed sharing his wealth with his friends and family. Of course, everyone accepted their invitations.

"Can we come during Sarasota's polo season?" Jean asked. "Gardner would love to see a few matches and perhaps even play in one."

"John and I'll drive up from Naples, anytime. I can arrange my tennis dates and our guests around your schedule," Pat said. "And maybe John can commute with you in your plane. He does have to run his business in St. Paul."

"How nice of you to invite us," Rhoda Jane said. "Wesley's new venture seems to be going well, but I'd better check with him."

Wesley had invested his inheritance from his mother in a wholesale building supply company. So far, so good. Hopefully, the housing boom would not disappear, like the need for frozen food lockers did after the war.

The Herrmanns

"Our boys need to be separated, John. They fight all the time, and you need to stop picking at them," Pat said, disgusted.

"I suggest the St. Paul Military Academy. Jack needs physical discipline and Judd mental discipline. Rules and order would develop their characters. Now, characters are all they are," John said.

"That kind of discipline will not work for Judd. Perhaps Breck, the Episcopalian Prep school, can entice him to use his fine mind."

"It's in Minneapolis!" John teased.

"The wrong side of the River?" Pat asked and laughed. "I find this continual ill will between Minneapolis and St. Paul to be so silly."

"Just so we don't live there," John replied.

The Dickinsons

"Great news from the doctor today, Wesley," Rhoda Jane said, much relieved. "Robert can resume his physical activity. Apparently, our keeping him quiet and confined helped. The doctor said the rheumatic or scarlet fever didn't injure his heart. Buying him that piano was the best therapy for him."

"What a surprise to discover he has a musical gift. We shouldn't have wasted our money on all those years of piano lessons for the girls," Wes said. "I can hardly wait to tell him he can sign up for bantam hockey."

"Is that for Robert or for you?" She teased.

"Robert, of course, Rhoda Jane. He loves hockey. It seems like all of our kids are doing well now, unless this is just the calm before another storm."

"Let's hope so. Thank God Joanie was put in that special class for gifted kids," Rhoda Jane said.

"Yes, she had too many low life losers for friends," Wesley agreed.

"Writing plays with her new friends is much better than hanging out at the mall, that terrible roller rink or bowling alley. She certainly has a mind of her own – full speed ahead. I'm glad we were able to redirect her energy away from those cigarette smoking boys with the greasy ducktails."

"I'll be happy when she outgrows her dance, acrobat and baton lessons. I'm too old to be sitting on street curbs watching those parades," Wes said and laughed. "This current walking group with parasols is the worst."

"Oh, you get a kick out of them. This winter, you'll be sitting on cold bleachers watching hockey," Rhoda retorted.

"I worried about Nancy, but her confidence has improved now that she's in high school. She enjoys her choir and intermural sports. I'm going to take her golfing next weekend. Who knows, perhaps that will strike her fancy. She is coordinated and likes sports."

"She must get her coordination from you." Rhoda Jane smiled. "I also think we should start looking at colleges for Susan."

"She can go to the University."

"Well, she wants to get away from home, study out of state – home economics."

"The AG campus is in St. Paul. That's almost out of state, on the wrong side of the river and certainly away from home. Who knows, she might end up back in Willmar with a farmer, sewing clothes and debeaking turkeys," Wes said, with a twinkle in his eye.

He delighted in his own clever humor, sometimes at others' expense, and only, sometimes, appreciated by others. It seemed that sarcastic mocking and knocking was the humor of many men his age - like Gordon, John and Gardner. The light, cleverness sometimes bordered on mean, sadistic teasing. And if they'd been drinking, it could be most cruel. If someone took offense, they'd just come back with, *Oh, can't you take a joke?* And thus their children, hurt and diminished when they were small, chose, when older, to be angry, tough, distant and sometimes cowed by their fathers' humorous barbs. If they challenged their authority or retaliated, they discovered their fathers could dish it out, but couldn't take it in return. They were the kings of their families and always right. And their wives excused them:

He didn't mean it. Or: *Just ignore it.* Or: *He had a bad day at work.* Or: *It's the grown-up cocktail hour - please go to your room or outside.* Or: *Please don't read the newspaper before your dad has seen it. You'll make him angry.*

The men all worked hard, so, of course, no one considered them alcoholics.

The Johnsons

"Jean, Patty is miserable living with you and Gardner. I just can't stand to see her so unhappy," Rhoda said. "If you'll agree, I will pay for her to go to a girls' boarding school. I've checked with some of my friends - they say we should consider the Episcopal school for girls, St. Katharine's Hall in Davenport, Iowa."

"That seems too far away, but yes, I'm open to anything. I'm tired of being the referee between Patty and Gardner. He actually yells at her, argues with a child. If you ask me, he's the child. And it certainly isn't fair to Jay to live with such dissention. He's four, not a baby anymore."

"Jean, I know it's none of my business, but you seem very unhappy. I worry about you. Gardner is drinking to excess. Are you certain you want to stay married?"

"Oh, Mother, everybody drinks too much, me included. And no one's marriage is fantastic. I certainly have not been talented at choosing good husbands, but I do not want to be divorced and single again with another young child. Jay needs his father. Perhaps with Patty away, everyone will be happier, Patty included."

The Campbells

"What were you thinking, Heather? Are you stupid?" Gordon asked, disgusted with his oldest. "You almost killed yourself!" And she almost did. Heather was teaching diving lessons at the Edina pool and hit her head on the concrete bottom.

"Gordon, can't you express less anger and more concern? It certainly wasn't intentional," Margaret said, defending her daughter. But it was too late for a little empathy. Heather dissolved in tears and ran to her room.

"She is too sensitive," Gordon remarked.

"Perhaps, but you are too critical. Heather is so conscientious. She tries so hard to excel at everything. How about a compliment once in awhile? Gordy, sometimes I believe you have become your very father," Margaret scolded. "Perhaps it's a good thing she is going away to Boulder for college."

"She could have gone to the University, if she wanted a big school. It has better credentials than The University of Colorado."

"Heather will be a fine student wherever she goes, Gordon. What she needs is more fun, laughter. I want her to go through sorority rush, live on campus, ski, make good friends, relax. She is too serious, takes everything literally. She tries too hard to please. All of our kids do. They need more smiles from you."

"At least Jim is a good worker, but he needs more exercise, a sporting interest perhaps. He's too fat."

"Stop it, Gordy, this minute. Jim is content working at the pet store and saving his money. Let him be, Gordon. And Scottie, too. Stop picking at them."

"I think Scott might be a good skier."

"Let's just enjoy our family. Soon, they'll be gone. You need to stop teasing them." Margaret was exasperated with her husband.

Vacations with Grandma

"Patty and Susan, it is time to dress for dinner," Grandma said. "You've had way too much sun. You both look like lobsters. I know you won't listen to me, but you will not like how your skin looks at my age, unless you start protecting it."

Were they having a good time? How could they not? Their grandmother had treated them to spring break in Bermuda. They didn't know what they enjoyed the most – the cruise or the beach.

1959
Delray Beach

"Nancy and Patty, it is time to dress for dinner," Grandma said. "We have to be back early because I am playing bridge tonight."

Were they having a good time? Of course, their grandmother was spending the winter in Del Ray Beach, Florida. Patty and Nancy had flown in an airplane, a first for both of them. Poor Joanie, her nose was out of joint. She was considered too young. Drat!

Minneapolis
The Hanscomes

"Please bring Aunt Mur a fresh glass of water," Rhoda Jane

yelled from the top of the stairs.

Joanie searched the cupboards but found every glass and dish in the cupboard grimy. She cleaned a glass, filled it with water and brought it up stairs. Rhoda Jane had promised to look in on Aunt Mur as Grandma was on another trip. Aunt Mur stopped working due to her bad eyes a few years ago. She could no longer type. Today, they found her resting upstairs in her bed, midday, and still in her nightgown. Rhoda Jane helped her get cleaned, dressed and sat her in a chair, near the light. She wondered how long she'd been lying in bed and sighed. This was not a good situation.

"Thank you, Rhoda Jane," Aunt Mur said as she headed for the stairs.

"I'm concerned about you walking downstairs. Can you see well enough to do that?" Rhoda Jane asked.

"Of course I can. I can still make out shapes. But would you please do me a favor and read Rhoda's letter to me?"

"What's wrong with Aunt Mur?" a bewildered Joanie asked after they left.

"She's blind, Joanie. I will have to tell your grandma she can no longer take care of herself. Aunt Mur can't live alone anymore. Her house is dirty, and this neighborhood has really gone to seed. Our next stop is Burnsville to visit Uncle Will. I hope he and Aunt Ethel are doing better than Aunt Mur. Thank you for going with me. This is hard for you to see, I'm sure. And, I must add, also me. I had no idea she was so blind. Only my mother seems to thrive as she grows older. Uncle Will has a mink farm, Joanie, like he had when he was younger. Let's hope they are taking care of themselves."

Burnsville

As they drove, Rhoda Jane wondered how her mother could gaily traipse around the world and leave Aunt Mur? Wasn't she her sister's keeper? But rather than be critical of her mother, she decided she would visit her aunt more often.

"Here, Joanie, you can feed the mink, if you'd like," Uncle Will said, handing her a food pellet.

"They look like big rats, Uncle Will. Are you sure they won't bite?"

"I can't promise, but I've never been bitten. Just lightly stroke their fur," Uncle Will kindly said.

"Soft! Their fur is so soft. And it tickles when they eat from my hand."

Joanie tried not to think of how many minks it took to make one of Grandma's coats. When they went inside to have cookies and lemonade, Joanie checked the glasses. They were clean. What a relief.

The Dickinsons

"Scratch, scratch," Joanie heard the familiar noise at her bedroom window. It was the middle of the night.

"Let me in," Susan whispered. Joanie struggled to get the bent screen off. Susan climbed in through the window, prom dress and all.

"You woke me up, Susan, again," Joanie said, disgusted. "It must be 3:00 in the morning. Nancy got in hours ago. Everyone is sleeping, like I was. And you smell like booze!"

"Shh. I don't want Dad to know the time, so I didn't ring the doorbell."

"I'll be happy when you go to college next year, so I get this room to myself, with a new screen that doesn't let in the mosquitoes."

"I think you'll have to share a room with Mary. Nancy is the next oldest and wants a room to herself."

"Joanie, how'd you like to take a trip with me?"

"Oh yes, Grandma. Where are we going?" Finally, her grandma was taking her somewhere.

"We're driving to Patty's high school graduation in Davenport. Won't that be fun?"

"Just me?" Joanie tried to hide her disappointment – no plane, no cruise, no beach. Iowa was definitely not an exotic vacation spot.

"Jean is coming, of course. Nancy has her high school *Mikado* performance the same weekend, so she can't make it. I hope I'll be able to catch her operatic debut before we leave. St. Katharine's has a lovely two-day ceremony. First, they coronate the Queen of the May, and the next day is graduation."

The pageantry was lovely, certainly unlike Susan's Bloomington High School graduation ceremony held in the football stadium. The magnificent old brick mansion sat on a hill overlooking the Mississippi River. The girls wore filmy, ethereal white dresses and flower tiaras with flowing ribbons in their hair, like princesses in a fairytale. When Patty's name was called, she presented herself like a debutante with a hint of a smile, gracefully floated through the flowering arbor and curtsied, accompanied by polite applause. She had been symbolically inducted into womanhood.

Later that evening, they took Patty's boyfriend to dinner. What did Grandma think of him?

"Jean, this just won't do. This boyfriend can't speak proper English and aspires to be a truck driver," Grandma said, horrified. "Where did Patty meet him? Does he come from a good home, Jean? I thought this school supervised the girls better."

"She'll be coming home with us, don't worry Mother." Jean laughed. "She plans to enroll at The 'U' this fall."

"You promised," Pat said. "I just love the River Road. It's nature at its best – the trees, the bluff. We can watch the change of the seasons from every window."

"Yes, I did promise," John said, good-naturedly. "It is now my turn to live on the wrong side of the River. You know what people say about living in glass houses, don't you?"

"Don't be silly, John. Just so you're not the one throwing stones at it. I think you protest too much. You'll love it. You can see your beloved St. Paul right across the bluff. It's close to your work, a quick drive across the Marshall Bridge, and just a few blocks walk for Judd to Breck. And with Jack driving, you won't have to drop him at the St. Paul Academy. I think I'll enroll Penny in the Minnehaha Academy for girls, also nearby. And the house is modern. There's a separate wing for the kids, and the upper level will be our own private suite. And, we each get our own special rooms!" The usually dry-witted, calm Pat was ecstatic.

"Slow down, Pat. I like it, too. And where is my special room?"

"It's your very own bathroom. You can be as messy as you want."

"And your special room?" he asked.

"I'm going to make the vaulted ceiling room that overlooks the Mississippi into my music conservatory and art gallery. All I need is another grand piano, so I can practice my duets with my friends. I'll find a used one at an estate sale. They're like white elephants, these days."

"I think I need another special room, then, for equality's sake."

"You can have the living room, one level down. It's near the refrigerator in the kitchen, you'll like that." Pat laughed. "And the kids have their own wing and a *rec* room on the lowest level that looks too indestructible for them to wreck.”

“So, we will all be separate, but not quite equal.” John laughed.

“You said you wanted more privacy. Now everyone has some.”

The Dickinson's turn of the century home

“You’re laughing, Mother. Don’t you like this house?” Rhoda Jane asked.

“Of course, I love this Minnesota River valley. It’s on Auto Club Road, not even a mile from my old house on Ferry Hill. But it’s a white elephant, Rhoda Jane - just like the old Automobile Club that the Audubon Society is using for bird-watching. Everyone wants modern these days, all glass and modern, like Pat. This is the old Chamberlain summer home, isn’t it? When was this place built?”

“1907. That’s why we can afford it. No one else wants it. It just takes my breath away, Mother. Ten acres on the bluff overlooking the Minnesota River. It has four bedrooms upstairs, three baths and a sleeping porch. And downstairs, it has three fireplaces - in the library, living room and dining room. It has two more bedrooms, for the help I would imagine, and two more baths. I am so excited to be resurrecting our old furniture from the basement of that cracker box. Do you see those intercoms behind the doors? If you blow in them, a corresponding bell rings in the kitchen to summons the servants. And the French doors all open onto this spacious screened porch and the gardens. We will probably live out here in the summer time. And the gardens! I love all the gardens! Then there’s the carriage house we can rent, if we want that hassle, attached to the two-car garage. It’s so charming with the tower.” Rhoda Jane was breathless with excitement.

"No doubt that garage was once used for horses and now houses bats. Rhoda Jane, I hear your enthusiasm, but look at this kitchen. The linoleum is old and coming up in spots, and the farmer's kitchen sink is so shallow. And that huge octagonal shower upstairs is antiquated. Do you plan to take family showers? I hope you have had a plumber check all the pipes - they might freeze in the wintertime. Do you really want this place? I fear you will become a slave to it. I do hope Wesley has agreed to a cleaning lady and renovations. You have no servants to answer those bells in the kitchen. It's a wreck, Rhoda Jane."

"Wesley loves it too, Mother. Where you see old, we see lovely. You should have seen him smile when he discovered the old balls in the carriage house tower for bowling on the green. Did you see that level field surrounded by the ornate concrete benches? It's charming! Wes can use it for a putting green, and we can hold our family softball games there on Sunday. But he does worry about the heating expense. He told me it was my money, and if I want it, we can buy it. He agrees to a cleaning lady, but no renovations, at least not now. Mother, I can look out at the view while I cook. I simply won't look down at the old floor."

"And a yard man?"

"No. Wesley says he and Robert can mow the grass. He already has a daily rotation planned out."

"Well, I'll love to visit you here. It will bring back memories of Ferry Hill. I can help you with the gardening."

Rhoda came every Sunday and sewed buttons and hemmed skirts while the girls helped make dinner. She believed in being useful, but she was now in her seventies and did not move as fast as she used to. She watched Rhoda Jane garden, the whole family play baseball and usually cornered one grandchild for a fourth for bridge. Wesley held firm to the family rule that Sunday was to be spent at home, with family. Of course, friends were welcome, but not vice versa.

Rhoda Jane humored Wes by allowing him to select an English hunt mural wallpaper for the grand front foyer. He did picture himself as a country squire and master of the hunt. It was gracious living, indeed.

The Campbells country-living estate

"Can we have horses, Gordon?" Margaret asked.

"Yes, we have five acres right on the Minnesota River bluff, not far from the Dickinsons. We can have a barn, tennis courts. What else do you want?"

"I want all the living areas and our master bedroom suite to open onto the swimming pool. What a view. What privacy! With Heather in Colorado and Jim at Carleton College, we don't have to worry about them. They can have bedrooms downstairs. But I worry about Scott."

"Why worry? He can finish out the school year at Edina while we build it and go to Eden Prairie High School next year. He'll have his driver's license by then."

"Eden Prairie? They have that one-room schoolhouse," Margaret said.

"That's not true. It has more than one room. This whole area will be a suburb one day, just like Bloomington is now."

"I don't think he'll like it. He has little in common with farm kids. It's too bad we couldn't find any River bluff property in Bloomington, closer to Rhoda Jane and Wesley. Their schools are great, like Edina's."

"Maybe we should send him to a private school, Margaret."

"Send him *down the River* to your old alma mater, Shattuck? I think there's a better solution, Gordy. Let's see if Bloomington or Edina would let us pay tuition."

"I'm glad you finally asked me where I want to go to school. I want to stay with my friends in Edina," Scottie said. And he did.

Was Scottie lonely? Hardly. His friends loved to ride their horses, play tennis, swim and marvel at the live animals his parents brought home from their African safaris.

"Joanie, that lion won't hurt you," Scottie said and laughed at a holiday gathering. The lion was kept in the billiard room, and when they were playing pool, it kept circling the table. "It's just a cub."

"You win the game. I'm leaving," Joanie said. "That lion is no longer a cub. That animal wants to eat me!" And she left only to see a monkey sitting on Aunt Margaret's shoulder. A monkey! Soon the lion went to the zoo, but the dirty monkey stayed.

And Jean? She didn't want a new house. She loved her tutor home in St. Louis Park, right on the border of Minneapolis. What she didn't love was her marriage. Now, she had enough of her own money to leave Gardner.

How, pray tell, did they afford all these new homes? Campbell Properties, the family holding company that JAC established prior to his death, was thriving, thanks to Gordon. He was the Executive, and Rhoda and his sisters were all on the Board of Directors. They decided to declare a healthy dividend. Why not? They wanted to feather their nests before the children flew the coop.

"Money won't bring happiness," Rhoda said to her children.

"No, but it certainly makes life easier," Gordon replied with a smile. "After all, you taught us the importance of gracious living, Mother."

Chapter 17

Two Down and One Remains
1961
Minneapolis

Not all was levity and gracious living. The old guard was changing; half a century had passed. The Hanscomes and Campbells needed to recalibrate. First JAC died. Who would be next?

"Oh no!" Rhoda cried. "Not my dear sister, my dear Mur!"

Aunt Muriel had declined living with her sister, in favor of a nursing home. December 10, 1961, she just failed to open her eyes. She was seventy-seven. Two days later, she was buried at Lakewood Cemetery next to her parents, Rhoda Baldwin Cooper Hanscome and William Kissick Hanscome.

Most of the nephews and all of the nieces came. Uncle Will and Aunt Ethel, and their children William Dixon Hanscome and Barbara Jane Munger came, but their other two sons, Thomas Dixon Hanscome and John Baldwin Hanscome had moved to California. It gave the Hanscome cousins a chance to catch up.

"How is your Dad doing, Barb?" Rhoda Jane asked. "He seems quite the gentle person, not how I remembered him as a child."

"You mean his fierce temper?" she asked and smiled. "His stroke in 1953 made him positively sweet. He used to scare us and his grandchildren with his tirades. He was part of that *children should be seen and not heard* generation. Perhaps your dad's death had a positive impact on him. All I know is we didn't expect him to outlive Aunt Mur. And here he is - Mr. Patience! If you ask him, he'll say his father bequeathed him his fiery temper."

"I don't remember Grandpa Hanscome as having a temper, but father's can be very hard on their sons. Mother says Uncle Will became bitter after his hardware store partner ran off with the money. Nonetheless, I have good memories of their place on Lake Minnetonka. I remember when he saved Tommy's son's life when he fell off the dock. Little Tommy must have been five or so. The same thing happened to our daughter, Nancy. She would have drowned, if our friend in Willmar hadn't pulled her from the drink by her hair."

"And I remember your family's Bone Lake bonfires, the weenie and marshmallow roasts. Those sleeping swings were the best. We are getting older, too, Rhoda Jane."

"It is too bad we don't see each other much anymore, Barb. Tell me more about your California brothers."

"Well, Tommy and Jack are both in California. Jack's is a funny story. He and Marge went out to the Rose Bowl Tournament. Jack was doing sports reporting then. They loved the paradise of California so much that they never came back. He's still in the newspaper business in Long Beach, not too far from Tommy."

"I wonder why Wesley hated California so. He thinks there's no place like Minnesota. And Tommy? How is he doing?"

"Tommy, our nuclear physicist, is still mitigating the effects of radiation from those nasty bombs, the atomic bombs he helped make. It has been his whole career. The Navy snapped him up from teaching at 'U of M.' After his Pacific tour of duty, he worked in Washington DC in the Defense Department. Do you know that in 1953 he and JoAnn drove from Washington DC to Toronto to visit Dad's Aunt Naomi?"

"Oh, I didn't think there were any relatives left in Toronto," Rhoda Jane said, puzzled. "Who is Naomi?"

"She's our great aunt, the last of all the sisters. She just died last year."

"All the sisters? My mother never mentioned any of them. What was Aunt Naomi like?"

"She was in a nursing home, dark complected like my dad with pure white hair and quite well-spoken. She never married. Tommy was so glad he went, and their kids were fascinated to visit that *foreign* country of Canada. Dad used to talk about all his Toronto aunts and uncles a lot. He was truly enamored with his grandfather from Charleston. Dad has the portraits of Thomas and his wife Mary Sophia from Charleston. Didn't you see them?"

"Oh. How could I have not known about them? Are you certain? No one from our family ever came from Charleston. This is so strange, Barb. I never heard Grandfather or Aunt Mur speak of them. Grandpa had a living family! And Aunt Mur said her grandfather came from Scotland. I don't believe I've ever seen the portraits. Did Aunt Naomi say anything about our Indian ancestry?"

"No. The portraits are in Dad's basement, getting moldy. He burned the old lovely frames in the stove, can you believe that? They were gilded with gold. But Rhoda Jane, where did you get an Indian connection? That's a new one on me."

"From my mother," Rhoda Jane answered, now very perplexed. "Where else did his dark complexion come from?"

"Intrigue and Hanscome skeletons!" Barb laughed. "I don't really know."

"Mother, may I speak to you?" Rhoda Jane asked later. "Why did you never tell us about Grandpa's brothers and sisters in Toronto? Barb said Tommy and his wife JoAnn made a special trip to visit an Aunt Naomi. She said they came from Charleston, not Scotland. How could Aunt Mur have said her grandmother was from Argentina?"

"Oh, Rhoda Jane, we began anew when my parents left Toronto. I knew them when I was younger, charming people, really. It just didn't seem important. The past is the past."

"But, Mother, we could have visited them! And Uncle Will never told Barb and her brothers about Indian blood."

"After your Uncle Will's stroke, he never had a good memory. Now, this is Aunt Mur's funeral, and I hate to see you so upset. We can talk later, if you'd like."

But they didn't. Rhoda Jane knew her mother well and knew the conversation was closed. Also, she was fearful of opening Pandora's box. She was afraid some things simply didn't add up.

When Rhoda found her brother Will, he was despondent.

"One down and two remain. First Mur, next it will be me," Will said.

"Or me," Rhoda said, giving him a hug. "We are getting older, too. Mur didn't enjoy the last few years of her life, being blind. I believe she was content to die. But don't think the Grim Reaper will be coming so soon for you, Will. There is life left to live. We need to be thankful for our health and our vision. It makes me want to travel more, see everything there is to see in this world. I don't want to have any regrets when I die."

"I do have one regret, Rhoda," Will said.

"And what is that?"

"I regret that I never went back to Toronto after our father died. Our last aunt, Aunt Naomi, died alone in a nursing home just last year. She was ninety-six. Of course, my children only have a smattering of our full family history. Did you ever tell yours? This secret is our shame, Rhoda."

"Well, you can do nothing about that at this late date," Rhoda replied briskly. "Regrets are a waste of time, Will." And with that, Rhoda curtly walked away.

The family gossip turned to Jean's solo appearance at the wake. Where was Gardner? Jean had filed for a divorce.

And where were the Campbell grandchildren? Heather was in Boulder, at the University of Colorado. Susan was in Fargo, attending North Dakota State University. Patty and Nancy were at The 'U'. Jimmy was at Carleton College. Why couldn't the younger children come? They were all busy, yes, but the truth was their parents didn't think it was necessary.

"Children, let's go back to my house. I've prepared a simple luncheon, if you have time," Rhoda invited. "I so want to get caught up on your lives, Barbara and Billy. And perhaps you can fill us in on your two California brothers."

The conversation was light and cheery as the adult cousins reminisced about Aunt Mur and their fun childhood family gatherings. Before they left, they promised to stay in better touch, but their families consumed their time - what with hockey games and finding Prince Charmings.

November 29, 1964

"Oh, Ethel, I am so sorry," Rhoda consoled at Lakewood Cemetery. Her brother Will had died. The marker read, *William Thomas Hanscome*. "I have found it very strange to visit JAC's grave and realize that in a few years I will occupy the space next to him. My name is on the head stone, just the final date remains to be engraved, for all eternity."

"I know people say Will had a good long life, he was 84, but I can't imagine my life without him. You seem to enjoy your life as a widow, Rhoda. How do you do it?" Ethel asked.

"You just need time to adjust to the shock. It seems death always knocks on someone else's door. I loved JAC, make no mistake about it, Ethel, but I have learned to enjoy my freedom. Life is for the living. You will go on, and I hope not dwell on the past. The nice thing is now I remember JAC as a vital young man, not how ill he was before he died. And I have my children and grandchildren. However, with Will's passing, I do realize I am next, or as he would say, two down and one remains."

"I don't know how I'll carry on Rhoda. I'll have to pray for guidance," Ethel lamented.

"Yes, we must always be spiritual," Rhoda affirmed as she patted Ethel's hand.

What did Rhoda mean by the phrase, *we must always be spiritual?* She never discussed it as she felt spiritual lives were private, not to be discussed glibly.

Did any of Rhoda's grandchildren attend their Uncle Will's funeral? No, but the Hanscome first cousins warmly exchanged news of their current, busy lives. None gave thought to tending their Hanscome connection, that now hung by the slim thread of Rhoda's selective memory.

"Soon, we must get together soon," they all promised. But they didn't.

The one remaining carried on, but not alone. Rhoda had her children, and they needed her help marrying off their children. She certainly would not shirk her duties as the matriarch. She truly intended to have fun. Enough of death. Onward to weddings. How romantic.

Chapter 18

Prince Charmings and Maid Marions
Fall 1959
Bloomington

Susan seemed to be thriving at North Dakota State University in Fargo. Like her mother and aunt, she pledged herself both to Kappa Kappa Gamma and fraternity boys. Had she fallen in love in Fargo? She was working on it.

"Absolutely, no farm boys for me," she declared. Her fall in the turkey dung in Willmar had jaded her for life. Then why on earth had she chosen an agricultural college? After all, wasn't the point of going to college to find a suitable husband? Her mother's words were firmly ensconced in her head.

"When you grow up, you will find a special man, fall in love, marry, and he will take care of you. An education is for you to develop your mind – and also to find your prince charming," Rhoda Jane said, a bit tongue in cheek, but that was how her parents sowed their wisdom, a bit subtly with humor. Regardless of the kind delivery, it was assimilated as a concrete order.

Susan's home economics pattern-making class was a snap for her. She designed a fine wool, camel hair coat and lined it with the fur of an old muskrat coat of her mothers. What a warm fashion statement that was. But when she stumbled through organic chemistry, she considered quitting. She was discouraged.

Fall 1960

"Vroom! Vroom! Vroom!" Dick screeched into the long arched driveway on his motorcycle, Nancy hopped on the back and off they went. She and Dick had been going steady for two years. Nancy was a senior and Dick a junior at Bloomington High School.

Wesley convinced himself that their romance wouldn't last when Nancy went to The 'U'. But he didn't like it when she sported Dick's new graduation ring around her neck. Yes, they were glued together.

"Oh no!" Wes said when he answered the telephone on a Sunday evening. "It's the police. Rhoda Jane, Nancy was in a car accident and is in the hospital. We must leave right now."

"And where is Joanie? She must have been in the car, too."

"They didn't say."

And neither did the police say that Nancy was in a coma, near dead. The two girls had been to a church youth group meeting, and friends were to have driven them home. Joanie was in the back seat and Nancy in the front when they hit a telephone pole. Nancy lay in a bloody heap on the floor of the front seat, but Joan seemed okay, disoriented, but okay. She kept asking the police where they were taking her sister, but the police wouldn't answer her questions. The ambulance whisked Nancy off, but no one else was examined. The police kept talking to the driver, who was also disoriented and complaining of a headache. The boy next to Joanie was crying, and the police insinuated there was some *hanky panky* going on. Didn't the driver know that the road didn't go straight? What made him drive right over a ditch into the telephone pole? True, it was a dark, rainy night, and the old church camp friends were from Richfield and unfamiliar with the roads. When the police finally drove Joan home, no one was there to help ice her bruises. And did anyone think to call Dick?

While Nancy was in a coma with severe brain injuries for several weeks, Rhoda Jane kept the nature of her injuries private. Yes, private from the other children, even Joanie. What a shock when they first saw Nancy in a wheelchair, minus all her teeth, talking with a lisp. Robert's eyes almost fell out of his sockets. Joan felt sick; it could have been or should have been her in the front seat. When they finally were able to bring her home, Wesley put his arm around his tearful wife and whispered, "We dodged a bullet, Rhoda Jane. Now our life must return to normal."

But it didn't, not for Nancy who was in danger of not graduating. The words she read just seemed to float meaningless on the page. She blamed herself, "Why am I so stupid?" Why didn't the school help her? Why didn't her family help her? Everyone just assumed her brain would heal with time. She sported a new set of Hollywood teeth and looked much better without those braces. Hopefully, Dick was her confidante.

Christmas 1960
Edina

"Heather is in love! Isn't that exciting, Gordon," Margaret exclaimed, clapping her hands. "I overheard her telling all her cousins about him last night when they came for dinner. I've never seen her so effervescent, so glowing!"

"We better meet him before this gets too serious," Gordon said with a frown. When they flew Heather back to Colorado, they met the handsome, bespectacled Alex. Heather had pledged Delta Gamma Fraternity and lived in the sorority house, when she wasn't exploring the mountain trails with Alex. It was difficult to choose between all her favorite things. But then, why shouldn't she have it all? Of course, it went without saying that she studied, but Margaret was right. Heather needed some light-hearted fun. What they didn't bargain for was a serious romance.

"It is serious, Sir. I am serious, Sir. I love Heather. I have given her an engagement ring, and she has accepted," Alex replied to Gordon's queries as to his intentions. For a tall boy, he felt suddenly quite small. His ball of courage had been pricked, deflated and flattened by the daggers in Gordon's eyes.

"I would have preferred if you would have asked for her hand, first. We will have to discuss your proposal, Alex," Gordon scowled as he stood up. The discussion was over. Alex had been summarily dismissed. The next day, Gordon sat down with Heather.

"Heather, your mother and I are leaving, as soon as you give that ring back. What were you thinking? That Alex will never amount to anything," Gordon said, disgusted.

"Who are you to talk? Did you graduate from college? Did you have lofty career goals?" Heather retorted. "I've been told by my aunts you were a wild fraternity boy, and you actually picked up mother on a street corner!"

Did Heather's explosion propel her out the door and forever into Alex's waiting arms? No, her father's demeaning glare cowed her into submission. She gave the diamond ring back. It was not only the end of her engagement. It was the end of her freedom. The next fall, she was safely back in Minnesota and enrolled at the 'U.'

Fall 1961
Bloomington

"Joanie, let's walk down to the River, I want to read my *Catcher in the Rye* book to you," her new next door neighbor, Mike, said with a gleam in his eye.

"What's it about?" she asked, feigning great interest. Yes, she cared, but not about the book.

"Ah, the loss of innocence," he mischievously grinned. "It's about being a teenager."

As they strolled through the fall leaves at the bottom of the river bluff, Mike touched her hand. If there had been a ceiling, Joanie would have bounced off it. He was a worldly twenty, tall, dark and handsome, the notorious wild man of her sister Susan's high school class, swooned over by every girl. Then, he kissed her. Did the earth move? No, but she swore the Minnesota River changed its course, right then and there. Was she an innocent about to be slaughtered by the demon of first love?

"Joanie, are you falling in love with Mike?" Bahariah, their foreign exchange student from Malaysia, asked. They shared a room together now that Nancy and Susan were both in college.

"You had better be careful. I don't think our mom and dad would like it. He's too old for you."

"Mike says he didn't mean to be my first love. We didn't mean to fall in love. He knows I am too young. He wants to do the responsible thing. He wants me to enjoy high school and date other boys - and I will. Don't worry, he's going away to college in California after Christmas. Please don't tell my sisters or my parents."

"You are fooling no one. I can tell. His parents can tell. Your parents can tell. Keep your wits about you. I saw him at the football game the other night watching you cheer. Then I saw the two of you leave together, right after the game, and he put his arm around you."

"Can you keep that a secret, Bahariah? We just can't stay away from each other. So, we meet on the sly."

"Yes, I will keep your secret, but I am afraid Mike will break your heart. He's too wild. He drinks. He smokes. He's handsome and a charmer, that's for sure. Ask your sister Susan. His wicked grin is more than dangerous," Bahariah counseled. "But at school, the cat is out of the bag. The two of you were noticed, by everyone, and the gossip is flying."

Christmas 1961

"Why don't I fix you up with Dan?" Nancy suggested when Susan came home for the Christmas holiday. Dan was a friend of Nancy's boyfriend, Dick, and home on leave from the Army. What a match. The sparks flew! Susan was in love.

"Well, Rhoda Jane, we have Nancy smitten with a grease monkey, motorcycle maniac, Susan wants to drop out of college, and starry-eyed Joanie is entranced by the pied piper next door," Wesley said. "I don't know that I like being a father of daughters. Our girls can't seem to separate the wheat from the chaff. There must be some true Prince Charmings out there."

"For our true Maid Marions? You're doing fine, Wesley." Rhoda Jane laughed. "Let's just enjoy this Christmas. Who knows how long all our girls will be home at the same time."

Let's Twist Again - Like You Did Last Summer... Mike drank beer and banged on his drums while Joanie and Bahariah twisted like pros. It was quite the going away party for Mike. Susan and Dan were on a double date with Nancy and Dick. Both sisters would be going back to college tomorrow. And Wesley was doing the evening countdown, waiting for his girls to come home, bourbon and water in hand.

Slam! went the front door.

Joanie and Bahariah danced their way upstairs. Good – two girls home, thought Wes. He toyed with the idea of fixing that front door, but then he'd never know when his girls came home.

Slam! went the front door, again.

Nancy and Dick came in and went directly into the kitchen to fix Dick his nightly peanut butter and jelly sandwich. Good - three down. Wes smiled. Where on earth did that Dick put those triple decker Dagwood sandwiches? He was as thin as a rail.

Slam! went the front door.

"Dad, I have something to show you," an effervescent Susan said, leading Dan and showing her sparkly diamond ring.

"You give that ring back, right now, Susan," her father ordered, giving them both his fiercest, beady-eyed look. "You hardly know Dan. He is leaving for active duty tomorrow, and you are going back to Fargo to complete your degree. And that's final! Do you hear me?"

Susan's lip trembled, but she obeyed and handed the ring back to an unbelieving Dan. Wow, that was fast - ring on, then ring off. There was absolutely no discussion. They both fled from Wes's wrath - Dan out the front door and Susan upstairs.

"Susan, what's wrong?" Joanie asked. "Why was Dad yelling? And why are you crying?"

"Dan proposed to me, and Dad made me give his diamond ring back."

"Well, go tell Dad to jump in the lake. It's your life. Get that ring back, if you want to marry Dan. Come on! Go right now, Susan. Go after Dan," Joanie prodded.

What a terrible thing their father had done. Did Susan go after Dan? No, she did not. Susan went back to Fargo instead, mastered chemistry and graduated.

Nancy went back to The 'U' wearing Dick's Christmas present, an olive green sweater that was identical to the one she had given him. How fun, twin sweaters. Wes was relieved there was no Christmas engagement ring to give back. After her dad's performance with Susan and Dan, Nancy and Dick decided to talk with him first. Wesley gave his consent to their engagement, with the stipulation Dick first graduate from college. Did Nancy and Dick agree? Yes. They grumbled, but they acquiesced. Wes patted himself on the back for his major coup. He had set the stage. They would never last for four years.

And Joanie settled into a weekly pen pal arrangement with Mike that lasted for years. She avidly read *Franny and Zooey* and discussed it and many more books with him. How dangerous was that? Very. Although she dated, flirted, went to prom, her heart was not available. Joanie went to Turkey the summer of 1962 as an AFS exchange student. Nine months passed until they saw each other. And then? Mike and Joanie started all over again.

1962
Eden Prairie

"Mr. Campbell, I am asking for your consent to marry Heather," Angus Wurtele said, who had recently met Heather on a Colorado ski vacation. He was a mature young man, a few years older than Heather.

"Well, well, well!" was all a surprised Gordon could say, but he was smiling. "Let me think about it, discuss it with Margaret and Heather, of course." Gordon had expected Angus' friend to propose. Heather had gone to Colorado with one guy but came back with another. What was she doing?

"Dad, I will be graduating from the 'U.' Angus meets your responsibility criteria. He just finished his MBA program and has joined the family business. We want to get married and start a family together. I know we haven't known each other long, but we love each other."

"Of course we consent, Heather," Margaret said, eyeing Gordon with her *don't you dare* stare. He'd better not ruin another proposal. "What did you have in mind for a wedding?"

"A small wedding, nothing pretentious, right here in the living room is fine with us." Heather beamed. "We want to have a relaxed day and have our families get acquainted, perhaps at the end of summer. We could have a lovely dinner catered by the pool. Simple. What do you think?"

"Couldn't be better. Congratulations!" Gordon smiled. Was his daughter actually asking for his opinion? And why should he object? Angus was a Yale graduate with a promising future in the family business, Minnesota Paints. An added bonus was that he was very personable and came from a good family. Heather had chosen well. Gordon breathed a sigh of relief, and Margaret was thrilled. One down, two more to go. Raising children was not easy, particularly headstrong girls.

Grandma Campbell was also most pleased. Heather's engagement was another party opportunity.

The Minnekahda Club

"Oh, thank you, Grandma," Heather said as she held up the filmy, white peignoir set for all to see.

"My pleasure, Heather. Every bride needs a lovely negligee and robe for her honeymoon."

Rhoda was giving a beautiful bridal shower for Heather, with all her aunts, girl cousins and Wurtele ladies.

"Rhoda Jane, you better help Joanie. She is wobbling on those high heels," Grandma whispered as they moved into the dining room for lunch. Apparently, as fast as Joanie dug the hazelnuts out of her daiquiri glass the waitress had refilled it. Was she drunk or just a novice on spiked heels?

And one good party needed a return engagement.

Lake Minnetonka

"Thank you, Mrs. Wurtele, for the lovely party," all the female Campbell cousins said as they left. The chuck wagon barbeque had been a success. The Wurtele's lovely old home on Lake Minnetonka was perfect for a swim and a bridal shower. This time, Heather received practical gifts for her kitchen. Of course, she would have to return the duplicates. After all, how many toasters did a homemaker need?

But Heather's was not the only engagement.

"Mom and Dad, I am going to propose to Lynn. I have decided to leave Carleton and enroll in the 'U's School of Business," Jim announced to his parents.

Jim and Lynn had met during their freshman year and had been together for two years. His parents had hosted Lynn many weekends as she was from faraway San Diego.

"Don't you think you should wait until you graduate, Jim? What's the rush?" Gordon asked.

"There's no rush. I've just found the girl I want to marry, and I don't want to lose her. She wants to graduate from Carleton. We won't get married until we both finish and have jobs. I thought you liked Lynn. What's the problem?"

"There's no problem. You're just too young," Gordon said.

"We simply love Lynn, Jim. She exudes such warmth and sincerity, and her eyes sparkle when she looks at you." Again, Margaret's glare warned Gordon to behave.

"I'll wait until Christmas to propose. I don't want to steal Heather's show. And by the way, Nancy has decided to live at home and commute to the 'U', so I offered to drive her."

"That's nice of you, Jim. We hear Nancy plans to marry her boyfriend, Dick," Margaret said. "I think she's had a hard time concentrating on her studies, but I think that's due to her brain injuries more than her love for Dick."

"Maybe we should just have one massive Campbell cousins wedding," Gordon offered. "It would save a lot of money and a lot of time." He laughed.

"Sometimes, you are not very funny, Gordy," Margaret said, miffed. But, of course, Gordon had that Hanscome trait of finding himself more amusing than others did.

• • •

Heather's wedding was a model for all. Simple and elegant.

"Do you, Heather, take Angus to be your lawfully wedded husband?"

"I will," she answered. With her blue eyes and sleek, Breck blonde hairdo, she was an exact replica of Princess Grace of Monaco. What a composed, beautiful bride – the WASP ideal.

The sunset over the Minnesota River Valley could not have been more perfect. And the wedding was almost perfect. Twelve-year-old Robert kept calling the bride and groom, *Heifer and Angus*. And who had put him up to that? Why his older cousin, Scottie, of course. He had been schooled well in the art of teasing by his father. It was also unfortunate that Jim's Lynn became ill and had to excuse herself. Was the culprit too much champagne?

"Will you be teaching German?" Aunt Jean asked, whose fear of German kept her from graduating from the 'U.' "I wish you could have been my tutor, Heather."

The Campbells had sponsored a friend Heather had met in Germany for citizenship. Barney had escaped over the Berlin wall and was homeless. He was also at the wedding with his wife-to-be, Sue. They were now considered family.

"Yes, I plan on teaching after the wedding," Heather answered. But did she? No, Heather was too busy entertaining and soon became pregnant. Rhoda was thrilled; she would be a great grandmother.

June 1963
St. Paul

"Jack, what are we going to do about us?" Shelly asked. She and Jack had just spent a beautiful day sailing on White Bear Lake, where the Herrmanns had a cabin.

"I don't know what to do, Shelly. You're going to Macalester College next year, and I'm joining the Green Berets, that is, if they take me. I could even be sent to Viet Nam, if that heats up. I have nothing to offer you right now."

"Do you love me, Jack?"

"Yes, you know I do."

"Let's tell our parents, please Jack."

"Oh, Shelly, no one is going to approve of us. Not our fathers for sure. And my mother? Well, even she's questionable. We are too young to get married. Let's wait."

"Fine," Shelly said as she broke into tears. "You may be a fine soldier, but I think you're a coward when it comes to us. I'm not going to wait for you."

"I understand, Shelly. Don't then. Don't wait." Did Jack mean to push her away? Yes and no. He didn't want her to leave, but he saw no future for them.

Was this just the end of a high school romance or did Shelly wait for Jack? Yes, she waited. She loved Jack with a passion.

July
Minneapolis

"Patty, why do you want to marry Bob?" Grandma asked. "You hardly know him. Last year, there was a boy at the 'U' you wanted to marry. Then you decided to leave the 'U' and go to the business college for secretarial training. Why don't you finish that program first, and then we'll talk about it."

Why had Patty come to her grandmother rather than her own mother? Because her grandmother was a soft touch and always interceded on her behalf.

"Jean, I've discouraged Patty from marrying that Bob. What do you think?" Rhoda asked.

"I don't recommend marriage for anyone, Mother. I am happy being divorced from Gardner. Bob seems nice enough, pleasant, cares for Patty, but is that enough to have a marriage last? He has no ambitions or career skills."

"You're her mother, Jean. Please talk with her. She's expecting a wedding at The Woman's Club, and she's determined."

August

"Do you like this silk dress, Grandma?" Joanie asked, modeling a bright turquoise party dress. Rhoda had taken her to Young-Quinlan's for her fall wardrobe and lunch. Rhoda sat drinking tea as Joanie pivoted and turned in front of the three-way mirrors. She was going to The University of Wisconsin in Madison and needed decent clothes for sorority rush. Her glossy, clipped, curly brunette hair, clear milky complexion and thin, muscular frame, made her the perfect sorority pledge, a true WASP. Rhoda was also picking up the tab for all her sorority expenses. She needed wool skirts and matching sweaters, a suit and a few party dresses. Slacks? Heavens no! Decent girls wore skirts to classes, even in the frigid winter.

"Yes, I like the dress, Joanie, but what are those disfiguring marks on your neck?"

"Oh, those rope burns? It was one continuous scab, but some crusty parts have fallen off. Now, I cover my neck with a scarf, so my customers won't stare at me like some immoral creature. I got it when I galloped our horse right into our clothes line, showing off for my date, who was speeding into the driveway. We were waving to each other and not paying attention. He was lucky his car didn't end up in the culvert. I catapulted off the horse, right over its rear. Luckily, the clothesline wasn't taut, and I didn't have my feet in the stirrups, or I would have broken my neck. You should have seen me, Grandma." Joanie smiled. Did her Grandma think she had suffered a love bite, one of those low-rent hickeys?

"I'm glad I didn't," Rhoda laughed, relieved. "Who was your date?"

"Oh, a guy from high school I dated this summer, but we're not serious."

"We'll take them all," Rhoda said, motioning to the sales clerk. And she wrote out a check. "Next stop is the shoe department. I can't tell you when I've had so much fun buying clothes."

Bloomington

What had happened to Mike? The stacks of love letters, indexed by date and bound with rubber bands, were worn and smudged by Joanie's cherished, daily rereading while she listened to Dinah Washington sing *Unforgettable*.

When Mike finally came home from California, he took her to the Guthrie Theatre with his older brother and his wife. Joanie wore her new, sorority rush suit and way too much of her mother's Chanel N°5. She felt so grown-up. She was eighteen. A few days later, she left for Madison. Never fear, they made no promises, but Mike called every vacation she came home. His parents were always thrilled to see her. And Wesley? He was not pleased, no, not pleased, at all. But he was even less pleased when Mike broke her heart after her sophomore year. He had moved home from California, right out of her life and into the Minneapolis bar scene.

Wesley held an impromptu lecture for Joanie and three of her high school friends on the evil intentions of boys. Unbeknownst to him, he was already too late. All three of her girlfriends were pregnant, dropping out of college and getting married. They had no choice.

Susan graduated from NDSU and drove off to the Mesabi Iron Range in northern Minnesota for her first teaching position in her brand new Chevy Nova, a convertible. The golden flecks in the metallic brown paint job perfectly matched her shiny, auburn hair. The tallest and darkest-haired, blue-eyed Nancy was bookkeeping at a foreign auto company, saving every dime and living at home, while dutiful Dick had given up his grease monkey job for college. The horse, a gift for Campbell soup-faced kid Robert, who didn't ride it, went back to the stables. And smiley, *Summer Blonde Baby Mary*, as she was affectionately called for the rest of her life, was content to have her big room all to herself.

June 1964
San Diego

"I, James Gordon Campbell, take you, Carol Lynn McCann, as my wedded wife."

The Campbells were represented by a small group in San Diego. Gordon kindly offered to fly Jean and Rhoda Jane in his private airplane for the special occasion. His mother, Rhoda, and Patricia were relieved to fly in a commercial plane. It took less time, was less noisy and Rhoda could exercise her legs. Rhoda hated to admit it, but she was getting older. She was seventy-eight, but didn't complain. *Mind over matter*, was her current motto.

Minneapolis

The cousins missed the wedding, but not Lynn's bridal shower at The Minnekahda Club. And what color was Lynn's peignoir? It was white, of course. A bride should always wear white. And who drank too much at the shower? Patty. She should have been the one to get married next, in the family pecking order.

"Oh, wait your turn, Patty," an unsympathetic Nancy said. They had become best friends during their year as dorm roommates at the 'U'. "You will be married next. If you want to feel sorry for someone, feel sorry for Susan. She seems to have lost her turn in the marriage line and is a good sport. I certainly hope she doesn't marry that golf pro. He gives her whisker burns, his chin juts out so, like Dick Tracy."

"That's very funny," Patty said and giggled. "How are your wedding plans, Nancy?"

"Lynn has already offered me her wedding dress, but I have yet to try it on. Susan has already said she will make all the bridesmaids dresses. What a nice sister. I can't believe my dad hasn't come up with another excuse to put off our wedding. We'll both be at Mankato State. I'm going to take some accounting courses, while Dick completes his Master's in economics. We've only waited four years. Ugh!"

February 1965

"I swear, Patty, you have chosen the coldest day of the year to get married. It was twenty below zero this morning. You should be wearing warm, white velvet. You'll freeze to death in that lacey dress," Jean laughed. "Perhaps we should buy you some long underwear to wear underneath."

"Forget about the underwear, Mother. Are you happy for me?" Patty asked.

"Yes, of course I am. What a silly question to ask. Just do a better job with marriage than I did."

And did Patty do that? The elegant wedding pictures in front of the Grecian marble pillars at The Woman's Club looked identical to her mother's and aunt's wedding pictures years earlier. Would the fate of Patty's marriage be similar to her mother's? No, it wasn't. Patty and Bob were devoted to each other.

The rehearsal was held at St. Patrick's Episcopal Church in Bloomington. Mary, just twelve-years-old, walked down the aisle first, followed by Joanie, then Susan, then Nancy on her father's arm. They all practiced the hesitation step, so they would appear to float. No running allowed. Dick was waiting at the altar with his brother, two friends and Robert.

"Just remember, Nancy, you don't have to get married. It's not too late to change your mind," her father said intently, before he put her hand in Dick's. "You can always come home."

Did Dick think Wes' offhand comment was funny? No, he was insulted. Wesley still didn't want Nancy to marry him. He had tears in his eyes as he stepped away. It wasn't that Wes disliked Dick, he couldn't bear to lose any of his girls. In spite of all his teasing, he loved his children.

Rhoda Jane shook her head and smiled. How was her husband going to make it through another three weddings? After all, as he always said, *You are my favorite daughter*, to each one, in turn. Wasn't he clever? Sometimes, he was thoroughly delightful, kind and loving, and Rhoda Jane remembered why she married him.

The wedding went off perfectly. Susan, the maid of honor, finished hemming the floor-length, silver blue bridesmaid dresses just the night before. She even made matching hats with the extra material. And Nancy? Her bright blue eyes and dark hair were smashing. And Lynn Campbell's dress fit like a glove.

"Joanie, can I talk with you? Privately?" her cousin Jack asked, back from his duty in Germany.

"Excuse me, Jim. I'll be right back." Who was Jim? He was Joan's boyfriend from Madison. They had been dating her sophomore year and were in love. Yes, she had finally found a love who was more devoted to her than himself. How could she have convinced herself that Mike was heaven sent?

"What's wrong, Jackie?"

"I don't know what to do. I have this girlfriend that I've been in love with for years. I want to marry her, but I'm afraid my father will disown me."

"Now, why would he do that? And why haven't I met her? You never before mentioned a girlfriend. You could have brought her to Nancy's wedding."

"Joanie, she's black."

"Oh, Jackie, you still could have brought her. I would like to meet her. Certainly, your parents will welcome her. What's her name?"

"Shelly. Her name is Shelly. She just graduated from Macalester College in St. Paul and wants to get married. You don't understand how racist my father is, and I don't know what my mother will do. Do your parents like your Jewish boyfriend?"

"I don't know how much my parents like Jim. I haven't asked, intentionally. I'm not giving my dad an opening to call another guy a *yo-yo* or *the missing link* or some other derogatory term. Don't allow your parents to discourage you, Jackie. If you want to marry Shelly, you should just do it."

"Do you know that it's only been a few years since interracial marriage has been legal in Minnesota?"

"Really, Jackie? No, I didn't know that - and here I'm a history major. The Civil War was over a hundred years ago. I know prejudice runs rampant, but how can such laws still exist?"

"They are most alive and well. They are called miscegenation laws, and, in many states, our marriage would be illegal and our children illegitimate."

"How ridiculous, Jackie. Miscegenation, what a terrible word. Why is it really necessary to differentiate between the races? What purpose does it serve, except to make a pecking order of good and bad? Differentiate and discriminate. I am better, you are less. And I also hate the term illegitimate. How can a young child be illegitimate or legitimate? Babies just are. We are really all quite similar, male and female, black and white. Don't you agree?"

"Yes, but tell that to my father. He's of German background, you know, ethnic purity and all."

"Now, that's not fair, your father is no Nazi, and he served admirably in the War, but I do see your predicament. My dad is prejudiced, too. When they argue, he calls my mother a *half-breed*, because of our Indian ancestor. What a hypocrite he is. He uses that trite expression - *You don't see blue jays marrying robins*. I cringe when he says to Jim, *people of your faith....blah, blah, blah*. But actually, as prejudiced as my dad is, I think he likes Jim. He gets a kick out of his theatrical banging on his guitar when he sings."

"Do you think you two will marry?"

"That's a long way off, but we talk about it. I can't imagine my life without him. First, I have to graduate, and he has to ask me. Then, I'm not so sure his mother will approve. In fairness to her, I don't think she'd even approve of a Jewish girl. Her Jimmy is that special. When he was born, his dad gave her a ring for his son, but no rings for his sisters, as if being a boy is somehow better. Jim says his father, who died last year, would have *sat shiva*, if he were still alive, and we got married. I guess that's not much different from your father's reaction. On the other hand, your parents might like Shelly, if they met her. What are you going to do?"

"We're thinking of going to San Francisco. I have the GI bill and can go to school for free. Shelly can get a job. Her major was international relations."

"Are you going to get married first?"

"I don't know, I really don't know," he said with a sigh.

Jackie left the reception early. He and Shelly moved to California, unmarried.

By the way, who drank too much champagne at the wedding? Well, the maid of honor, Susan, of course. As the oldest, she should have gotten married before Nancy. Who would get drunk at the next wedding was becoming a family joke. Robert promised to take bets at the next wedding.

"Will you marry me?" Jim asked at Christmas. Surprise, it was not Joanie's Jim, but Susan's.

"You'd better ask my father first," Susan replied, with a knowing smile. "And if he says *No* or *Wait*, we'll get married anyway." Yes, these Dickinson girls were starting to assert themselves. Finally.

And who was this Jim? He was an art teacher at the same school as Susan. She had given up on her Iron Range teaching position after one year of living over the town grocery store, staying in at night and protecting her schoolteacher reputation from the rough, tough, and yes, wild miners, used to having their way with women. She rewarded her *Up Nord* survival by traveling in Europe for three months before settling down again. Where did she land? Safely back in Bloomington. She taught at the same high school she graduated from, side-by-side with her old teachers. Imagine that.

Was there a scene between Wesley and Jim? No, Wes was quite cordial, but he did ask the *twenty questions*, about Jim's family, religion, future goals, etc. Finally, he gave his blessing. And why not? Susan was twenty-five, Jim twenty-three, and both were gainfully employed. Had Wes accepted the notion he could no longer control his children's lives? No, not really, but he was making progress with his empty nest syndrome.

"Just hang on, Wes," Rhoda Jane encouraged. "You're going to make it. Two down, two left to marry and no shotguns, yet."

"Why do you want to get married in March, Susan?" Rhoda Jane asked. "That's such a bleak and dreary month. It will be too cold to use the porch or the gardens, like we did for Nancy's wedding. And worse, we could have a blizzard."

"I've found the right guy. I don't want to wait another day, neither does Jim, but I convinced him that it would take three months to plan a decent wedding. We have to register for gifts at Dayton's and Donaldson's. I want to sew my own wedding dress, the bridesmaids' dresses, send out the invitations. There's a lot to do."

"Oh, Susan, you work too hard," her mother said. "I'll help you, and we'll buy your wedding dress."

However, Susan insisted on making the hot pink, floor-length bridesmaid dresses. Hats? Jackie O hats were way too passé. Instead, they glued fresh flowers on headbands. How creative, how smart and how aromatic.

March 1967

The wedding was at St. Patrick's Episcopal Church, followed by a catered reception at the Dickinson home for one hundred and fifty guests. There was no blizzard, but the recent snow had melted, making their driveway a mud hole and the grass a soggy, squishy bog. Where could they park the cars? Bethany Fellowship, an evangelical Christian Church right across the road with a huge paved parking lot, saved the day - for a small donation. Dick, Nancy's husband, and Jim, Joanie's boyfriend, served as valets. At the end of the reception, Jim had made enough money in tips to take her to dinner.

Jim enjoyed her family of WASPs, as he called them. In return, her family really got a kick out of him. What an entertaining comedian, but his jokes were many times at Joanie's expense. She hated it when he would tease and embarrass her. Jim was the practical joker, and Joan was his fall guy. "You are so adoringly gullible," he confessed.

"Why aren't we getting married when I graduate, Jim?" Joanie asked.

"I'm just getting myself squared away, but I do want to marry you. Why don't you look for teaching jobs in Milwaukee for next fall, then we can set a date?"

June
Madison, Wisconsin

"Open your graduation present, Joanie," Jim coaxed.

"A watch? Well, thank you Jim." Joanie tried not to look too disappointed. She guessed she would not be looking at *June Bride* magazines with the rest of her Kappa Kappa Gamma sisters.

"My mother thought you could use a watch for your teaching. She helped me pick it out," Jim said proudly.

Minneapolis

In spite of no engagement ring, Joanie trusted his intentions and found a position teaching history right outside of Milwaukee. She was so excited. She bought her first car - a brand new, candy apple red, Galaxy Ford 500 to drive to Milwaukee. Her father was pleased she had bought such a big, safe car.

"What were you thinking? Why did you buy that car? You didn't even ask me. I thought we were getting married. I would have advised you to get a Volvo, not that Ford," Jim said.

"I thought it was my decision. You know... my job, my money, my car. And are you planning this wedding for anytime soon?" She wasn't angry, she was excited. He had mentioned marriage.

August 1967
Milwaukee

Joanie found an apartment on Milwaukee's West side, closer to her school. What a surprise to find out her two new roommates were both ex-nuns. They loved her Jewish Jim and his thoughtful bouquets of long-stemmed red roses.

His *apt*, as he called it, was downtown on State Street in a black neighborhood where they had been barricaded in, along with Father Grappi, during the race riots. For five days, they played gin rummy, practiced for the Green Bay Packer half-time entertainment and sang every song from *The Sound of Music*. Some couples had a song; they had whole albums. She listened to his troubles and his serenades. They were inseparable best friends and deeply in love.

"Jim talked to me about you two getting married," his mother said, after they returned from Temple one Friday night. "You know, if his father were alive, he would have wanted Jim to find a Jewish girl. I know you were raised Christian, but I'd like you to consider converting to Judaism. It is important for us because children follow the religion of the mother. If you aren't Jewish, Jim's children will not be considered Jewish."

"I know, Jim told me."

Joanie had fallen away from her Christian beliefs after her priest declared that the Muslims she lived with in Turkey were all going to hell unless they accepted Christ as their Savior. How small minded, she thought.

"I see. I don't know how to say this, but I don't see converting. I'm truly not too crazy about Christianity, but I'm not interested in any religion. I consider myself agnostic."

Joanie swallowed hard, trying to be tactful, yet truthful. She had wanted Jim's mother to accept her, but in spite of Jim's reassurance, she didn't feel any warmth from her. She was pleasant, not rude, but not welcoming. Joan also thought converting to Judaism was ridiculous, a sham. She knew she would never be accepted as *really Jewish*.

"I see. Well, that is unfortunate," Jim's mother said, icily.

By Christmas, Joan was depressed and decided to quit teaching, but her sister Susan talked her out of it. She stuck it out, but in June, she moved to Denver to live with her best friend Judy. She wanted friends, laughter and a job she loved. Was that the end of Jim and Joan? No, it was not. He always said he had a *master plan*.

March 1968
St. Paul

Wedding bells, again!

"I, Jack, take you, Rachelle, to be my lawfully wedded wife."

It was a small wedding in St. Phillips' Episcopal Church in St. Paul. Shelly's sister Pearl was her maid of honor, and her father proudly walked a glowing Shelly down the aisle.

"Jean, thank you for coming," Pat whispered to her sister. "Please sit with us."

"I think it's a shame, just a shame, Pat. I am the only Campbell at Jack's wedding. I am sorry. I thought for sure Rhoda Jane would come, but Wesley threw a fit when she suggested she go by herself. And our mother? I thought she would change her mind," Jean whispered.

"Don't worry, Jack and Shelly have gotten used to being snubbed," Pat replied. "This wedding is for them, and I intend to celebrate it. I don't even care that John has disowned Jack."

"Mom, why don't they mix?" thirteen-year-old Penny asked. "All the black people sit on one side and all the whites on the other."

"It's customary to have the family and guests of the bride on one side of the aisle and the groom's friends and family on the other side," Pat replied. "Don't make too much of it, Penny."

"Oh," Penny said. "It is the strangest wedding I've ever seen. It's my first black and white wedding," she said, laughing at her own cleverness, like the rest of her relatives.

Only Jack caught a glimpse of his father standing in the rear of the church, hiding behind dark glasses.

And where was Rhoda, the matriarch? She was stunned, shocked and almost speechless when Pat told her Jack was marrying Shelly, a black girl.

"Oh no!" Rhoda said, putting her head in her hands, distraught. "Oh no! Why, Pat? Why that girl? He surely could have found someone more suitable!"

"They have loved each other since high school. They went to California together and decided to come back home to be married. She's really a talented, beautiful girl. I like her, Mother. I hope you will, too."

"I see, Pat. I understand, but if you don't mind, I am feeling ill. Please excuse me. I think I'll lie down."

"Will you come to their wedding, Mother?"

"No, Pat, I don't think I can, and I don't want to discuss it. I am exhausted. I believe I need to rest."

After Pat left, Rhoda picked up a picture of her father and wept, first softly, then she wailed violently as the floodgate of years of denial and tears opened deep within her soul. Her pride of always being in control of her emotions was lost. Her very foundation cracked as she quaked and shook.

"What was all our effort for, Father? What was all Grandpa Hanscome's effort for? For whiteness! For opportunity! Our sins of omission! Our lies! And now this! My grandson Jack, dear Jack, has ruined his life!"

Spring 1970

"We're all going to need wheelbarrows," Lynn Campbell said, pregnant with her second child.

"Yes," Nancy agreed, pregnant with her first.

"Yes, you all are big as houses," Heather said and laughed, greeting Shelly with a hug.

Where were they going? Why to The Minnekahda Club, of course. And the occasion? Grandma was giving a baby shower for Shelly. Yes, Shelly walked in, chest held high, as though she had a diamond on it. She fit right in with all the other Maid Marions.

Joan couldn't attend. Why? She was going to graduate school in Boulder, Colorado. What happened to Joan and Jim? Their love simply wasn't enough, but they would meet again.

1971
St. Paul

"I, Judd, take you, Susan, to be my lawfully wedded wife."

It was a small wedding in St. Paul, but this time, the Campbell's attended in fuller force.

"Let me hold the baby, please," Grandma said to Shelly.

Little Danielle, with her lovely golden skin, was special to her great grandmother. Did she ever say why? No, but somewhere deep inside her, a major shift had occurred.

"Let me hold, Danielle," Grandpa John said. Yes, he was still racist, but he loved his granddaughter and discovered Shelly to be quite charming. If only one of his sons would be as ambitious and successful as Shelly, but he wasn't holding his breath.

Chapter 19

Money! Money! Money!
January 1972
Minneapolis

Campbell Properties Board of Directors Meeting
Present: Gordon Campbell, executive director, Rhoda Campbell,
Rhoda Jane Dickinson, Jean Johnson and Patricia Herrmann

"As we discussed at the last Directors' meeting, I have liquidated the assets of Campbell Properties that will be distributed at the end of next quarter. I will continue to manage your shares, Mother, but Jean, you will have to find a financial advisor. The holding company has served its purpose. We need to thank our father for our financial well-being. Each of us is now responsible for our separate prosperity."

"Thank you for your years of service to us," Rhoda Jane said. "What advise do you suggest we give our children?"

"I recommend that you safeguard Jay's, Mary's, Robert's and Penny's inheritance until they reach twenty-five or become married. For the older children, I suggest they buy a house or another piece of property. The key is to use the capital wisely, but I'm sure most of them will fritter it away."

"I wish you would be more optimistic, Gordon. Money means new opportunities. I think this is exactly what the children need. And I still want to exert control over mine," Rhoda said firmly.

"Mother, as we discussed, you will receive a monthly allowance to spend as you like, but your fixed bills, our accountant will pay."

"I am capable of managing my own money, Gordon," Rhoda huffed. "Next, you'll be taking my driver's license or declaring me senile."

"We've been through this before, Mother. You are eighty-five, and I agree, quite capable, but at any date, you could have health issues. We need to have our ducks-in-a-row for your care. As long as you are interested, you are welcome to visit the accountant and discuss your financials. However, I suspect you may find our arrangements freeing. Dad did not want you to worry about money. And lately, you have been. If the situation were reversed, I'd be happy to have you take care of me," Gordon said.

And the truth of the matter, if the truth can ever be seen in the same light by all concerned, was that their mother was slipping. Rhoda was giving money to television evangelists and sometimes paying bills twice. She was still driving her big black Bonneville to her clubs, bridge parties and every Sunday out to Rhoda Jane's. The neighborhood service station owner always smiled and said, *There goes that driverless car, again.* How could she see the road? All that was visible was the very top of her hat; she must have shrunk five inches.

And more of the truth was that Gordon was tired of hearing his mother's lifelong refrain: *Gordon, you must watch after your sisters!* He had heard that since he was three years old. But there were other undercurrents that motivated him to end his duties:

Jack has ruined his future by marrying that black girl. What was he thinking! No one, and I mean no one, will hire him if they know he executes such poor judgment.

Is it fair to have your family own more shares, because you have five children, Rhoda Jane? I think Dad made a mistake giving equal shares to each grandchild individually, rather than dispersing it equitably by family. It's as though he was rewarding your lack of family planning. Wesley didn't have to keep you strapped to that bed post.

You are all adults, fend for yourselves. I'm tired of Wesley's and John's armchair critiques of my oversight. All the money has been divided equally, but is it fair that I received no payment for my diligent management?

Am I the only one making money in this family? Are all of our boys doing drugs, dropping out, living in communes, not working! And that awful long hair is disgusting!

Who was Gordon referring to? His son Scott had done nothing with his respectable business degree from the University of Denver. Scott barely eked out an existence in Aspen and lived in a converted garage with his girlfriend. Robert had dropped out of Mankato State after six years of tuition, with no degree, no job, unless skinning muskrats trapped on the Minnesota River bottoms counted. He had moved home. Or Judd and Jack, with no college education to speak of, new marriages, surly critiques and unfulfilled dreams in their bright heads. Except for Jim, who escaped the *Sex and Drugs and Rock and Roll* era, all the family boys were struggling.

"What an era of enlightenment," Gordon sarcastically commented. "Our sons are lazy. Well, I'm done with providing the silver platter."

Yes, Gordon was done harkening to anyone else's call. And about time. He was sixty and wanted to play more himself. Why not? He deserved it. Flying became his passion. He and Margaret bought an island on the Canadian border, only accessible by plane. Rainy Lake was to be their retirement haven. Did they become hermits? Hardly. They entertained, flew in friends, food, and yes, even Gordon's sisters and their husbands. Complaints aside, gossip aside, critical teasing aside, the Campbell clan enjoyed and even loved each other. Gordon may have been semi-retired, but Margaret worked even harder.

August

"What a lot of money," Mary Dickinson said. She was nineteen and just finished with her freshman year at Mankato State. "What are we going to do with my inheritance, Jerry?"

And who was Jerry? Jerry Dexter had been Mary's high school boyfriend and was soon to be her husband.

What? Young Mary married, at nineteen? Had Wesley slacked off in his fatherly duties and given his consent? Yes, he had. Perhaps he was tired of being an ogre, but more probably, Rhoda Jane was concerned that Mary might get pregnant.

"Joanie, would you talk to Mary about birth control?" Rhoda Jane asked, when Joan visited for a holiday.

"What makes you so sure I know anything about that, Mother," she teased. Joan had taught sex education in Colorado, as a single person. Unheard of! *The times they are a changing.*

"Sure, I'd be happy to, Mom."

"Mary, are you on birth control pills?" Joan bluntly asked.

"Yes, I am. Why do you ask?"

"Mother asked me to talk with you. Good. Consider your sex education talk finished."

Goodbye church wedding. Hello informal wedding under the flowering arbor in the yard. Joanie was maid of honor. Susan, again, made their matching dresses, this time summer floral dresses with bright yellow cummerbunds. And the wide-brimmed, summer hats were oh, so stylish.

"Joanie, I want you to know how proud I am of you," her grandma said during the reception. "Getting your master's degree is quite an accomplishment. Rhoda Jane also tells me you hold a responsible position at the University of Colorado - the only woman with a big office. It is such a blessing for a woman to be able to financially take care of herself. In my day, unless a girl inherited wealth, one's only recourse was to marry well."

"Why, thank you for the compliment, Grandma. My family doesn't think too much of my feminism. My mom unbelievably said, *A lady gets married and her husband takes care of her*. My Dad commanded me to *come home*, after I'd finished my degree. And Nancy thinks I am *too bossy* for any man to want me. She even gave my old boyfriend, Jim, a paddle one Christmas, *to make me mind*. I laugh at the nonsense, but I so appreciate your encouragement. Sometimes, I feel I'm swimming against the current."

"Times change, and yet, they don't. They cycle - move forward, then backwards, then surge forward again, hopefully with improvements," she remarked with a knowing smile. "Do you know we suffragettes called ourselves feminists? How we fought for the right to vote. The Minneapolis Woman's Club is not called The *Lady's* Club for a reason. Ladies can be thought of as children, with other people taking responsibility for their welfare. I like that your feminist movement has returned to the term woman. Women have always worked and worked hard - on farms, raising children, in factories, doing double-duty during wars, but never been fairly compensated. A woman's place isn't necessarily in the home."

"Your viewpoint amazes me, Grandma. I always think of you as a lady, a fine lady."

"Ah, yes, I was determined to have the best, be my best. But I know I am a lady only because JAC provided well. My father was quite the gentleman, but he was not financially astute. The Hanscome money ran dry. JAC always appreciated my contribution to our success. I pushed him. My mother was a team with my father. I come from a legacy of strong women, in spite of our male-dominant society, as you label it. And I am glad you show some spunk."

"Did you love Papa?" Joanie asked. "You sound quite calculating, Grandma."

"Of course, I loved him. I chose him. But now, young women are obsessed with the romantic notion of love. I never abdicated my soul to JAC. I was taught to give my allegiance first to God, before my husband. Now, it's as though women are the slaves to their men's desires, as if they have no brains or God to guide them."

"I am puzzled. What do you mean, *God is first*. I don't even know if there is a God."

"It has to do with respect. In respecting God, who is greater than us all and a part of us all, we also find self-respect. Don't make a god out of romantic love."

"Why did you never talk about this before, Grandma?" Joanie was used to playing bridge with her grandma, exchanging pleasantries and hugs, but they never talked about anything of substance. She was amazed at her wisdom.

"I tried to instill backbones in my girls, a sense of self, but their era was not mine. Pat has that sense of self more than Jean or your mother. In their generation, to love a man meant to obey him, put his needs first. Of course, the Church has reinforced that, but the Church is not God. I read the Bible daily, to extract meaning for my life. I became a Unitarian and a Christian Scientist to expand my horizons. God's spirit is everywhere and difficult to miss. Churches are run by men."

"But you are Episcopalian, and our priests are so rigid."

"Yes, that is true, but I find the rituals familiar and comforting. However, I choose what to believe. Remember, Joanie, your choices will define you."

"I floated my way through life, lucky, I guess, but now I take responsibility for my choices…and credit for my accomplishments."

"And what do you want, Joanie?"

"I want to have a career, help people be their best, Grandma. I want to make a difference. I want my life to have some meaning. And, like you, I want to marry a partner, not a boss."

"It is possible to love a man and be a strong person, Joanie. Just don't marry someone who is so insecure, he is afraid of your talents. In a good marriage, the need to control fades, and you learn to trust. JAC was strong. I was strong. We trusted each other. I call that love. I like to think when I die, we will be together again."

Had Joan made a god out of love? Perhaps so. Love was the theme of every popular song. Love was the lyrics, the agony, the ecstasy, the meaning of life. And she definitely had not given up on fun. She loved to flirt, dance and drink.

Joan and Robert both tied for the best drunk prize at Mary's wedding reception.

Why? Joan was twenty-seven, and her internal wedding bell was torturing her. Robert? He was a lost soul. He had wanted to quit college and become an Air Force pilot, but his parents feared for his life.

"No, Robert. Stay in school!" Wesley pleaded. "This Viet Nam War is not worth fighting."

Robert couldn't stand up to his parents, so he continued to party at Mankato State. Part of his bartender's job was to lead the patrons with chants of "Beaver, Beaver!"

Before Joan went back to Colorado, next door neighbor Mike called. Did her heart still beat for him? She smiled. Perhaps it always would. Who forgets their first love? But she also knew he put his desire for many women over her need for a special one. Accept his invitation? Of course, she did.

"What time will you have her in, Mike?" Wes asked.

"Wes, I'm not bringing her home," Mike replied with a grin.

"What do you mean, Mike?"

"Just what I said, Wes. I'm not bringing her home tonight." Mike waved as he quickly ushered Joan out the door. Wes uttered not one word. For the first time, he was speechless. Dumbfounded.

"That wasn't very nice, Mike. Now, why did you say that to my dad?" Joan asked, with a broad smile. No date had ever stood up to her father. Never.

"I've been waiting to say that to your dad for eleven years."

Was that the last surprise of the evening? No, it was just the first.

"I knew it. I knew it!" Mike's mother shouted as she jumped out of the backseat of his car, where she had hidden after he refused to tell her who his date was. Yes, Mike had driven out of his driveway only to turn into Joan's. Now, who was embarrassed!

They laughed their way to Mike's new bar and restaurant in Downtown Minneapolis. Everyone who was *anyone* knew Mike, and he loved being the ringmaster of the circus. He had earned the biggest prize money when he was raffled off as one of Minneapolis' Most Eligible Bachelors. And Mike's secret for success as a restaurateur? He made the person he was with feel special, if just for the moment. He asked about them. He listened to them. Above and beyond that, in his electric bon vivant style, he was also kind. What a special knack.

Joan smiled. Her father thought Mike would never amount to anything, but then that's how he viewed all of his daughters' boyfriends. After they laughed all the way back to her house, he properly kissed her goodnight. Were they still in love? No, but it was not the last time they would see each other.

The money

"Would you please look at these condo plans, Dad? I can easily afford to make two, big, down payments. I will get a roommate for the house in Boulder. And the Vail condo? It's only $32,000. West Vail is just opening up. The value on both should soar."

"Oh, this is a big financial commitment, Joanie. Why don't you wait? You may still get married."

"And if I do? So what?" Well, she had asked for her dad's opinion, so there was no reason to get testy. But, unfortunately, she did listen to him.

"Dick and I are saving our money," Nancy said as she forcefully whacked six-month-old Kelly on her back, as she did after every feeding. Kelly had been three months premature, weighed two and a half pounds at birth, but was finally gaining weight. "Dick isn't sure how long we'll be in Madison, and with Kelly's health, I don't even want to think about a new house."

"Why do you have to burp her so hard?" Susan asked. Her son Ryan was the same age as Kelly, but twice as large.

"If you think I whack her hard, you should see how the doctors do it. Otherwise, she'll throw up. She won't break," Nancy replied.

"What are you doing with your money, Susan?" Mary asked.

"Jim and I are going to build a house. We're looking at river bluff property now," Susan said. "We can hardly wait to get out of the carriage house. It's too small and too close to our mom and dad."

"Jerry and I are looking at a building in Sturgis, SD, for a western wear store. His parents want to help us," Mary said.

"Are they putting in money, too?"

"No, they just want to help us in the store." Now, what did that mean?

"My bike! My bike!" Robert yelled as he ran across the yard to pick up his brand new 750 Honda. "I thought you knew how to ride it!"

Joanie had taken it for a ride, spun out and was pinned to the ground, underneath Robert's prize possession. She wasn't hurt but was flabbergasted he was more concerned about his new purchase than her.

What did the rest of the Campbell cousins do with their money?

Jim, Patty and Jack took Gordon's advice and purchased lovely new homes. Judd bought a bookstore in Stillwater and Scott a business in Snow Mass, CO. Young Penny and Jay were left waiting until their next birthdays.

All intended to manage their money smartly. But truly, it was hard to say what happened to it. After all, it wasn't considered polite to ask. The family had an attitude of discounting the importance of money.

Shelly asked Joan once at lunch, "What happened in your family? The boys learned all the right sports, fine manners, how to live well, but not one of their dad's taught them how to be successful. They are allergic to work. Money is not evil! What are they going to do when the money runs out? What is important in your family?" She was fed up with being the breadwinner.

These were the unspoken values:

Be frugal
Be humble; do not brag
Contribute to the welfare of others
Take care of your family
Be a good sport
Be a leader, not a follower
Be pleasant and smile
Practice fine manners
Don't be selfish; devote yourselves to others (that was for the girls)
Excel. Do something significant with your life (that was for the boys)
Put the needs of the group first (as dictated by the fathers)
Be spiritual! What, pray tell, did Grandma exactly mean by that?

Did these scripts for successful living take? Well, not exactly.

"Dad would be happy, and let us both alone, if I were you, Joanie, and you were me," Robert said. "You are ambitious, and I don't care."

What Robert did care about was hockey, kids and coaching. He had natural patience. Too bad he wasn't encouraged to be an elementary school teacher, but that was not a manly profession.

"Do you, Joan, take you, Richard, to be your wedded husband?"

"I do."

They said their vows in front of the living room fireplace, witnessed by the thirty-five guests, mainly relatives. Mary was her matron of honor, and Richard's brother was best man. Aunt Pat played the piano and a friend of Joan's sang Cat Stevens' *Morning Has Broken* – fitting, as it was an eleven o'clock wedding, followed by a champagne brunch.

"No other alcohol, Dad, please. I don't want this to be a drunken brawl," Joan said.

"Wow, that was fast," her sister Nancy said. Was she referring to the quick ceremony or the fact that they had only met four months ago?

"How did they meet?" Heather asked. "He's very distinguished looking with his salt and pepper hair, but how old is he?"

"He's older than we are, Heather," Susan replied. "They were fixed up, met at a conference at the Air Force Academy last December. He was married before and has two little boys."

"Oh, that's too bad."

"Joan is crazy about them."

"Has she given up on her career aspirations?"

"Time will tell. She's applying to law school."

"And does Richard support her?"

"Yes. They share a similar philosophy about affirmative action and equality for women and minorities. He's a Dean of Student Services, and they both are advocates for the Chicano population."

"Why didn't his parents come to the wedding?"

"They are poor, oil field folk. Joan has yet to meet them. Richard grew up very poor, at the end of Route 66 in Bakersfield; they actually lived in a tent. His family lived the

Grapes of Wrath life. Joan's a sucker for the Horatio Alger story; a fierce champion for the underdog."

"Oh."

"She should have married Jim," Nancy said. "I think she's lost her sense of humor; so serious about her mission in life."

The next morning, the wedding couple was gone, but Nancy was throwing a fit! Why? Her three-year-old son had found Robert on the pullout couch in the library, sleeping buck naked with his wedding date, Mary. What a disgrace! Robert didn't think so. He had won the prize for the most alcohol consumed, which also predicted his marriage would be next.

1975

"Do you, Robert Campbell Dickinson, take you, Mary Margaret Whitlock, to be your lawfully wedded wife?" the Justice of the Peace asked in Owatonna, Minnesota.

"I do."

Robert and Mary had eloped. Her parents had taken Mary's five-year-old son, Justin, by her first marriage, for the day. Robert had not told anyone in his family that he was getting married.

1978

"Do you, Scott Campbell, promise to honor, love and cherish Barbara Hart?"

"I do." *Finally!*

They had a lovely wedding in the mountains in Durango, Colorado, where Scott owned a bar and restaurant. Only his immediate family attended. Scott was now thirty-two-years-old, but he was not the last Campbell cousin to be married.

"Do you, Penny Lou Herrmann, take you, David Eden, as your lawfully wedded husband?"

"I do," Penny replied.

They were married in St. Paul. At twenty-eight, Penny was the last Campbell cousin to marry. She was a lovely bride, fine-featured, with her mother's captivating, pale green, iridescent eyes. Those relatives who still lived in the Twin Cities came, except for Rhoda Campbell, who was ninety-five and in a nursing home with that dreaded Alzheimer's Disease.

"I'm surprised to see that Penny's husband looks older," Heather remarked. "She's such a beauty, and he looks, well, middle-aged. How did they meet?"

"They met at *The Minneapolis Star and Tribune*, where they both worked. After Penny's car accident and long recovery, David was her sane savior," her Aunt Jean replied.

"That's a strange word to use for a Jewish guy," Penny's brother Judd said and smiled.

"That may be, but we were all happy to see she rejoined the living," Rhoda Jane added. "David is good at taking care of her needs."

"Just so she hasn't confused love with kindness," her brother Jack said.

Penny eventually went back to school to finish her elementary education degree.

And who else became a teacher? Jay Johnson. He had become ensconced in the Episcopal Church and joined the faculty as an English and drama teacher at an academy similar to his alma mater Breck, in Oklahoma City. A few of his cousins thought he might become a priest, but he did not. Neither did he marry.

Chapter 20

Transformation
September 30, 1982
Minneapolis

Rhoda Hanscome Campbell's name was deeply etched into the granite Campbell headstone right next to James Arthur Campbell's. The permanency of death could not be denied. Her final transformation was most sobering to her family.

It was a sunny, warm day and the colorful leaves were falling at Lakewood Cemetery. How apropos. Rhoda had finally captured, to her deep satisfaction, the glory of these *Indian summer* days on her canvases. Had she intentionally selected such a beautiful day to close her final chapter? Was her spirit intentionally rustling those leaves to summon her family's appreciation, one last time, of the beauty that surrounded them?

Pay attention, children, to the miraculous lessons of nature. How can I ever be alone amid this glory?

She was slowly lowered into the ground in ominous silence, surrounded by her four children and most of her thirteen grandchildren, their spouses and the older great grandchildren. She was one-month shy of her ninety-sixth birthday.

"Is GG really in that box?" one of her great grandchildren asked.

"I think I'll have the same songs at my service," Marie Campbell, Rhoda's oldest and only living friend, remarked. "We used to laugh so when people thought we were related, but as you know, we weren't." She sighed. "We lived too long – Rhoda and I."

And had she? Her children appreciated that Rhoda had made her own decisions in the last few years of her life. Rhoda Jane offered to have her live with them, but she declined. She placed herself in the Edina Care Center at age ninety, gave her car to Rhoda Jane and, year-by-year, graduated herself to higher levels of care.

"I won't have any of you taking my freedoms from me, little-by-little. Let the Care Center make those nasty determinations!" Rhoda laughed.

"I don't know why they call them higher levels of care…they should be lower levels, the last one being lowered in the ground," Pat said, with her dry sense of humor.

A few tears were shed, but most were thankful she had died. Finally. The last four years were not how Rhoda would have liked to live. It seemed unfair and unkind that such a vibrant, larger-than-life matriarch shriveled up, lost her memory, outward dignity and inner sense of self before she exhaled for the last time. Her complete transformation seemed relentless torture, a pinch of life excised slowly, daily.

Had Rhoda divulged her family secret before her death? No. She took it to the grave where she thought it would remain. Perhaps she didn't even remember it herself.

"We are next in line," Jean said to her sisters, breaking the silence.

The Campbell cousins adjourned to Margaret's and Gordon's home overlooking Lake Calhoun. They laughed, reflected on their lives, told Grandma stories and renewed their bonds. Wasn't that the purpose of funerals?

How are your children? Of course, that was the opportunity to brag about their accomplishments. It wasn't really bragging, if you were asked. And the honored reply was: *How wonderful!*

How are you? Of course, that was the opportunity to brag about your accomplishments. And the appreciative response was: *How smart of you!*

How is your husband/wife? Of course, that was the opportunity to brag about their accomplishments. *Oh no! You got divorced? How awful!*

Yes, several Camelot unions had bitten the dust. Heather, Joan and Judd were divorced. Of course, according to each of them, their respective spouses were to blame, but the undercurrent in the family was that there was something terribly wrong with each one of them. They should have bitten the bullet - that was the rule. Yes, except for Jean, their parents remained married, in spite of their many *for worse* years. What was the unspoken message?

Lower your expectations of marriage, please, dear children. Validate us and stay together. Have another drink, inhale your feelings and cigarettes, deny your pain, and, above all else, smile.

How could you be so dissatisfied with the man who owned Valpar Paints, Heather? He gave you everything - wealth, social position and three beautiful children. Well, she gained a large portion of their assets.

If you'd taken better care of your husband and not gotten your doctorate, Joanie, he wouldn't have strayed, and you wouldn't need that stupid Equal Rights Amendment! Well, she lost half of her inheritance to her husband.

So what if Sue isn't the love of your life, Judd. Love isn't everything! Think about your boys. Well, he lost his bookstore.

"Let's drink a toast to Grandma!"

"Hear! Hear!"

And what wasn't said:

Thank you, Grandma, for your joie de vivre!

Thank you, Grandma, for your appreciation of beauty.

Thank you, Grandma, for your appreciation of the finer things in life.

Thank you, Grandma, for teaching us to expect we can fulfill our desires.

Thank you, Grandma, for your generosity.

Most of all, thank you Grandma, for your love.

Cheers to Grandma!

Chapter 21

The Whistleblower
Spring 1988
Irvine, California

"Hello, Thomas? Is this Thomas Hanscome?"

"Yes?"

"I am so pleased to have reached you. Please allow me to introduce myself. I am a cousin of sorts, from nine generations back - back to Salem in 1629, and then nine generations forward again. My name is Robert Hanscom, but friends call me Bob. I have been studying the Hanscom genealogy."

"Well, I'll be. Let me sit down. I need to absorb this. And please, call me Tom."

"I am an attorney from Maine, where your namesake settled in the 1650's."

"My namesake?"

"Yes, the first Thomas Hanscome. Well, at least the first Thomas Hanscome in America. I have been studying our genealogy since I was a teenager, and I finally discovered the missing link of our two Hanscom family branches."

"I have been studying genealogy, too, but of my grandmother's Rhoda Baldwin Cooper Hanscome's family, the Baldwins, Pages and Popes. We seemed to have hit a dead end with our Toronto Hanscome lineage. My wife, JoAnn, and I went to Toronto in the 1950's and met my great Aunt Naomi, who was the last surviving sister of my grandfather, William Kissick Hanscome. She died in 1960 at ninety-six.

"That's quite a long life."

"Indeed, but she had two other sisters who lived as long. Unfortunately, we only found out from my father about our relatives in Toronto after the other aunts had passed. It was a big family secret. I remember my grandfather well. He lived until the end of the war, was close to ninety."

"Secret? Then, you are familiar with the Charleston Nancy Randall - Thomas Hanscome story?" Bob asked.

"No, the secret was, we discovered our Toronto relatives who were never discussed. I've never heard about Nancy Randall and Thomas Hanscome. Naomi talked about her parents coming from Pennsylvania, but said she had never met her grandparents. Why don't you tell me about that missing Charleston love story?"

"It would make a great book or movie. Theirs is a love story between a freed black woman, Nancy Randall, and a wealthy planter, Thomas Hanscome. They are Naomi's and your grandfather's grandparents."

"A slave owner? A freed black woman? I'm not sure I like that news or believe it. You must have the wrong Hanscomes. We have four Hanscome portraits from the early 1800's, and they are all white, as white as one can be. One portrait, of Thomas Hanscome, has sandy-colored hair, a long, pointed nose and ears that stick out, definitely English looking, but my Great Aunt Mur said he came from Scotland."

"Really? How fascinating. He could be Thomas Hanscome, the third generation South Carolinian planter who died in 1831. There are so many Thomas Hanscome's, it gets confusing. And the other portraits?"

"The other three we had refurbished at the Smithsonian when we lived in DC in the 1950's. I'm a retired nuclear physicist and worked for the Department of the Navy for years. There is a woman with reddish brown hair who Aunt Mur identified as her grandmother, Mary Sophia Hanscome and a handsome, black-haired man with a goatee who she said was her grandfather, also Thomas Hanscome. The third portrait is of a James, who according to Aunt Mur moved to New York, a nephew, an uncle or a brother of her grandfather, the Toronto Thomas. Now that I think about it, he does have black, kinky hair, but also the English nose and fair complexion. I am quite skeptical of your information, Bob. I don't think we have any colored people or slave owners in my family," Thomas bristled. *What ridiculous and erroneous information!* "Perhaps you mistake us for another Hanscome family."

"Believe me, there are many Hanscoms, with a variety of spellings, and I have found us all to be related. All of them came from the original Maine line. Thus, I am very excited to find your South Carolina branch, which is quite small in number, just you and your cousins. I don't mean to be a whistleblower and discredit your Aunt Mur's story, but Nancy Randall is the mother of the Toronto Thomas Hanscome. Her colored status, relationship to the planter Thomas Hanscome, and legacy of wealth and slave ownership are all documented in wills I have located in Charleston. She actually changed her name to Ann Hanscome, but of course, legally, they could never be married. I hope this isn't too much of a shock. I thought Naomi would have told you."

Silence.

"I find this hard to believe. Yes, Aunt Naomi did mention that her parents came to Toronto from Pennsylvania, not Scotland, which is Aunt Mur's story, who also alluded to her grandmother as being Argentinian."

Silence.

"I can see this is puzzling to you. I certainly didn't mean to upset the apple cart," Bob said in his most tactful tone. "Why don't I send you the family tree, and we can talk about it again. You are correct that they did live for a few years in Pennsylvania. Perhaps there is an error, but, as I said, I've checked the court documents and the wills."

"Or maybe it is not an error. It is just difficult to grasp. It would explain why my grandfather and Naomi both had darker complexions, as did my father."

"What did your father tell you about his background?"

"Oh, he just laughed and said he had some Indian blood."

"And Naomi?"

"She agreed with my Aunt Mur that her grandmother was from Argentina, a bit dark from Indian influence. She said her own mother, Mary Sophia, had red hair, just like the portrait. I've been staring at those portraits hanging on my wall for years and not given their background much thought."

"Families are interesting, aren't they," Bob said, with a laugh. "I believe Nancy Randall to have been mulatto, thus she could have been quite fair. I'd certainly like to have photographs of your portraits for my collection."

"Let's trade information, then. I'll send you copies of the portraits, and you send me your documentation. I have much to digest, Bob. I still don't believe it."

"I'll see if I can find an Argentinean tie. Many family stories have some basis in fact."

November 1988

    "Dear Bob,

    Thank you for your condolences regarding my
    dear husband, Tom. I know how much he
    appreciated your correspondence and telephone
    calls. It was quite a shock for him to accept his
    Hanscome or, as you spell it, Hanscom lineage,

but it made us both reflect. You see, I come from the original Mayflower stock and it makes me wonder how embellished or truthful my family stories are.

We both reread Alex Haley's book, 'Roots.' All my Tom could say is, 'My God, My God! This all seems so personal to me - now.' He so wished his family had not white-washed their background. Of course, Tom knew their intentions were good. Like all parents they just wanted the best opportunities for their children. Both Tom and I felt fortunate to have lived such fine lives.

As you know, Tom had been ill for awhile before he died, but he passed your genealogy information on to our son, Tommy. Tom also made me promise to send a copy of your genealogy to his cousin, Gordon Campbell in Minneapolis, Rhoda Hanscome Campbell's son. His wife Margaret has always been very curious about the Toronto Hanscome story, and we correspond frequently. Gordon and Margaret can pass your information on to his sisters, Rhoda Jane, Jean and Pat. We have also mailed copies of your family tree to Tom's sister Barb Munger and his two younger brothers, Billy and Jack. They were equally shocked, but welcomed the information. They are still uncertain if it is the truth. This is hard for them to digest.

I was sorry to hear of your divorce, Bob. My best to you with your new life in Massachusetts. Thank you again for your kindness to my husband.

Sincerely,

JoAnn Hanscome

And what were the Campbell reactions to JoAnn's news?

December 1988
Minneapolis

"My mother was a black beauty!" Gordon exclaimed. "Well, I'll be damned." He was grinning from ear-to-ear. "What a hypocrite! What affectation! What pretense!"

"Don't talk like that Gordy," Margaret chastised. "She was like a mother to me, and it is not kind to speak ill of the dead."

"I'm not speaking ill of her, just speaking the truth, which for all her higher than mighty morality, she apparently had difficulty doing."

"She had good reason. She was trying to protect us all," Jean said, also with a huge smile. "Nonetheless, I do see the humor. I guess we never truly know someone."

Margaret Campbell had called a meeting of the Minnesota Hanscome cousins. Barbara Hanscome Munger and her brother William Dixon Hanscome both lived in Minneapolis. Their brother John Baldwin Hanscome lived in Long Beach, California, not far from Tom Hanscome in Irvine.

"What are we going to do with this genealogy information?" Barb asked.

"You mean our family secret?" Jean asked. "I just can't believe Mother got away with her little *white* lie for as long as she did."

"Yes, it was a little *white* lie," added clever Pat, also with a grin, "but Grandpa, Aunt Mur and Uncle Will were also complicit. Her commands to *Stay out of the sun, Pat* now make sense. I just can't stop smiling. What a different side of our mother. I think I even like her better."

"What I can't believe," Barb said, "is why Tom and JoAnn never suspected a colored link? They visited Great Aunt Naomi several times in Toronto. She must have been of fairer complexion than our grandpa."

"Perhaps even lighter than I am." Pat laughed.

"I can't believe it. All the years we were growing up, we actually had living aunts. What a shame we weren't able to meet them," Rhoda Jane said.

"I didn't think you could choose your family, but our omnipotent mother apparently did. I'm still in shock," Gordon added. "Does anyone else need a stiff drink?"

"I knew about Dad's aunts and uncles," Billy Hanscome said. "My father told stories about his youth and visiting his grandparents in Toronto, but only when we were older. He also told me about his Uncle Harry who was an artist, like your mom. I just assumed you knew, too, but then the last time we saw each other was at your mom's funeral. Let's see, Aunt Rhoda died six years ago."

"We promised to get together, but we just don't. I didn't even hear about Tom's death, until today. I have great memories of Tommy," Rhoda Jane said, sadly. "We had so much fun. He was young, only seventy-four. I'm sure you miss your brother."

"And Tommy is younger than I am," Gordon said. "Death and taxes are the only certainties in life. Now, I'll add lies as the third certainty."

"I still can't get used to Tom's passing," Barb said, ignoring her cousin Gordon. "It's like a part of my childhood died."

"So, what are we going to do with mother's secret?" Pat asked, always cutting to the quick of issues. "That's why you invited us, Margaret, isn't it?"

"Yes. Tom gave Bob Hanscom's genealogy to their son, before he passed, and JoAnn mailed a copy to me," Margaret explained. "I thought I would wait until we had a chance to meet to see what you want to do."

"For heaven's sake, let's have no more silly secrets. I can hardly wait to tell Jack, Shelly and my granddaughter. Danielle should know she's not the only brown person in our family. She's always thought her dad was pure white. And John will be dumbfounded, but he'll adjust. This is 1988. I'm sure Tom's California granddaughters found it interesting, no big deal," Pat said.

"Yes, my nieces actually thought it was *neat*," Billy said.

"If being mulatto is so *neat*, so desirable, why are we all laughing about this? Would we be laughing if we had English royalty in our lineage?" Rhoda Jane asked. "No, we'd all be puffed up, feeling more elite than Mother made us feel. This humor is a poor way of handling our own prejudices. Remember yours, Gordon, when Jack married Shelly?"

"Yes, I do. That's why I'm smiling, Rhoda Jane. I actually wanted to disinherit Jack from our colored family! Quite ironic, isn't it? It's nice to think that now my grandchildren might be able to use affirmative action to their advantage, get a job or maybe even a scholarship."

"Stop it, Gordon. Stop it!" Margaret said. "Rhoda Jane is right."

"I suppose laughter and jokes are better than ridicule. I know Wesley will not like this news. We just had our 50th wedding anniversary - and thank you all for coming. In retrospect, the past few years of our marriage have been the most harmonious. I don't want to tell him – he is so racist. He'd have to replace his *half-breed* diatribe with even worse phrases for me. We're all in our seventies, except for Pat. Let's just honor our mother's wishes, and let it be. It was so long ago, so many generations ago. Our children all look more Scottish than anything," Rhoda Jane said, with her unique ability to smoothe things over. The truth was, she hated conflict more than anything.

"I agree with Rhoda Jane," Gordon said. "Divulging this information, if it is true, serves no purpose. But remember, if you tell Wesley, and he wants to divorce you, tell him the money he's been living on is yours."

"I agree with Gordon and Rhoda Jane," Jean said. "Why bother? Patty likens our mother to a queen. I don't want to cast any aspersions on our mother, tarnish Patty's memories of a fine lady."

"Why should this tarnish anyone's view of our mother? This information helps me view her in a more humane way, Jean. She was not perfect; she simply lied. Who hasn't? What are you Hanscomes going to do?" Pat asked of her cousins. "Certainly, you cannot uphold the lies of the past when your brother has told his whole family?"

"I think I will go the truth route. What do you think, Billy?" Barbara asked.

"I agree," Billy said, with a smile. "However, you Campbells do what you want. I just think that the *black* cat's out of the bag, and it's only a matter of time before all our kids will know."

"I'd prefer to continue Mother's sin of omission," Rhoda Jane said. "Pat, you do what you want. Our kids hardly ever see each other. They're all scattered to the winds. What about you, Margaret? What do you think?"

"This is your family," Margaret said. "I agree with Pat, Barb and Billy that truth is usually the best way to go, but do we really know what the truth is? I think I'll write some letters to Toronto and see if I can find out more information. I'd like conclusive proof. We're just taking a stranger's word that Grandpa's grandmother was Nancy Randall, a mulatto freedwoman. I'd like to see the wills. Until then, I'm not going to tell my children."

That was the last meeting of the Hanscome cousins. All left in amazement, some chuckling, some smiling and a few worried. No policy on *The Truth* was ever formulated. No one contacted the whistleblower, Bob Hanscom, to thank him for his discovery.

June 1991
San Luis Obispo, California

"Do you feel any different, now that you've graduated, Danielle?" her Grandmother Pat Herrmann asked. Jack, Shelly and Pat all flew out to California to see her graduate from Cal Poly.

"I feel just the same, Grandma. No lightning bolt of wisdom has struck me, but I do feel proud of my accomplishment. There is something I want to tell you. I am very interested in a job offer in Atlanta."

"I had hoped you would come back to St. Paul," Shelly said, disappointed.

"For once, your mother and I are in agreement," Jack added. Shelly and Jack had been divorced for only two years, but they tried to celebrate their daughter's milestones with civility.

"I want a new beginning, Mom. Atlanta has great job opportunities for blacks. Educated minorities in Minnesota stand out like a sore thumb. I'd like to be in a majority, for once."

"I still don't know why you call yourself black, when you're half white," Pat said.

"Probably even more than half, given the white in my family." Shelly smiled. "Most blacks have lots of white in them. I have a great uncle who passed for white and was on the St. Paul police force. But we've gotten rid of the measuring stick, the percentage of this and that. It used to be the whiter a Negro was, the better he or she was, like differentiating between a house slave and a field slave. There was a pecking order that divided us. Black is beautiful has united us. We fight discrimination together. We're all African-American."

"Why not just garden variety American?" Pat asked. "Why not focus on the similarities? We are going to have difficulties as a nation if we keep noticing the differences, like the Hatfields and McCoys. Soon we'll be shooting each other."

"That's ridiculous, Mother," Jack said. "This is the 90's."

"After true equality comes, perhaps we can be one," Shelly agreed. "We're not there yet."

"If the black separatist stuff continues, equality will never happen." Pat disagreed. "Jews separate themselves from the majority, and people distrust and discriminate against them, in part, because of their aloofness. This dilemma is a double-edged sword – maintain a proud cultural or religious identity or assimilate. In our era, the immigrants could hardly wait to assimilate. Be American, WASPish, if not a bonafide WASP. Now, you want to be African-American. I can hardly keep up with all the proper terminology."

"What would you have Danielle call herself?" Shelly asked. "Mulatto? That is out-of-date and derogatory."

"I'd like you, Danielle, to call yourself my granddaughter and to be your own person," Pat said and laughed. "Would you consider me black, if you learned I had an African ancestor?"

"But we don't, Mother," Jack said.

"Oh, yes, we do. I just recently discovered our family secret."

"Really!" Jack, Shelly and Danielle replied in unison. Then the light went on in Jack's eyes.

"I see. Your Grandfather Hanscome was not Indian at all. He was black!" Jack had a huge smile. "Amazing!"

"His birth certificate says *White*, but he wasn't, not totally, maybe three-fourths white, maybe less. The Hanscome's had a big 'M', not for Minnesota, but 'M' for mulatto in the 1850 census in Pennsylvania. My great grandparents became white in Toronto."

"Here comes the percentage stick again," Shelly said, "and that dreadful term, mulatto – a hybrid, a mule."

"Yes. So what do you call me? The just one drop makes me what?" Pat asked.

"White, Pat. You are white," Shelly answered with a smile. "But I find this whole story fascinating. It just doesn't fit with the image I have of Grandma Campbell, the elegant WASP matriarch. I'd love to hear the full story."

"And furthermore, the mulatto Hanscomes, African-Americans as we would call them today, were wealthy slave owners."

"No!" all three exclaimed, again, in unison.

"Yes!" Pat said.

"That, I don't find too amusing," Shelly said. "I'd need some proof of that."

"So, listen to my story and decide what you want to do with it," Pat said. And she had a truly captive audience as she drew the Hanscome family tree.

"I think that's despicable, Mother," Jack said. "This whole slave owner story makes me cringe."

"You don't have to condone slavery in order to accept your lineage. I don't believe we are responsible for our ancestors' actions. They lived in another time period, another reality, and I imagine them loving, as well as inhumane. To me, that is the nature of human beings. No one is totally good or evil. That's the hardest part to accept. And we must guard against these continual inhumanities, because they keep repeating in our history. Next time, we Whites could be the slaves," Pat postulated with her tongue-in-cheek humor. "In truth, your, and I should say our, African-American roots are quite varied. I hate to see us adopt the *poor field slave* mentality as our only origin. It's a victim consciousness that no longer serves a purpose. I like to think we may have come from Islamic royalty and wealth in Timbuktu. Our ancestors may have owned slaves in Africa as well as here. But, for certain, we can add wealthy slave owners of all shades to our legacy."

"I don't believe I will ever mention this to anyone," Jack said.

"Then you will live in denial as Grandma did. Yes, deny those wealthy mulattos who loved their families and bought and sold slaves. No one wants to be related to a Nazi either, but many are."

"It just seems wealth rules, and wealth makes right," Jack said. "That's the WASP rationale, isn't it?

"What would you choose if faced with the opportunity to have wealth and whip backs or to grovel and be whipped?"

"Slaves didn't have a choice! I would have been an abolitionist, like the Fortens, not cowards, like the Hanscomes!"

"Perhaps. Or perhaps you would have accepted your parents' circumstances and viewpoints as right and would have chosen to be white, too. You don't have to like your relatives, Jack."

"Perhaps Nancy Randall was raped, taken advantage of by Thomas Hanscome," Danielle said. "That is the most common scenario."

"You can play the story that way, but according to South Carolina history, theirs was a true love story played on the stage of slavery."

"Think of it as an earlier version of your Mom's and my love," Jack offered.

"Really, Jack? I fail to see the parallel, except in the skin tones." Shelly laughed.

What was John Herrmann's reaction? Maybe Pat decided it was not his business to know and simply retreated with Penny to Mackinac Island for her usual summer of tennis and piano duets. Or perhaps, he called Pat demeaning names. Or perhaps, John said he was glad they had separate but equal bathrooms. The Herrmann/Campbell sarcastic humor was, at times, quite sick. Or perhaps, Pat just moved on, went into the world of denial that her mother had carefully taught her and said, *No big deal. I like my tan.*

Chapter 22

We Have to Stop Meeting Like This
September 22, 1991
Walker, Minnesota

"Have some orange juice, Joanie," Rhoda Jane said after she and Joanie discovered Wesley had died during the night. "It's important to get your Vitamin C."

"Are you okay, Mom?" Joan gave her mother a hug, amazed that it was just *life as usual* for her. Perhaps her daily routine would ground her grieving process, steady her for the next hard days and weeks to come. One thing at-a-time.

"Yes, I'm fine. I'll have a little cereal, before I take my bath." But first, she went to the door, looked out over her husband's beloved Leech Lake, a place he'd spent his summers since he was six years old. She yelled for their dog. "Tasha! I wish Tasha would come home."

Joan made no comment, but she had a feeling that old, arthritic Tasha had wondered off to die in the woods. Uncanny, what animals know, she thought. Joan stared at the orange juice, that dreadful, canned concentrate her parents had downed dutifully every morning for fifty years, and decided to drink her coffee and smoke a cigarette as she sat on the couch where she had slept the night before. She looked at her dad, lying so quiet in the hospital bed in the living room. She got up, gently kissed him on his bald head and wondered - *Where have you gone, dear Dad?*

Go home! were his last angry words to her, just last night. He had been crying out in pain, and she had given him a dose of morphine, against his will.

"I want to be alert, not a zombie!"

A battle of wills, that's how Joan characterized their relationship. Had she killed him with that morphine?

"It's too late now," she said and sighed. "I'm sorry, Dad. If you could stand the pain, I should not have stepped in to orchestrate your last day. In truth, you were the tough one. I'm the one who couldn't stand your pain."

She phoned the medical examiner, also his doctor. He had made a house call yesterday and told her what to do *when the time comes*, out of earshot of her mother. Soon, a van arrived for his body. Dad was zipped up in a bag and whisked away, along with the hospital bed. How simply, how quickly, all traces of him were erased, she reflected. The end of a life - efficiently zipped up and hauled away in fifteen minutes.

Joan poured the rest of the morphine down the toilet, before they headed to Walker to pick out his casket.

I guess it's up to me to help Mom plan the funeral. It's okay, it will give me something to do, instead of crying, like the non-essential boiling water for a birth. Actually, I feel relieved, not sad, that your ordeal is over. Good for you, Dad, you finally let go and made it to the other side, wherever that is.

"My sympathies," the mortician said in his practiced, sincere way, as he took Rhoda Jane's elbow and escorted her to a room filled with coffins. "This white satin lining and pillow embossed with pine cones is very North Woods and so soft. Don't you think Wesley would like to rest his head here?"

Before her mother could agree, Joan interrupted, "How much?" followed by, "Dad always mentioned a pine box, Mother. How about the real pine and skip the satin pine cones? He wouldn't want you to spend so much money on a casket."

"Yes, he'd like that plain pine box better," her mother said and sighed.

Where had the time fled? Six months from healthy to dead, from colon cancer to cancer everywhere, in spite of chemo and radiation. What was left of his life was consumed by trips to the doctor. Almost blind from macular degeneration, Rhoda Jane searched for the white line at the edge of the road while she drove. Wes directed her, *Steer a little more to the right, Rhoda Jane.*

That's a marriage, Joan thought with a sigh. *They each had some good parts left to contribute to their joint body. And her last act of love was to help him die.*

Gordon flew Margaret, Pat, John and Jean up the next day in his pontoon plane and landed smoothly on the lake. Jean was recovering from lung cancer. The family was gathering. Mary flew in from Anchorage, Nancy and Dick drove from Kansas City, Susan and Jim from Chanhassen and Robert from Mankato. When it was time for dinner, all the grandkids fought over who got to sit in Grandpa's big-armed chair at the head of the old round mahogany table. They knew the throne of power had been vacated.

"Grandpa's spirit is here, mind your manners," Nancy said, for a little comic relief. "No commotion at the dinner table, or you will be excused." The adults smiled. Yes, Wes was a force to reckon with.

Wesley Adsit Dickinson was buried at Evergreen Cemetery in Walker, Minnesota. He was seventy-eight. The same day, Robert buried Tasha on a bluff overlooking the lake. How fitting.

Jean died in a hospice, attended by Patty, her husband Bob from Madison and Jay from Oklahoma City. Joan visited, but was too late to say goodbye. Jean's bed was empty, and the staff was playing *angel music* to swiftly send Jean's spirit on her way. Gordon and Margaret, Pat and John and Rhoda Jane all sat solidly, shoulder-to-shoulder together at the memorial service.

After the burial at Lakewood Cemetery, the Campbell cousins caught up on their lives in hushed tones at Jean's home.

"We have to stop meeting like this," Jack said.

"I'm afraid this is only the beginning," Heather said.

"It's nice to meet you, Debra." Yes, Jim had divorced and remarried.

And where was Judd's new wife, Linda? Not present. Was he getting divorced again?

"We are next," Nancy said to her cousins.

"Let's toast to our long lives," Jack chortled, raising his glass high.

"And let's pray my mother is enjoying heaven," Jay said and smiled.

"Hear! Hear! Here's to Jean and Wesley, leading the way!" Patty said.

"We've got to stop smoking, Judd," Joan said. "Or, we'll end up like Aunt Jean."

"Yes, one day I will. Maybe tomorrow." But neither one quit.

Why was it so hard to accept their parents would soon all be dead and their lives were more than half over?

Jean Hope Campbell Johnson was seventy-five.

July 1, 1994
Carefree, Arizona

What happened? Gordon had recently been riding his horse,
flying his plane, commuting between Arizona and Minnesota.
Heart disease, passed on from his father JAC, was named the
culprit. Margaret held a memorial service later that year for her
Gordon at The Minnekahda Club, attended by many friends and
family. His ashes were buried in Lakewood Cemetery on a
beautiful summer day.

James Gordon Campbell died in Carefree, Arizona. He was
eighty-one.

February 29, 1996
Edina, Minnesota

Rhoda Jane died, after struggling with life ever since her Wesley
died. What happened? She gave her last ounce of energy caring
for her husband, *a privilege*, she said. She died of everything:
congestive heart failure, strokes, kidney disease, uterine cancer,
stomach cancer, to name the worst. Was it really pneumonia or a
broken heart? She would sing along to *When a Man Loves a
Woman* on the radio and stifle a cry, because tears were not
allowed. No one ever mentioned what a jerk he was to her at
times.

"Joanie, I heard the loveliest birds today!" her eternally
positive mother said.

She was blind, chipper and determined to live, in spite of not
having any stomach to digest her food. Rhoda Jane showed
courage, but to her children, her life looked like torture. Susan's
and Joan's eyes had long ago glazed over from witnessing the
gradual demise of their mother. Every three or four months, they

waited together in the hospital's family waiting room for her to survive another surgery.

"We have to stop meeting like this," Susan said.

Rhoda Jane was so special, she had two memorial services, one in Minneapolis at her old St. Luke's Episcopal Church and one in Walker. And she was buried twice, or almost twice. The family waded through deep snow to the gravesite, and the minister began the 23rd Psalm, *The Lord is my Shepherd, I shall not want...*

"Stop!" Joan yelled. "This is the wrong place. Dad is over there, next to the tree!" And he was, but of course all the cemetery markers were hidden in high, February snow drifts. Two days later, they had thawed the correct grave site, dug the hole and lowered her casket.

"Rhoda Jane always had a hard time leaving any party," one of her son-in-law's joked.

"Dad is rubbing his bald head and smiling," Mary said.

"Yes," Robert added. "Can't you get anything right, Rhoda Jane?" Yes, it was cold outside, but the comic relief warmed their spirits.

She was fun, receptive, bright, artistic, thoughtful, humble, non-judgmental, loving and kind. She smiled and laughed her way through life, just as her mother, Rhoda, had taught her. No wonder everyone liked her.

Rhoda Jane Campbell Dickinson was just shy of being eighty-one.

June 22, 2001
Minneapolis

John Alvin Herrmann's memorial service was held at Becketwood in Minneapolis, just across the Mississippi River from his beloved St. Paul. He was eighty-five.

It was the saddest of funerals. Why? His sons delivered eulogies that roasted rather than toasted their father. Joan and Susan cringed in their pew. Hopefully, this nasty send-off was necessary before Jack and Judd could begin to forgive their father. Didn't they know that resentments poison the holder, never the transgressor? Joan decided to remember her Uncle John's Secret C.C. Society badges, humor and charming smile.

And Pat Herrmann? Undaunted by her sons' unkind words, she graciously thanked all the friends and relatives who paid their respects to her husband of fifty-nine years.

August 20, 2007
St. Paul

Miriam Patricia Campbell Herrmann died at age eighty-eight, with Jack, Judd and Penny close at hand.

Joan, in town from Florida, called to invite her to lunch with their Aunt Margaret and her second husband, Bill.

"No, she can't come," Judd said when he answered her phone. "She's too busy dying."

Judd had a sense of humor like his mother, dry. So Susan and Joan visited her instead. Susan made Pat the Willmar caramel cinnamon rolls she loved. Pat's eyes were bright, and her spirits high. She didn't look unhappy to be dying.

"Aunt Pat," Joan said. "I want to ask you something."

"Well, it better be quick, I may be dead tomorrow." Pat laughed and Joan smiled.

"I want to know the family secret. Are we Native American, East Indian or what? What was your grandfather's Toronto background? Why the secrecy?"

"Bastards. We are all bastards!" Pat's eyes lit up, and she laughed. "There was no East Indian princess. There was no Hanscome fleet that sailed the world looking for the perfect wife, as your grandmother led you to believe. My grandpa's father got his upstairs Indian maid pregnant and sent Grandpa away with money, bought him off as it were, when Grandpa was a young man. He was a source of embarrassment to his legitimate children…And here we are. Not royalty, but bastards! *Pure half-breeds*, as your father said."

"Really, Pat?"

"Yes, really!"

"I'm so glad I asked you." Joan laughed. "It's a relief to finally know the truth. Thank you, Pat."

Pat was remembered well in her obituary for her "generosity of spirit, endearing frugality, personal warmth and understated sense of humor." Judd must have written that.

January 12, 2013
Scottsdale, Arizona

Margaret Fuge Campbell Wearly died at age ninety-four.

What a full life. Margaret thought her nieces would abandon her when she remarried, but who could abandon an aunt of a lifetime? Her eyes could twinkle as fast as she talked, and her second husband, Bill, was as charming as Gordon. Her children, Heather, Jim and Scott, gave her an August memorial weekend tribute that also served as a family reunion for the Campbell cousins. First, a Friday night dinner cruise on Lake Minnetonka, followed by a luncheon the next day. And where was that held? The Minnekahda Club, of course!

Chapter 23

"If You Don't Like Something, Just Deny It!"
Rhoda Hanscome Campbell
Fall 2013
Anna Maria Island, Florida

What a relief to finally have the mystery solved. Was Pat's deathbed recollection, as Walter Cronkite would say - *The end of the story?* No, oh no, it was not. Apparently, Pat had received a large dose of her mother's ability to deny the truth.

Email from Jim Campbell:
November, 2013

Dear cousins,

Remember being told we were Indian? Messing around with the Family Tree maker on Ancestry, I managed to connect with a woman who has the answers. Turns out our great great great Grandmother was a black named Nancy Randall and a slave.

The 1850 census shows the Hanscomes as mulatto. We are 1/32 black.

Jim

Email from Mary Dexter:

Don't you remember when I told you all at Aunt Margaret's memorial luncheon that Adam had made the same discovery? You all laughed when I told you he sent his sister Michelle a mahogany birthday card. He deserves some credit for his research.

Love,
Mary

Email from Joan Dickinson:

What happened to Aunt Pat's story? She looked me directly in the eye, just weeks before she died, laughed and divulged her truth! Perhaps she just wanted to be Indian; she certainly didn't seem demented. Perhaps she promised my mother not to disclose the truth. I am amazed as I look at the family tree Jim sent. Aunt Margaret had this same family tree from Bob Hanscom in her possession since the 1980s. Why didn't our parents tell us about our lineage? Apparently, they felt the family secret was worth keeping. How ridiculous!

I sat down as thoughts raced through my mind: *Grandma, Grandma, Grandma! Who were you, my loving Grandma? A liar, a hypocrite, a racist? And, even more important, who am I? I'm black, not Indian, black. I want to be part Indian, and it's gone.*

I stood up. I looked in the mirror, and I said it again. *I'm black.* I looked at my black pupils in my white eyeballs. And I said that every day for several weeks. *I'm black.*

What was the result of my intentional consciousness raising? I came face-to-face with my own brand of racism. Yup, I was a white liberal, who denied any prejudice. I knew I would have puffed up if I'd discovered I was English royalty. But images of poor ignorant slaves and scumbag slave owners, both white and black slave owners, were not visions of my ideal relatives.

Comments from my family:

I can sing and I can dance. Ha, ha, ha.
I wonder if I can apply for reparations. Ha, ha, ha
You know, this information may be suspect. I don't know if I believe it.
I don't know why my mother told Shelly and me but no one else, not even Penny and Judd. I thought you all knew! Courtesy of Jack Herrmann, may he rest in peace.
How could our parents have hid this from us?
Of course, I'm not prejudiced.

Did I raise my consciousness, integrate my soul, end my prejudice or that prejudice we inhale via osmosis just living in America? I don't know. I do feel different and act different. When I pass a brown face, I directly meet their eyes, smile and wonder - *Are we related?* When I recently filled in a blank for ethnicity, I checked them all and smiled.

My Hanscome ancestors need not define me. I am not responsible for them. I don't love their evil doings, but they gave me my most precious life. I own them as mine. I did my best to understand their motivations and find their humanness. They are reminders to me that the evils in society can and do happen again. I wonder how the grandchildren of Nazis feel? In my case, just a few relatives away from slavery, I intend to be vigilant.

I have a lot of wants these days, thank you, Grandma, for teaching me that wanting is okay, just not at other's expense.

I want to get past the labels, colors and see only equality.

I want to applaud the oneness of humanity and embrace our enriching differences.

I want to own, not deny, the atrocities of our ancestors – slavery, genocides, holocausts – by recognizing they stem from simple, daily feelings of superiority.

I wanted to document the WASP ideal culture that still poisons minds, yes, in 2019, and insidiously permeates our American cultural and political system. I want my Hanscome Trilogy to make a difference.

My grandmother always implied we were the cream of the crop, the top of the heap, better than others. Yes, of the best family. Superior in character. Light of face. Not common. Special. WASP. White Anglo-Saxon Protestant.

What's the harm in that?

Here is my secret. It is very simple. It is only with the heart that one can see rightly. What is essential is invisible to the eye.

The Little Prince - Antoine de Saint-Exupéry

William Kissick Hanscome and James Arthur Campbell holding Heather
Campbell, two, and baby Susan Dickinson, circa 1942

William Kissick Hanscome, 1942, age 87

Muriel Hanscome and her father William Kissick Hanscome, 1942

Dickinsons, 1035 Hill Road, Willmar MN, 1950
Upper left: Nancy (7), right: Joan (5), Center: Robert (6 mos.), Susan (9)

Secret Campbell Cousin Society Pin
Christmas gift from John Herrmann, 1952

Joan Adsit Dickinson, age 9, 1954

Hanscom(b)e Genealogy

First Generation:

Children of Thomas Hanscombe and Katherine Alcock Bedfordshire, England:

> 1. Joan Hanscombe b.1597? England d.1670? Salem, Massachusetts Bay Colony m. 7/29/1627 Richard Claydon b.1594 England d.1640's Salem, Massachusetts Bay Colony.
> 2. Thomas Hanscombe b.1618 England d.1696? Kittery ME m. 5/16/1664 Ann (Downing?) b.1646 Kittery ME d.1719? Maine.

Second Generation:

Child of Joan Hanscombe and Richard Claydon:

> 1. Katherine b.1627? England d.1629 on ship Talbot crossing to Salem.

Children of Thomas Hanscome and Ann (Downing):

> 1. Thomas Hanscome b.10/17/1666 Kittery ME d. 2/1713 Kittery ME m. Alice Rogers. Five children. After her death m. Tamsen Gowell Sheares. Six children.
> 2. John Hanscome b. 9/15/1668 Kittery ME d.? No known marriages or children. He was a mariner.
> 3. Alice Hanscome b. 3/12/1671 Kittery ME d.? m. 1690 John Mederille who abandoned Alice after the birth of her first child by Black Will, a slave. Both were flogged for fornication. Black Will was the first slave to buy his freedom and

settle in Maine. Alice had two more children, no identified fathers. Her first child, William Black Jr. b. 1690 Kittery ME d.? m. Elizabeth Turbot b.? Kittery ME d.? Settled Bailey's Island. Several children.
4. Samuel Hanscome b. 4/10/1675 Kittery ME d. young adult?
5. Job Hanscome b. 1679 Kittery ME d. 9/3/1779 Saco ME m. Mary Gowell b.? Kittery ME d.? Ten children.
6. Moses Hanscome b. 1680 Kittery ME d. Cape Elizabeth ME between the dates of 1748 and 1760 m. Hannah Rackliff b.? Kittery ME d.? Seven children.
7. Aaron Hanscom(b)e b. 1685 Kittery ME d. 1760 John's Island SC m. name unknown Two sons.

For further generations of New England Hanscoms consult Robert Hanscom's extensive genealogy on Face book: Family Hanscom Reunites.

Third Generation: South Carolina Branch

Children of Aaron Hanscom(b)e and unnamed wife:

1. Thomas Hanscome b.1723 John's Island SC d. 1787 John's Island SC m. Elizabeth, unknown surname b.? d. before husband Thomas. SC Assemblyman 1785-1786.
2. Moses Hanscome b.1730 John's Island SC d. 11/1771 South Edisto plantation at Ferguson's Ferry, St. Bartholomew's Parish SC m. 6/2/1761Mary Brown b? d. after husband Moses.

Fourth Generation:

Children of Thomas Hanscome and Elizabeth, unknown surname:

1. Ann Hanscome b. 1757 John's Island SC d. between 1777 and 1786 John's Island SC m. 4/24/1777 Col. Robert Rivers b. 1725? d. between 1777 and 1786. John's Island planter. No children.
2. Thomas Hanscome, Jr. b. 1760 John's Island SC d. 12/29/1831 Charleston SC. Never married. He challenged SC society by having six children with Nancy Randall, his colored mistress of twenty-five years. b. 1792 SC d. between 1850 - 1865 Charleston SC?
3. Mary Hanscome b. 1763 John's Island SC d. 2/1783 m. 1782? John Geyer, John's Island planter. No children.
4. James Hanscome b. 1774 John's Island SC d. 1812 Charleston SC. No will, marriage or children recorded. He was a South Carolina Assemblyman 1800-1801, physician and planter.

Children of Moses Hanscome and Mary Brown:

1. Thomas Hanscome b.1760's Ferguson's Ferry, South Edisto SC d.? m. Elizabeth Jenkins b. 1786 John's Island SC d. 1850? No children. Widow Elizabeth Jenkins Hanscome m. Paul Chaplin Grimball b. 1788 John's Island Longwood Plantation d. 1864. Several children.
2. Moses Hanscome b. 1760's Ferguson's Ferry, South Edisto SC d. after 1787 m.? Children unknown.

3. John Hanscome b. after father Moses' death in 1771, Ferguson's Ferry, South Edisto SC d. after his Uncle Thomas in 1787. Children unknown. His Uncle Thomas Hanscome's will provided for John's care until age 21. Moses' two older sons were not named in their Uncle Thomas Hanscome's will, but were included in their father's will.

Fifth Generation:

Children of Thomas Hanscome and Nancy Randall:

1. Joseph Hanscome b. 7/24/1812 Charleston SC d. 8/4/1838 Charleston SC m. 1834 Mary, unknown surname. d. 1876? Philadelphia PA. Joseph died of fever as did their toddler daughter, Ann.
In 1845 widow Mary Hanscome traveled with Thomas and Mary Sophia Hanscome to Bucks County PA where she married well-known abolitionist Robert Forten, son of James Forten, wealthy Philadelphia freedman sail maker and businessman. Robert d.1864 Philadelphia PA.
2. Louisa Rebecca Hanscome b. 1815 Charleston SC d.? Charleston SC m. 2/12/1833 William P. DeCosta b. 1808 Charleston SC d. 1873 Charleston SC. William was cotton gin maker and member of Brown Fellowship Society and part of Jewish Community.
3. Elizabeth Sarah Hanscome b. 1817 Charleston SC d. 1877 Toronto Canada m. 1839 John George Garden b. 1812 Charleston SC d. 1880 Toronto Canada. John was the son of the wealthy mulatto Hermitage Plantation owner and Brown Fellowship Society member, John Garden. The

Gardens bought a farm in Bucks County, Warminster PA near brother Thomas, sister-in-law Mary Hanscome (Joseph's widow) and sister Mary Ann Lee and their families in 1845.

4. Mary Ann Hanscome b. Charleston SC 1819 d. Toronto Canada? She purchased the family St. James' Cemetery burial lots in 1877, but not buried there. m. 1840 John Lee b. 1821 Charleston SC d.? Canada. John was son of Eliza, restaurateur, and John Lee, tailor, also Charleston Brown Fellowship Society members.

5. Thomas Hanscome b. 1821 Charleston SC d. 1894 Toronto Canada m. 1841 Mary Sophia Inglis b. Charleston SC 1823 d. 1899 Toronto Canada. Mary Sophia was daughter of Martha Sophia and Thomas Inglis, wealthy Charleston barbershop owner, Brown Fellowship Society member and son of white plantation owner Thomas Inglis.

6. James Randall Hanscome b. 1822 Charleston SC d. after 1898, possibly Charleston, Toronto or New York m. 1841 Serena Elizabeth Walker, wealthy mulatto slave and slave owner, daughter of wealthy white planter John Walker and his slave mistress Ann Jones Walker, another famed Charleston love liaison similar to Thomas Hanscome and Nancy Randall. John Walker was unable to manumit his mistress or any of their eight children. Serena divorced James before 1844. James m. 1856? widow Harriet (Hetty) E. Geary b. 1816 Savannah GA. James divorced Hetty. James m. 1865? Charleston SC Emma, unknown surname. In 1872 James was Charleston police officer.

No further information for Moses Hanscome and Mary Brown lineage.

Sixth Generation:

Child of Joseph Hanscome and Mary, unknown surname:

1. Ann Hanscome b. 1835? Woodland Plantation SC d. 1837 or 1838 Woodland Plantation SC.

Children of Mary Hanscome (Joseph's widow) and Robert Forten:

1. Wendell Phillips Forten b. 1847 Bucks County PA d. 1860 London, England.
2. Edmund Quincy Forten b. 1849 Bucks County PA d. after 1875 England?

Children of Louisa Rebecca Hanscome and William P. DeCosta:

1. Joseph Hanscome DeCosta b. before 1841Charleston SC d.?
2. Five other unnamed children.

Children of Elizabeth Sarah Hanscome and John George Garden: (St. James' Cathedral Cemetery source: nine children.)

1. Daniel Garden b. 1840 Charleston SC d.?
2. Walter Garden b. 1842 Charleston SC d.?
3. Amanda Garden b. 1844 Charleston SC d. 1911 Toronto Canada.
4. Ellen Garden b. 1846 Warminster, Bucks County PA d.? Toronto Canada.
5. Joel D. Garden 1847 or 1850 Warminster, Bucks County PA d. 1894 Toronto Canada.
6. Johanna Garden b.1848 Warminster, Bucks County PA d.? Toronto Canada.
7. Thomas Garden b.1850? Warminster, Bucks County PA d.? m.? Toronto wife unknown, but he

is listed as father of two infant daughters buried in Hanscome St. James' Cemetery plot.

1) Sadie Garden b. 1883 Toronto Canada d. 1885 Toronto Canada.

2) Helena Frances Garden b. 1885 Toronto Canada d. 1886 Toronto Canada.

8. Iona Butler Garden b. 1852 Warminster PA d. 1876 Toronto Canada.

9. Helena Garden b. 1853 Warminster PA d. 1918 Toronto Canada m.? Gallagher.

Children of Mary Ann Hanscome and John Lee:

1. John Drayton Lee b. 1844 Charleston SC d.?
2. No other Lee children recorded. Mary Ann Hanscome purchased St. James' Cemetery plots in 1877, but her last name of Lee was not used in those records.

Children of Thomas Hanscome and Mary Sophia Inglis:

1. Alice Constantia Hanscome b. 1842 Charleston SC d.1929 Toronto Canada. Unmarried.
2. Edwin Hanscome b. 1843 Charleston SC d. 1845 Warminster PA.
3. Martha Sophia Hanscome b. 1845 Philadelphia PA d. 1906 Toronto Canada. Unmarried.
4. Anna Louisa Hanscome b. 1846 Warminster PA d. 1943 Toronto m. 1888 William Philip Marston b. 1821 d. 1901. William had child(ren) by first marriage. Anna Louisa no children.
5. Virginia Emeline Hanscome b. 1849 (twin) Warminster PA d. 1929 Toronto Canada. Unmarried.

6. Eugenia Angeline Hanscome b. 1849 (twin) Warminster PA d. 1942 Toronto Canada. Unmarried.
7. William Kissick Hanscome b. 1856 Toronto Canada d. 1945 Minneapolis MN m.1880 Toronto Rhoda Baldwin Cooper b. 1844 England d. 1919 Minneapolis MN. Rhoda Cooper was a widowed school teacher who moved to Toronto with her Baldwin family from England.
8. Thomas Henry Hanscome b. 1861 Toronto Canada d. 1891 Toronto Canada. Artist. Unmarried.
9. Naomi Helena Hanscome b. 1864 Toronto Canada d. 1960 Toronto Canada. Unmarried.
10. Arthur Randall Hanscome b.1866 Toronto Canada d.? Vancouver Canada? m. unnamed English woman in Vancouver Canada. No known children.

Child of James Randall Hanscome and Serena Walker:

1. Sarah Hanscome b. 1841 Charleston SC m.? d.?

Child of James Randall Hanscome and Harriet Geary:

1. Peter Hanscome b. 1858 Savannah GA d. 1916 Charleston SC m. Phoebe DeLyons b.? d.? Charleston SC.

Children of James Randall Hanscome and Emma, unknown surname:

1. Perhaps three or four unnamed children.

Seventh Generation:
No further lineage information for seventh generation Hanscomes, other than William Kissick Hanscome, below.

Children of William Kissick Hanscome and Rhoda Baldwin Cooper:

1. William Thomas Hanscome b. 1880 Toronto Canada d. 11/20/1964 Minneapolis MN m. 1912 Ethel Dixon b. 11/4/1881 MN d. 10/23/1969 Minneapolis MN.
2. Muriel Hanscome b. 1/1884 Minneapolis MN d. 12/10/1961 Minneapolis MN Never married. No children.
3. Rhoda Hanscome b. 10/30/1886 Minneapolis MN d. 9/30/1982 Minneapolis MN m. 5/22/1911 James Arthur Campbell b. 1884 Minneapolis (Camden) MN d. 7/5/1954 Minneapolis MN.
4. Robert Hanscome b.? Minneapolis MN d. as young child. Minneapolis MN.

Eighth Generation:

Children of William Thomas Hanscome and Ethel Dixon:

1. Thomas Dixon Hanscome b. 7/2/1914 Austin MN d. 11/01/1988 Irvine CA m. 11/8/1940 JoAnn Elizabeth Chandler b. 5/27/1920 Glidden IA d. 2/27/2012 CA.
2. Barbara Jane Hanscome b. 11/25/1916 Austin MN d. 2/13/2005 Richfield MN m. Detroit MI 7/13/1942 Edward Allen (Jack) Munger b. 8/27/1907 Anaconda MT d. 9/20/1983 MN.
3. William Dixon Hanscome b. 5/29/1925 Minneapolis MN d. 12/09/2011 Anoka MN m.

7/7/51 Donna Mae Sundberg b. 5/26/1930 Robbinsdale MN d. 5/11/2012 MN.
4. John Baldwin Hanscome b. 1928 Minneapolis MN d. 1994 Santa Maria CA m. 9/9/1948 Marjorie Ann Timm b. 1927 Omaha NE d. 2012 San Francisco CA.

Children of Rhoda Hanscome and James Arthur Campbell:

1. James Gordon Campbell b. 6/08/1912 Minneapolis MN d. 1/06/1994 Scottsdale AZ m. 12/29/1939 Minneapolis MN Margaret Fuge b. 11/23/1918 Minneapolis MN d. 1/12/2013 Scottsdale AZ.
2. Rhoda Jane Campbell b. 4/17/1915 Minneapolis MN d. 2/29/1994 Minneapolis MN m. 6/23/1939 Minneapolis MN Wesley Adsit Dickinson b. 12/6/1913 Hastings MN d. 9/22/1991 Walker MN.
3. Jean Hope Campbell b. 8/27/1917 Minneapolis MN d. 2/17/1992 Richfield MN m.1939 Minneapolis MN William Gage Donald b. 1915 Pittsburgh PA d. 1960's, div. 1945 m. 1950 Edina MN Clifford Gardner Johnson b. 1/2/1918 Valley City ND d. 1978 VA div. 1962.
4. Miriam Patricia Campbell b. 4/9/1919 Minneapolis MN d. 8/20/2007 St. Paul MN m. 8/25/1942 Minneapolis MN John Alvin Herrmann b. 6/29/1916 St. Paul MN d. 6/20/2001 Minneapolis MN.

Ninth Generation:

Children of Thomas Dixon Hanscome and JoAnn Elizabeth Chandler:

1. Thomas Chandler Hanscome b. 07/02/1943 Washington DC m. 11/18/1966 Sherry Lee Maxwell b. 11/17/1945 Visalia CA div. 8/1/1971 m. 8/25/1973 Margaret Lee McDonald b. 3/11/1948 Fayetteville NC.
2. Cheryl Dixon Hanscome b. 2/5/1948 Washington DC d. 7/27/1966 Santa Ana CA. No marriage or children.

Child of Barbara Jane Hanscome and Edward Allen (Jack) Munger:

1. Edward Allen Munger, Jr. (Ned) b. 4/3/1948 Minneapolis MN m. 7/15/1972 Hopkins MN Jeanne Ruth Stevenson b. 1/18/1949 Grand Island NE.

Children of William Dixon Hanscome and Donna Mae Sundberg:

1. Craig William Hanscome b. 5/20/1953 Minneapolis MN m. 8/31/1974 Marilyn Ruth Phillips b. 9/ 5/1953 Toledo OH.
2. Geniene Marie Hanscome b. 2/14/1957 Robbinsdale MN m. 7/30/1983 Chetek WI Peter Allen Haack b. 2/17/1957.
3. Ronald Edward Hanscome b. 7/4/1960 Robbinsdale MN m. 1982 Elk River MN Crystal Schlosser b. 2/17/1957 div. 1987 m. 7/23/1988 Christine Eve Meinhardt b. 12/24/1964.

Children of John Baldwin Hanscome and Marjorie Ann Timm:

1. Jann Melanie Hanscome b. 1955 Minneapolis MN Unmarried. No children. Physician in Petaluma CA.

2. Barbara Christine Hanscome b. 1964 in Long Beach CA m. Matthew Todd Mumper b. 1963 Hayward CA.

Children of James Gordon Campbell (Gordon) and Margaret Fuge:

1. Heather Campbell b. 10/19/1940 Minneapolis MN m. Eden Prairie MN 1962 Christopher Angus Wurtele b. 9/24/1934 Minneapolis MN d. 8/30/2017 div. 1976.
2. James Gordon (Jim) Campbell b. 10/17/1942 Minneapolis MN m. 6/18/1964 San Diego CA Carol Lynn McCann b. 7/3/1942 div. 1987 m. 5/23/1991 Duluth MN Debra Lee Oftedahl Smoter b. 12/29/1954.
3. Scott Arthur Campbell b. 6/26/1946 Minneapolis MN m. 1978 Durango CO Barbara Lynn Hart b. 6/17/1952 Wildwood NJ.

Children of Rhoda Jane Campbell and Wesley Adsit Dickinson:

1. Rhoda Susan Dickinson b. 7/03/1941 Willmar MN m. 3/18/1967 Bloomington MN James Eigel Pedersen b. 6/1943 Tyler MN.
2. Nancy Jean Dickinson b. 8/23/1943 Willmar MN m. 6/18/1966 Bloomington MN Richard Raymond Dowell b. 6/6/1944 Minneapolis MN.
3. Joan Adsit Dickinson b. 5/17/1945 Willmar MN m. Bloomington MN 4/21/1973 Richard Allen Laughlin b. 10/18/1938 Bakersfield CA div. 12/29/1979.
4. Robert Campbell Dickinson b. 2/8/1950 Willmar MN m. 9/27/1975 Blooming Prairie MN Mary Margaret Whitlock b. 9/28/1951 Mankato MN div. 9/2000.

5. Mary Jane Dickinson b. 4/03/1953 Willmar MN m. 8/12/1972 Bloomington MN Jerry Dexter b. 9/22/1951 Ft. Collins CO.

Child of Jean Hope Campbell and William Gage Donald:

1. Patricia Donald b. 9/8/1942 Minneapolis MN m. 2/27/1965 Minneapolis MN Robert Ruble b. 10/4/1944Minneapolis MN.

Child of Jean Hope Campbell and Clifford Gardner Johnson:

1. James Richards (Jay) Johnson b. 9/23/1953. Unmarried. No Children.

Children of Miriam Patricia Campbell and John Alvin Herrmann:

1. John Heck (Jack) Herrmann b. 3/5/1944 Minneapolis MN d. 12/2016 St. Paul MN m. 3/1968 St. Paul MN Rachelle (Shelly) Mitchell b. 8/9/1044 div. 1989.
2. Judd Campbell Herrmann b. 6/11/1946 Minneapolis MN m. 1971 Sue Ellingson b. 2/1952 div. 1981 m. 1992 Linda S. Lee div. 1994 m. 2006 Marcia Gage b. 1/26/1955.
3. Penny Lou Herrmann b. 5/16/1954 St. Paul MN m. 1982 St. Paul MN David Eden b. 5/2/1952 div. 2009.

Tenth and Eleventh Generations: (Eleventh Generation Incomplete)

Child of Thomas Chandler Hanscome and Sherry Lee Maxwell:

1. Heather Chandler Hanscome b. 06/06/1970 Newport Beach CA m. 9/30/2000 William Matthew Artukovich b. 11/2/1969 Sierra Madre CA.
1) Barrett Matthew b. 3/26/2011 Newport Beach CA.

Children of Thomas Chandler Hanscome and Margaret Lee McDonald:

1. Jennifer Chandler Hanscome b. 8/6/1974 Cincinnati OH m. 5/10/2015 Robert James Bermudez III b. 10/28/1967 Orange CA.
1) Addison Rose Bermudez b. 5/22/2007 Laguna Hills CA
2) Ashlyn Rachelle Bermudez b. 1/27/2011 Laguna Hills CA.
3) Robert Brandon Bermudez IV b. 1/27/2011 Laguna Hills CA.
2. Kimberly McDonald Hanscome b. 3/30/1978 Newport Beach CA m. 9/28/2003 Keith Frank James Wojciechowski b. 1/6/1971 Patchogue NY.
1) Taylor James Wojciechowski b. 3/6/2001 Newport Beach CA.
2) Tanner Chandler Wojciechowshki b. 11/24/2008 Newport Beach CA.
3. Lindsey Anne Hanscome b. 6/19/1980 Newport Beach CA m. 8/10/2012 Aaron Wesley Lee b. 3/8/1983 Modesto CA.
1) Camryn Mackenzie Lee b. 3/4/2011 Laguna Hills CA.
2) Danielle Anne Lee b. 7/21/2014 Laguna Hills CA.

Children of Edward Allen (Ned) Munger Jr. and Jeanne Ruth Stevenson:

1. Sheila Ann Munger b. 12/5/1967 Kenosha WI
m. Melvin Loveday 04/12/1990 Div. 9/01/1998
m. 10/13/2001 RobRoy McGregor b. 05/16/1965.
    1) Adam Wade Rassmussen b. 2/8/1988 St.
Paul MN.
    2) Emily May Loveday b. 7/1/1990 Fort
Francis, Ontario Canada m. Cameron Block
6/21/2014 Niagara on the Lake, Ontario Canada.
    3) Jered David Loveday b. 4/21/1994 Fort
Francis, Ontario Canada.
    4) Matthew Gerald Loveday b.11/23/1995 Fort
Francis, Ontario Canada.
2. David Ned Munger b. 11/3/1968 Kenosha WI
m. 12/20/1995 Angela Lynn Visage b. 5/2/1971.
    1) Madelyn Grace Munger b. 1/25/1999 Dallas
TX.
    2) Emma Isabella Munger b. 12/18/2001
Dallas TX.
3. Derek John Munger b. 06/22/1980 St. Paul
MN.
4. Stephanie Jeanne Munger b. 9/30/1988 St. Paul
MN.

Children of Craig William Hanscome and Marilyn Ruth Phillips:

1. Joanna Ruth Hanscome b. 4/24/1978 Hicksville
OH.
2. Rachel Marie Hanscome b. 4/5/81
Ferkessedougou, Ivory Coast, West Africa m.
6/3/2006 Willis Gray III Toccoa GA b.
11/21/1979.
    1) Joshua Evan Gray b. 3/10/2013.
3. Daniel Paul Hanscome b. 3/17/1983
Ferkessedougou, Ivory Coast, West Africa m.
8/6/2005 Amy Chrissy Fincher Toccoa GA b.
6/27/1983.

1) David William Hanscome b. 7/12/2012 Birmingham AL.
2) Abigail Jean Hanscome b. 9/25/2014 Birmingham AL.

Children of Geniene Marie Hanscome and Peter Allen Haack:

1. Kelsey Lynn Haack b. 6/4/1987 Anoka MN m. 11/24/2012 Christopher Frank Millette b. 5/4/1983.
2. Collin Matthew Haack b. 6/30/1990 Anoka MN m. 8/13/2015 Katelyn Elizabeth James b. 5/13/1990 Minneapolis MN.
3. Karina Noelle Haack b. 2/17/1993 Anoka MN.

Children of Ronald Edward Hanscome and Christine Eve Meinhardt:

1. Nicolas Blake Hanscome b.7/20/1995 Minneapolis.
2. Ryan William Hanscome b. 9/26/1998 Anoka MN.

Children of Barbara Christine Hanscome and Matthew Todd Mumper:

1. Jackson John Mumper b. 2004 San Francisco CA (twin).
2. William Jeremiah Mumper b. 2004 San Francisco CA (twin).

Children of Heather Campbell and Christopher Angus Wurtele:

1. Christopher Campbell Wurtele b. 1/30/1964 Minneapolis MN.

2. Andrew Lindley Wurtele b. 5/7/1965 Minneapolis MN.
3. Heidi Wurtele b. 12/17/1967 Minneapolis MN m. 2000 Napa CA Caley Castelein div. 2015 m. 5/21/2016 Alex Fisher San Francisco CA.

Children of James Gordon Campbell and Lynn McCann Campbell:

1. James Charles Campbell (Jamie) b. 3/18/1969 Minneapolis MN.
2. Kevin Bryant Campbell (Casey) b. 11/18/1970 Minneapolis MN m. 7/24/2004 Boulder CO Anne Armstrong.
3. Robert Scott Campbell (Bobby) b. 3/18/1976 Edina MN.

Child of Scott Arthur Campbell and Barbara Lynn Hart:

1. Elijah (Eli)Fuge Campbell b. ? Steamboat CO m. 2010 Erin Elizabeth Di Santi b. 3/14/1984

Children of Rhoda Susan Dickinson and James Eigel Pedersen:

1. Ryan Wesley Pedersen b. 3/17/1972 Minneapolis MN m.1992 Chanhassen MN Jordon Greer Dolentz div. 2005.
2. Erik Eigel Pedersen b. 10/17/1975 Minneapolis MN m.11/11/2016 Phoenix AZ Katie Peters.

Children of Nancy Jean Dickinson and Richard Raymond Dowell:

1. Richard Raymond Dowell, Jr. b. 12/30/1970 Minneapolis MN m. Phoenix AZ 8/20/1992 Nichole Anderson b. 2/11/1972.

2. Kelly Rhoda Dowell b. 3/23/1972 Madison WI
m. Kansas City KS 6/7/1997 Chad Ingram b.
2/16/1971 Topeka KS.

Child of Joan Adsit Dickinson:

1. Sarah Adsit Dickinson b. 11/03/1975 Greeley
CO m. 7/11/2008 Boston MA Brian Harry Berejik
b. 1/04/1978 Boston MA.

Children of Robert Campbell Dickinson and Mary Margaret
Whitlock:

1. Justin Friend Johns Dickinson b. 6/22/1971
Mankato MN m. 1990? Stephanie Daunche b.
1974 MN div. 1992?
2. John Wesley Dickinson b. 1/8/1977 Austin
MN.
3. James Robert Dickinson b. 12/16/1977
Mankato MN. m. 2004 Mankato MN Catrina
(Trina) Kote b. 1980 Mankato MN.
4. Robert Whitlock Dickinson (Jake) b. 8/17/1990
Mankato MN.

Children of Mary Jane Dickinson and Jerry Dexter:

1. Adam Wesley Dexter b. 8/26/1980 Apple
Valley MN.
2. Michelle Marie Dexter b. 7/8/1983 Apple
Valley MN m. 2/11/2007 Spokane WA Kevin
Gawenite b. 4/3/1975 div. 2015, m. Joshua Sutton
Spokane WA 8/19/2017.
3. Scott Campbell Dexter b. 5/31/1987 Anchorage
AK m. 2/23/2014 Spokane WA Valentina (Tina)
Romanchuk b. 12/15/1987 Ukraine.

Children of Patricia Donald and Robert Ruble:

    1. Steven Ruble b. 7/9/1966 Minneapolis m. 6/27/1993 Spooner WI Susan Meyer b. 6/18/1967.
    2. Elizabeth (Beth) Ruble b. 11/12/1968 Sioux Falls SD m. 10/28/1999 Ronald Blanchar b. 9/16/1965 Madison WI.

Child of John (Jack) Heck Herrmann and Rachelle (Shelly) Mitchell:

    1. Danielle Herrmann b. 10/2/1970 Lake Tahoe NV m. Jamaica, Trevor Busby b. 1971 TN.

Children of Judd Campbell Herrmann and Sue Ellingson:

    1. Trevis Herrmann b. 7/20/1973 Stillwater MN.
    2. Jaymik Herrmann b. 8/26/76 St. Paul MN 2004 m. Nicole Cervantes.

Child of Penny Lou Herrmann and David Eden:

    1. Max Campbell Eden b. 11/5/1988 Cleveland OH.

Hanscom(b)e Genealogy

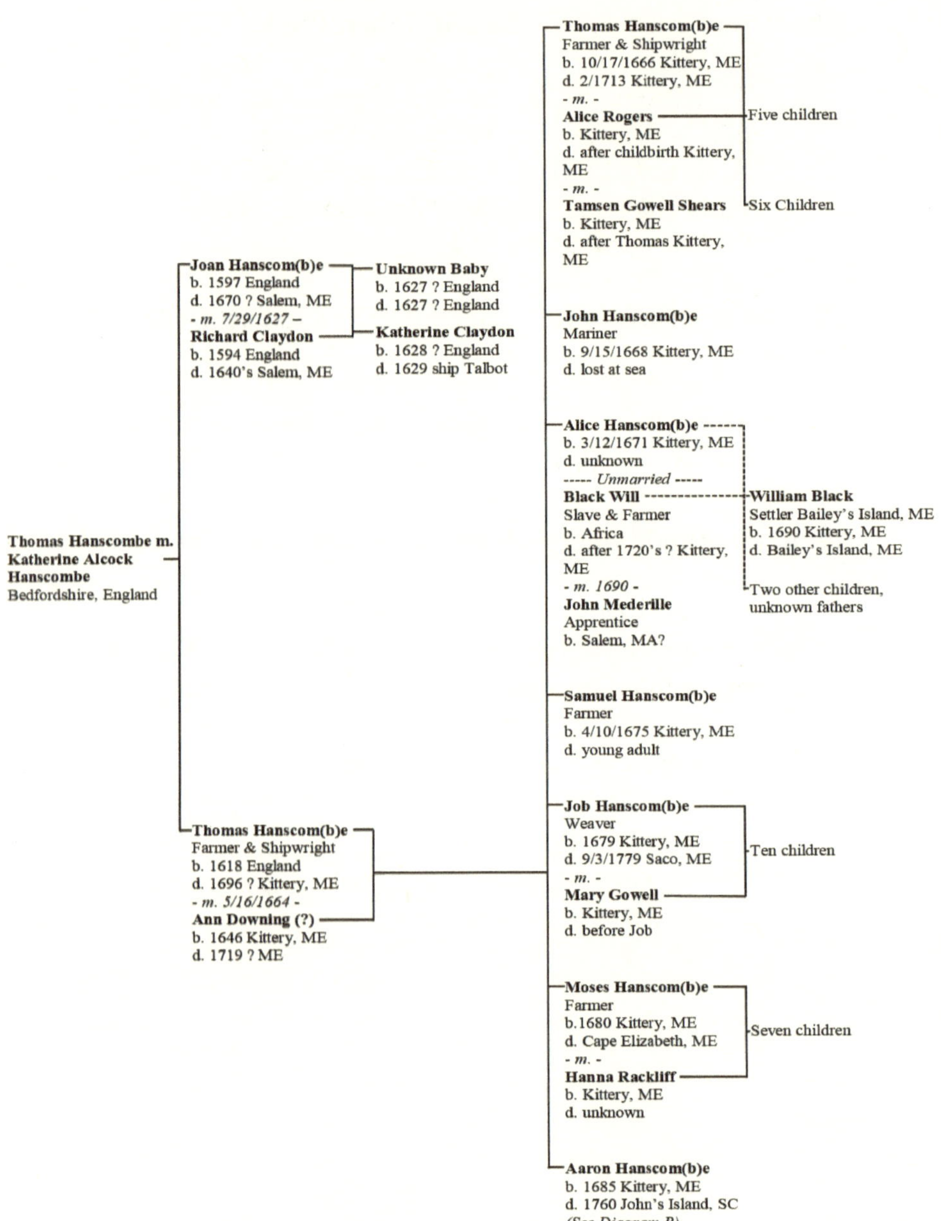

Diagram A

Hanscom(b)e Genealogy

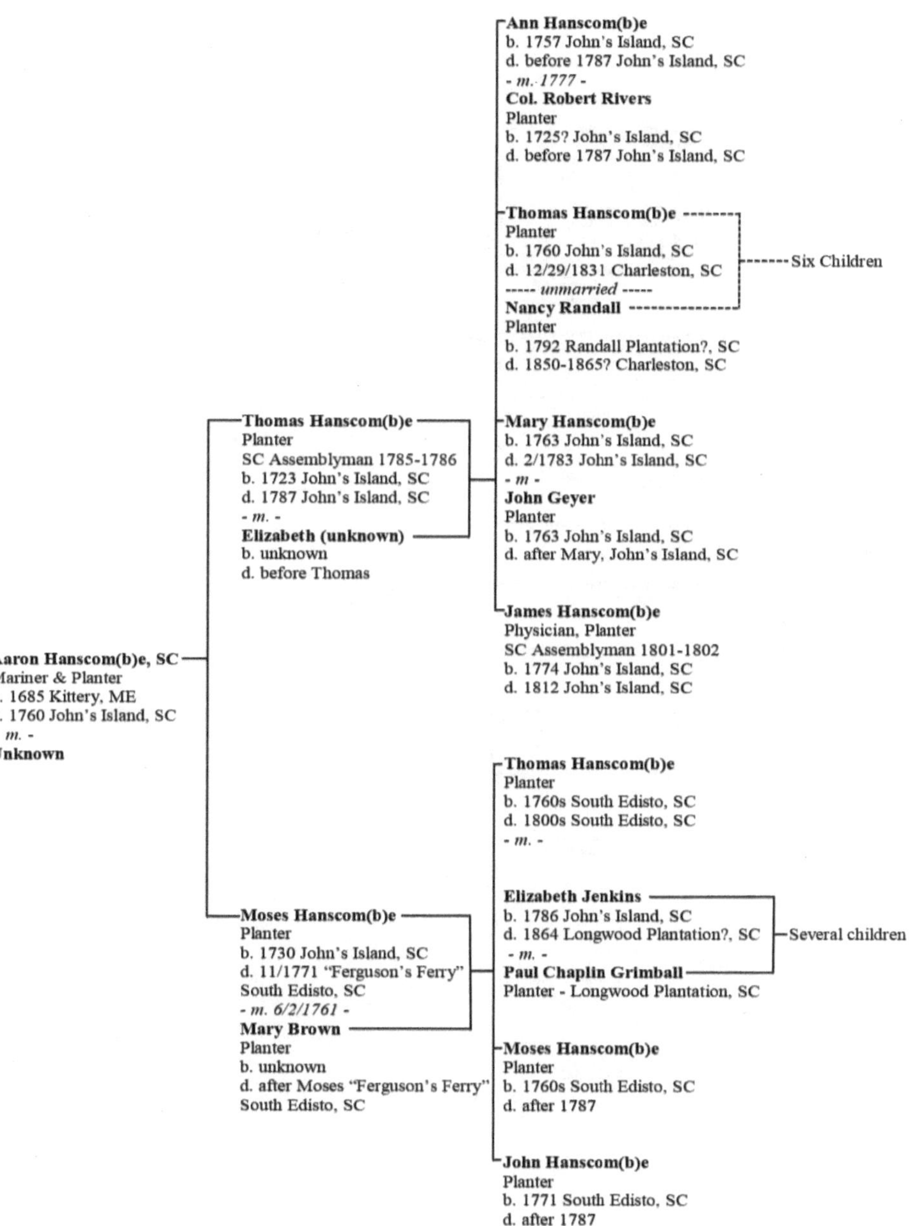

Diagram B

Hanscom(b)e Genealogy

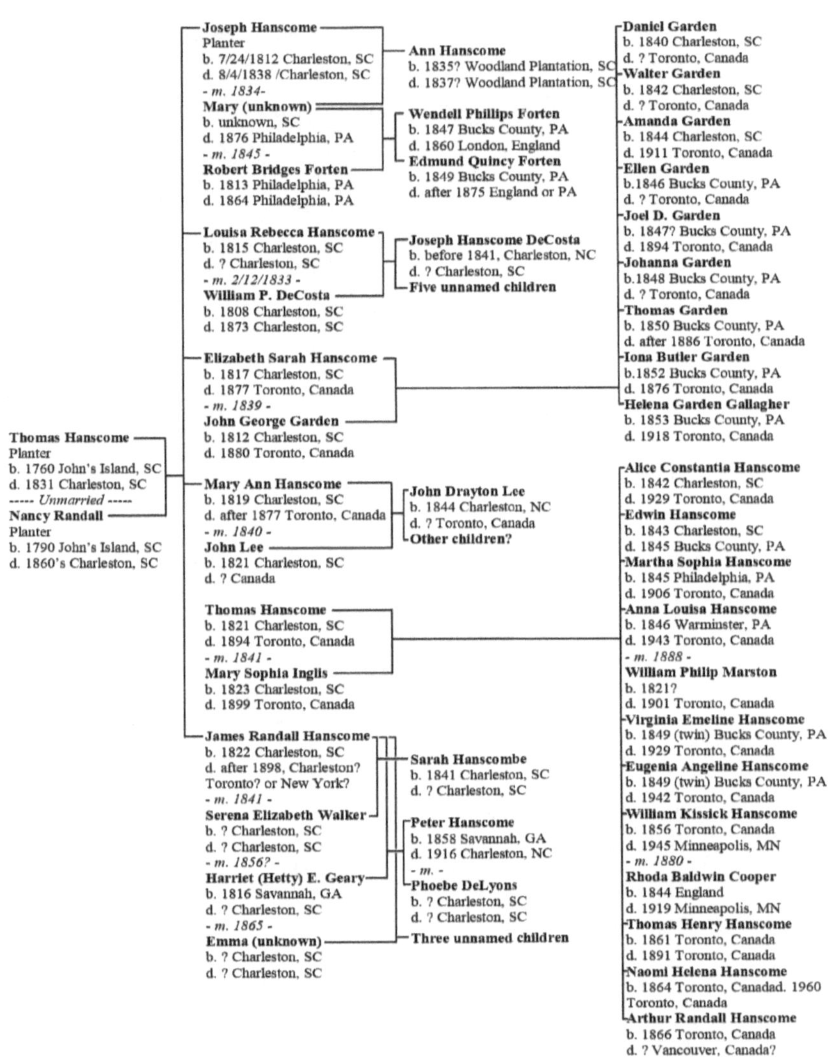

Diagram C

Hanscom(b)e Genealogy

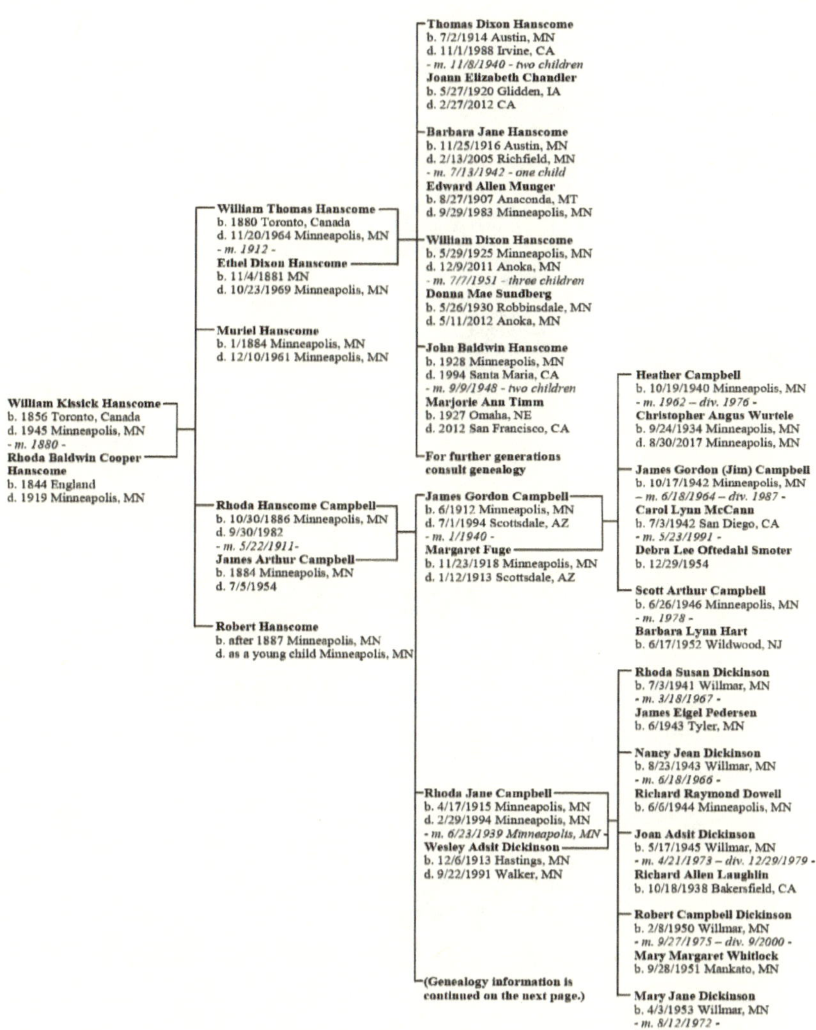

Diagram D
Page 1

Hanscom(b)e Genealogy

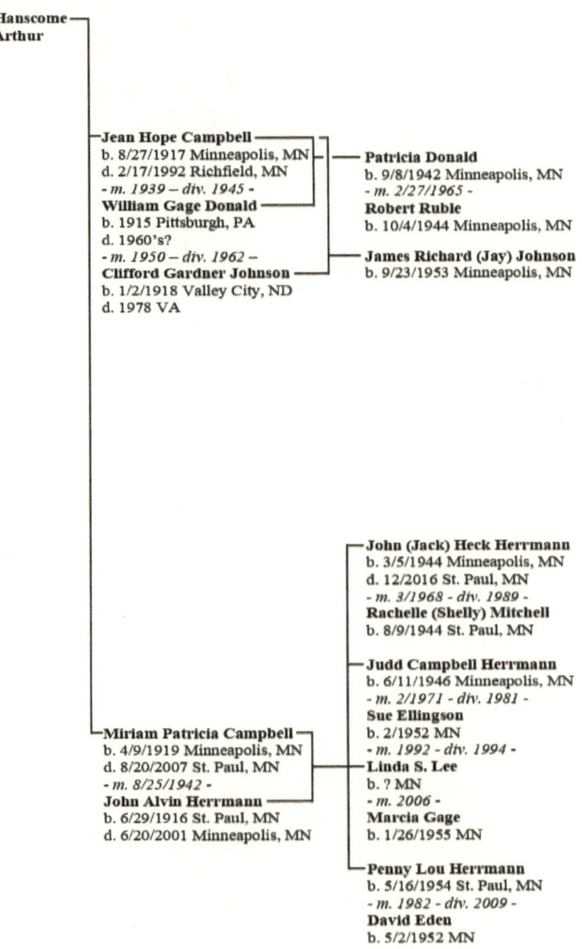

Diagram D
Page 2

Acknowledgments

Thank you, ancestors, friends and family!

Discovering my grandmother's secret took my breath away, hit me right in the sternum, sort of like my heart attack - thud! I inhaled deeply, began this research project, and five and a half years later finally exhaled. I took in all my ancestors - the pious, the afraid, the courageous, the lovers, the indentured servant, the Native American (Chepi was fictitious, alas, I wanted to be Indian), the slave, the slave master – both black and white, the young, the old, the greedy, the kind, the male, the female, the angry, the joyful, the meek, the hypocrite, the do-gooder, the rich, the poor and the *for better and for worse*. I birthed, married and buried them with joy and tears. I tried to raise my consciousness, mix their spirits with mine and did my best to have you catch a glimpse of history via the Hanscomes. They are all a part of me. Because of them, I am a bit different and a whole lot richer.

Thank you, Campbell Cousins for simply being a part of my life. I hope you will smile, perhaps even chuckle, at my portrayal of our families, even if it doesn't match your memories. Underlying the Waspiness, the alcoholism, the teasing, there was a great love of family that I attribute to our matriarch Grandmother, Rhoda Hanscome Campbell. I can't remember holidays without your fun presence. We knew who we were: The Campbell Cousins.

Jim Abrahams, you made me laugh, not uncommon in my fifty plus years of knowing you, when I asked for your help with the name of the title and you said: *The WASPs. Your family was the WASPiest family I ever met.* Something so obvious to you was too close to even be recognized by me. When I laughed, I knew you nailed the focal point, the meaning of the third novel and the social history of the 20th century as lived out through my family. There is so much truth in laughter, but then, you know that. Thanks!

Thanks to DD Scott for the lovely and most professional reformatted second editions of *The UnPuritans* and *The Lost Mulattos* and the first edition of *The WASPs* and their respective ebooks. You did teach me you can judge a book by its cover!

Freida Scalafani Williams: Thank you for initiating me into *Old Florida* culture, loving the water as much as I did, getting out of bed in the dead of night to fry up that snapper I caught fresh, the heroic kayaking to Egmont Key, the continual digging out the ditch during tropical storms, your genuine, honest friendship and generosity for twenty years. May you rest in peace.

Kappa Kappa Gamma sorority sisters, my friends for over fifty years, I thank all of you. A special thanks for support of my writing Lindalea Ludwick, Nancy Solar, Lucy Crichton, Joanne Hayes, Sally Fleming and from the beginning of my project, Alex Rose.

Friends, who are like family: Dianne Brown and Cheryl Beamer. And family who are like friends: Susan Pedersen, Nancy Dowell, Robert Dickinson and Mary Dexter. Thanks for your support.

And most of all, thanks to my daughter, Sarah Dickinson Berejik, for being a team with me.

About the Author

Joan Dickinson has worn many hats - history teacher, psychologist, professor, behavioral health director and international consultant, wellness columnist, public speaker, yoga and meditation instructor. She hails from Minnesota and kayaks with the dolphins near Anna Maria Island, Florida.

She loves to connect with her readers on Facebook: Https://www.facebook.com/joan.dickinson.52

Books by the Author

The Hanscome Trilogy:

The UnPuritans
The Lost Mulattos
The WASPs

9 781691 041268